Building Automated Trading Systems

With an Introduction to Visual C++.NET 2005

The Financial Market Technology Series

Series Editor

Ben Van Vliet

The Financial Market Technology Series is a partnership between Elsevier, Inc. and the Institute for Market Technology (i4mt) to publish cutting-edge books covering topics concerning the integration of technology with financial markets, including:

- automated trading,
- building trading and investment systems,
- operational issues in back office processing,
- clearing and settlement, and
- compliance and governance issues as they relate to technology.

The goal of the series is to promote increased understanding and competency with technology in the finance industry through publishing high-quality books on the latest areas of research and practice for professionals working in the financial markets.

Series Editor: Ben Van Vliet is a Lecturer in and the Associate Director of the M.Sc. in Financial Markets Program at the Stuart Graduate School of Business, Illinois Institute of Technology. Within this program, he teaches graduate courses in quantitative finance and automated trading system development using Visual Basic.NET, SQL, XML, ISO C++ and Visual C++.NET and UML. He is also a co-inventor of TraderDNA™, a real-time trading performance evaluation software package, as well as being a Director at TraderDNA LLC. He also serves as Vice Chairman of the Institute for Market Technology (i4mt), a not-for-profit organization that provides educational programs in financial markets and technology, where he also chairs the Market Technology Committee for the Certified Trading System Developer (CTSD) program. Please see www.i4mt.org for further information. Mr. Van Vliet also consults extensively in the financial industry. He is the author of *Building Automated Trading Systems* (Academic Press, 2007) and co-author of *Modeling Financial Markets* (McGraw-Hill 2004).

We welcome proposals for books for the series; please go to
www.books.elsevier.com/finance
where you will find a link to send us your proposal.

Building Automated Trading Systems

With an Introduction to Visual C++.NET 2005

Benjamin Van Vliet

AMSTERDAM • BOSTON • HEIDELBERG • LONDON
NEW YORK • OXFORD • PARIS • SAN DIEGO
SAN FRANCISCO • SINGAPORE • SYDNEY • TOKYO

Academic press is an imprint of Elsevier

Academic Press is an imprint of Elsevier
30 Corporate Drive, Suite 400, Burlington, MA 01803, USA
525 B Street, Suite 1900, San Diego, California 92101-4495, USA
84 Theobald's Road, London WC1X 8RR, UK

This book is printed on acid-free paper. ∞

Library of Congress Cataloging-in-Publication Data

British Library Cataloguing-in-Publication Data
A catalogue record for this book is available from the British Library.

ISBN 13: 978-0-7506-8251-0
ISBN 10: 0-7506-8251-5

For information on all Academic Press publications
visit our Web site at www.books.elsevier.com

Printed and bound by CPI Group (UK) Ltd, Croydon, CR0 4YY

Transferred to Digital Print 2011

Contents

Acknowledgments   xiii

CHAPTER 1   Introduction   1

  1.1.   ISO C++   2
  1.2.   Structure of This Book   2

Section I: Introduction to Visual C++.NET 2005

CHAPTER 2   The .NET Framework   5

  2.1.   MS Visual Studio 2005 Project Structure   5
  2.2.   What is C++/CLI?   5
  2.3.   Why Visual C++.NET?   6
  2.4.   The VC++.NET Compiler   7
  2.5.   What About Speed?   7
  2.6.   The .NET Framework   7
  2.7.   Sample Code: MessageBox_Example   9
  2.8.   Sample Code: StringConcat_Example   11
  2.9.   Sample Code: Debug_Example   12
  2.10.   Versioning   14
  2.11.   Summary   14

CHAPTER 3   Tracking References   15

  3.1.   Sample Code: TrackingReference_Example   15
  3.2.   Sample Code: TemplateFunction_Example   16
  3.3.   ^Managed Handle   16
  3.4.   Sample Code: RefType_Example   17
  3.5.   Summary   17

CHAPTER 4   Classes and Objects   19

4.1.   Abstraction   19
4.2.   Encapsulation   21
4.3.   Inheritance   21
4.4.   Polymorphism   21
4.5.   Memory Management in .NET   21
4.6.   .NET Types   22
4.7.   Unmanaged Types   23
4.8.   Mixed Assemblies   23
4.9.   Summary   23

CHAPTER 5   Reference Types   25

5.1.   Sample Code: RefType_Example   26
5.2.   Delete and Dispose   27
5.3.   Finalize   28
5.4.   Sample Code: Finalize_Example   29
5.5.   Stack Semantics for Ref Types   30
5.6.   Nullptr Reference   30
5.7.   This is Important   31
5.8.   Summary   31

CHAPTER 6   Value Types   33

6.1.   Sample Code: ValueTypes_Example   34
6.2.   Sample Code: PassingValueTypes_Example   35
6.3.   Summary   36

CHAPTER 7   Unmanaged Objects   37

7.1.   Sample Code: UnmanagedObject_Example   37
7.2.   Summary   39

CHAPTER 8   Composition   41

8.1.   Sample Code: Composition_Example   41
8.2.   Sample Code: UnmanagedComposition_Example   44
8.3.   Sample Code: ManagedComposition_Example   46
8.4.   Summary   48

CHAPTER 9   Properties   49

9.1.   Sample Code: Properties_Example   49
9.2.   Summary   50

CHAPTER 10   Structures and Enumerations   51

10.1.   Sample Code: ValueStructure_Example   51
10.2.   Sample Code: ReferenceStructure_Example   52
10.3.   Sample Code: Enums_Example   53
10.4.   Summary   53

CHAPTER 11   Inheritance   55

11.1.   Access Modifiers   55
11.2.   Object Class   56
11.3.   Abstract and Sealed Classes   56
11.4.   Sample Code: Inheritance_Example   56
11.5.   Interfaces   58
11.6.   Sample Code: Interface_Example   59
11.7.   Runtime Callable Wrapper   60
11.8.   Summary   60

CHAPTER 12   Converting and Casting   61

12.1.   Converting   61
12.2.   Sample Code: Convert_Example   61
12.3.   Static Casting   62
12.4.   Sample Code: StaticCast_Example   62
12.5.   Dynamic Casting   62
12.6.   Sample Code: DynamicCast_Example   62
12.7.   Safe Casting   64
12.8.   Sample Code: SafeCast_Example   64
12.9.   Summary   65

CHAPTER 13   Operator Overloading   67

13.1.   Sample Code: OpOverload_Example   67
13.2.   Summary   69

CHAPTER 14   Delegates and Events   71

14.1.   Delegates   71
14.2.   Sample Code: Delegates_Example   72
14.3.   Multicasting   73
14.4.   Sample Code: Multicast_Example   73
14.5.   Events   75
14.6.   Sample Code: Event_Example   76
14.7.   Wrappers   78
14.8.   Sample Code: Wrapper_Example   78
14.9.   Asynchronous Method Calls   80
14.10.   Sample Code: AsynchEvent_Example   80
14.11.   Summary   82

CHAPTER 15   Arrays   83

15.1.   Sample Code: ManagedArray_Example   83
15.2.   Sample Code: PassingArrays_Example   84
15.3.   Summary   85

CHAPTER 16   Generating Random Numbers   87
16.1.   Sample Code: Random_Example   87
16.2.   Sample Code: StdNormRandom_Example   87
16.3.   Summary   89

CHAPTER 17   Time and Timers   91
17.1.   Sample Code: Milliseconds_Example   91
17.2.   Stopwatch   92
17.3.   Sample Code: Stopwatch_Example   93
17.4.   Timers   93
17.5.   Sample Code: FormsTimer_Example   93
17.6.   Sample Code: ThreadingTimer_Example   95
17.7.   Sample Code: TimersTimer_Example   96
17.8.   Summary   98

CHAPTER 18   Input and Output Streams   99
18.1.   FileStream Class   99
18.2.   StreamWriter Class   99
18.3.   File and Directory Classes   99
18.4.   Application Class   100
18.5.   FileMode Enumeration   100
18.6.   Sample Code: StreamWriter_Example   100
18.7.   Sample Code: StreamReader_Example   101
18.8.   Summary   101

CHAPTER 19   Exception Handling   103
19.1.   Sample Code: Exceptions_Example   103
19.2.   Catching Unmanaged C++ Types   104
19.3.   Summary   105

CHAPTER 20   Collections   107
20.1.   Sample Code: Hashtable_Example   107
20.2.   Sorted List Class   109
20.3.   Sample Code: SortedList_Example   109
20.4.   Thread Safety   110
20.5.   Generics   110
20.6.   Sample Code: LinkedList_Example   110
20.7.   Sample Code: Generics_Example   111
20.8.   Summary   112

CHAPTER 21   STL/STL.NET   113
21.1.   Sample Code: STL.NET_Example   113
21.2.   Sample Code: STL_Example   114
21.3.   Summary   114

CHAPTER 22   DataSets   115
22.1.   Sample Code: DataSet_Example   116
22.2.   Rows, DataRowCollections, and DataRows   116
22.3.   Summary   117

CHAPTER 23   Connecting to Databases   119
23.1.   Database Connection   119
23.2.   DataAdapter   120
23.3.   Sample Code: ADO.NET_Example   120
23.4.   Enumerating Through All the Data in a DataSet   122
23.5.   Using Excel as a Data Source   123
23.6.   Writing XML from a DataSet   123
23.7.   Updating a Database with Changes in a Dataset   123
23.8.   Retrieving Data with a DataReader   124
23.9.   Summary   124

CHAPTER 24   Structured Query Language   125
24.1.   Data Manipulation Language   125
24.2.   Updating a Database with Changes in a DataSet   138
24.3.   Data Definition Language   138
24.4.   Summary   140

CHAPTER 25   XML   141
25.1.   Well-Formed XML Documents   141
25.2.   Valid XML Documents   141
25.3.   XML Schema Documents   142
25.4.   Parsers   142
25.5.   Sample Code: Traders.xsd   142
25.6.   Sample Code: XmlWriter_Example   144
25.7.   Sample Code: XmlReader_Example   144
25.8.   Summary   146

CHAPTER 26   Financial Information Exchange Protocol   147
26.1.   XML Protocols in Financial Markets   147
26.2.   Overview of FIX   148
26.3.   Summary   151

CHAPTER 27   Serialization   153
27.1.   Serialization_Example   153
27.2.   Summary   154

CHAPTER 28   Windows Services   155
28.1.   Sample Code: WindowsService_Example   155
28.2.   Summary   159

CHAPTER 29   Setup and Installation Packages   161

29.1.   Sample Code: Installation_Example   161
29.2.   Summary   162

Section II: Concurrency

CHAPTER 30   Threading   165

30.1.   Threading Namespace   166
30.2.   Sample Code: Thread_Example   166
30.3.   Sample Code: ThreadAbort_Example   167
30.4.   Thread Priority   169
30.5.   Sample Code: ThreadPriority_Example   170
30.6.   ThreadState Enumeration   170
30.7.   ThreadPool Class   171
30.8.   Sample Code: ThreadPool_Example   171
30.9.   Updating Forms from Other Threads   172
30.10.   Sample Code: FormUpdate_Example   172
30.11.   Thread Safety   174
30.12.   Summary   175

CHAPTER 31   Synchronization Classes   177

31.1.   Sample Code: Synchronize_Example   177
31.2.   Mutex Class   178
31.3.   Example Code: Mutex_Example   178
31.4.   Semaphore Class   180
31.5.   Sample Code: Semaphore_Example   180
31.6.   Monitor Class   182
31.7.   Sample Code: Monitor   182
31.8.   Summary   182

CHAPTER 32   Sockets   183

32.1.   Sample Code: SynchronousServer_Example   184
32.2.   Sample Code: SynchronousClient_Example   187
32.3.   Summary   189

Section III: Interoperability and Connectivity

CHAPTER 33   Marshaling   193

33.1.   Marshal Class   193
33.2.   Sample Code: StringToCharArray_Example   194
33.3.   Summary   194

CHAPTER 34   Interior and Pinning Pointers   195

34.1.   Sample Code: InteriorPointer_Example   195
34.2.   Pinning Pointers   196
34.3.   Sample Code: Pinning_Example   196
34.4.   Summary   198

CHAPTER 35   Connecting to Managed DLLs   199

35.1.   Example Code: DLL_Example   199
35.2.   Summary   201

CHAPTER 36   Connecting to Component Object Model (COM) DLLs
                        with COM Interop   203

36.1.   Sample Code: MyCOMLibrary   203
36.2.   Sample Code: UsingCOMDLL_Example   207
36.3.   Summary   207

CHAPTER 37   Connecting to C++ DLLs with Platform Invocation Services   209

37.1.   Calling C-Style Functions   209
37.2   Sample Code: MyWin32Library   209
37.3.   Sample Code: UsingWin32DLL_Example   211
37.4.   Creating Objects   212
37.5.   Sample Code: MyWin32ClassLibrary   212
37.6.   Sample Code: UsingWin32Class_Example   214
37.7.   CallingConventionEnumeration   215
37.8.   Summary   216

CHAPTER 38   Connecting to Excel   217

38.1.   Sample Code: ControllingExcel_Example   217
38.2.   Sample Code: ExcelChart_Example   220
38.3.   Summary   221

CHAPTER 39   Connecting to TraderAPI   223

39.1.   TraderAPI Overview   223
39.2.   FillObj   224
39.3.   InstrObjClass   224
39.4.   InstrNotifyClass   225
39.5.   OrderObj   225
39.6.   OrderProfileClass   225
39.7.   OrderSetClass   226
39.8.   Sample Code: TraderAPIConnection_Example   227
39.9.   Summary   230

CHAPTER 40   Connecting to XTAPI   231

40.1.   Sample Code: XTAPIConnection_Example   231
40.2.   Summary   233

Section IV: Automated Trading Systems

CHAPTER 41   Building Trading Systems   237

41.1.   Buy vs. Build   237
41.2.   Data Mapping   239
41.3.   Speed of Development   240
41.4.   Ten Things that Affect the Speed of a Trading System   241
41.5.   Getting It Right   242
41.6.   Logic Leaks   243
41.7.   Ten Things that Affect the Profitability of a Trading System   244
41.8.   Summary   245

CHAPTER 42   KIV Trading System Development Methodology   247

42.1.   The Money Document   249
42.2.   Research and Document Calculations   249
42.3.   Back Test   252
42.4.   Implement   253
42.5.   Manage Portfolio and Risk   255
42.6.   Summary   257

CHAPTER 43   Automated Trading System Classes   259

43.1.   Instrument Class   259
43.2.   Order Class   263
43.3.   Order Book   264
43.4.   Bracket   264
43.5.   Tick   264
43.6.   Tick or Bar Collection   264
43.7.   Bar   264
43.8.   System Manager   265
43.9.   Graphical User Interface   265
43.10.   Summary   265

CHAPTER 44   Single-Threaded, Technical Analysis System   267

44.1.   Sample Code: TechincalSystem_Example   268
44.2.   Summary   277

CHAPTER 45   Producer/Consumer Design Pattern   279

45.1.   Sample Code: ProducerConsumer_Example   279
45.2.   Summary   287

CHAPTER 46   Multithreaded, Statistical Arbitrage System   289

46.1.   Sample Code: Spreader_Example   291
46.2.   Summary   304
46.3.   Conclusion   304

Acknowledgments

This book began as the class notes for a course I teach at the Illinois Institute of Technology called Advanced Object Oriented Programming for Financial Markets. In this class we cover automated trading system design and development using Microsoft Visual C++. When I started teaching this course several years ago, I could not find a book that covered all the topics necessary to build real-time, automated trading systems and so, as a result, this book attempts to do just that—it brings together programming and technology-related topics for the development of trade selection, order routing, order management, and position management algorithms. I do hope that more schools will offer courses on automated trading system design in the future and that this book will be helpful in their instruction.

Furthermore, this book is a foundation text for the CTSD Certified Trading System Developer program offered by the Institute for Market Technology (www.i4mt.org). This is a new certification program that consists of three examinations, one in quantitative finance, one in securities and derivatives trading strategy, and one in ISO C++/C++.NET programming and market technology. This rigorous self-study program is designed to bring together the skillsets in demand in the financial industry today. Candidates who achieve the CTSD designation will be talented people indeed.

As one can imagine, additional credit for the completion of this project must be given to many friends, family, and colleagues: in particular to my wife, Julia, Mark McCracken, Dr. Andrew Kumiega, Andrew Acosta, Sagy Mintz, Jason Malkin, Larissa J. Miller, Derek Walther, Niraj Chokshi, Julian Mulla, Mike Hermanson, David Norman, Dr. Deborah Cernauskas, Dr. Joe Wojkowski, Pamela Reardon, Edward Wang, Alex Deitz, Andrew Robinson, and all my colleagues at the IIT Center for Financial Markets—Russell Wojcik, Dr. Michael Gorham, Keith Black, Dr. Michael Ong, Dr. John Bilson, Dr. Michael Kelly, and Jodi Houlihan. Also I would like to thank the many students who have taken my course and have all provided valuable feedback. Without their help and the help of many others this book would never have been completed.

This book is written for people with knowledge of ISO C++ or possibly Java, .NET, or COM. For financial engineers and aspiring financial engineers with a general programming background, this book will provide an in-depth discussion of higher level programming concepts such as event handling, interoperability, data feed connectivity, and concurrency. For experienced C++ programmers, you may find that this book provides a good introduction to the use of C++ within the .NET Framework. Whatever the case, I hope you learn from it and are inspired to delve deeper into the topic of automated trading system development. Please provide me with any feedback you have. I pledge to update my website, www.benvanvliet.com, regularly with corrections to errata and additional examples.

CHAPTER ◆ 1

Introduction

Automated (or algorithmic) trading systems consist of many parts, both hardware and software—clients, servers, networks, databases, calculation engines, application programming interfaces, real-time data feeds, and graphical user interfaces. However, the business logic of trading systems, which consists of trade selection algorithms, order management, and position management logic, is contained within software, and this book is concerned with the encapsulation of trading system business logic in software that controls the flow of market data. (There is no quant in this book.)

An automated trading system consists of the rules for entry into and exit from a position or positions and the technology, both hardware and software, used to make them happen. These rules are a set of logical or mathematical operations that can be based on qualitative, technical, or quantitative research.

If we want to build an automated system that executes trades on electronic exchanges, we need to learn how to work with data, both real-time market data and historical data, in code. After all, "data is the lifeblood of electronic markets," according to David Norman in his book *Professional Electronic Trading*.

That's just what this book is about, using Visual C++.NET to manage financial markets data (and there is a lot of it) in trading system applications. Generally speaking, this book covers three things:

1. Managing data in memory.
2. Storing data in and retrieving from databases.
3. Communicating data.

Front office programming in financial markets is largely concerned with connecting to databases, real-time data feeds, order execution platforms, quant libraries, optimization engines, charting software, report generation engines, legacy technologies, and Excel, just to name a few. In order to successfully manage real-time and historical data, we will need to understand:

1. Event-driven architecture.
2. Concurrency.
3. Connectivity and interoperability.

1

While this book addresses dozens of important technological issues that you will face when building real-world automated trading systems in .NET, it does not show you how to build a profitable trading system. (It is important nevertheless to recognize that technological superiority can be a major competitive advantage.) There are four disciplines that go into automated trading system development—computer science, quantitative finance, trading strategy, and quality management—and this is a computer science book. Development and testing of trade selection and risk management methods are topics for other books.

This book covers the basics of what a financial engineer should know about programming in .NET—objects, SQL, multithreading, interoperability, messaging, order selection algorithms, and order management techniques.

In this text, I have tried to include market-driven, job-relevant information. Today's employers in the financial markets demand job readiness. If you want to get a job in the trading and money management industry, which more and more every day is driven by automated systems, you will have to have a competitive level of knowledge of programming. You should realize that this book is an overview, however. It will not teach you everything. Technology as a topic is obviously far too vast to cover in one book. Even narrowing it down to VC++.NET for trading system development is still far too vast. Over the pages, I will present several important ideas, try to point you in the right direction, and hopefully in the end inspire you to do additional research on the topic of automated trading system development. From there, the diligent financial engineer must investigate further on his or her own.

1.1. ISO C++

This book covers the programming aspects of trading system development and assumes that you are familiar with ISO C++ programming concepts, including pointers, functions, objects, and the Standard Template Library.

1.2. Structure of This Book

Automated trading systems find their purest form in high-frequency strategies where speed of calculation and execution are the competitive advantage. Other systems, where milliseconds are not necessarily of the essence, may be fully automated or partially automated. This text will focus on introducing programming and design concepts for higher frequency systems.

Discussion of all the alternative technological concepts of trading system design and presentation of a complete trading system are beyond the scope of a book. The trading systems presented in this book are drastically simplified in order to illustrate common programming and design concepts.

This book is divided into four sections. The first section focuses purely on an introduction to Visual C++.NET types and programming techniques. The second section focuses on multithreading. The third focuses on interoperability and connectivity and the fourth on objects, design patterns, and architectural concepts for automated trading system development.

In the end, simply reading this book will not make you an expert. To really learn the material in this book, you should also work through the code samples presented. Only by involving yourself in the process, and furthermore going beyond it, will you gain understanding and intuition. It's hard work, but it will pay off.

SECTION · I

Introduction to Visual C++.NET 2005

CHAPTER • 2

The .NET Framework

2.1. MS Visual Studio 2005 Project Structure

In MS Visual Studio 2005, your software application is called a solution, and a solution can be made up of one or more projects, where each project could potentially be in a different Visual Studio language.

Over the course of this book, I will present solutions developed for the most part in MS Visual C++ 2005 for "managed" or .NET applications for reasons that I will explain shortly. However, be aware that Visual C++ 2005 is not a new programming language, but rather a full development environment that provides increased support for many C++ project types, including:

- Active Template Library (ATL) projects.
- MS Foundation Classes (MFC) projects.
- .NET or "managed" console, Windows or DLL projects.
- Win32 Console projects for ISO C++ projects.
- Win32 API projects and DLLs.

As a result, Visual C++ for .NET or "managed" projects is just one of several C++ languages offered within Visual Studio 2005, and this is one of the things that sets the new VC++ 2005 apart from the others in the .NET family—it provides essentially five independent C++ languages in one package. So if you want to continue making MFC applications, you can do that just like before. In fact, support for MFC and ATL has actually been improved in VS 2005.

In previous versions of Visual Studio, the .NET extension was added to the name in order to differentiate it from even earlier versions, such as Visual Basic 6.0. With the advent of VS 2005, the .NET extension to the name is usually left off and we can refer to them as VB, C#, and Visual C++.

2.2. What is C++/CLI?

C++/CLI (Common Language Infrastructure) is a derivation of C++. According to Stanley Lippman of Microsoft:

CLI refers to the Common Language Infrastructure, a multitiered architecture supporting a dynamic component programming model. In many ways, this represents a complete reversal of the C++ object model. A runtime software layer, the virtual execution system, runs between the program and the underlying operating system. Access to the underlying machine is fairly constrained. Access to the types active in the executing program and the associated program infrastructure—both as discovery and construction—is supported. The slash (/) represents a binding between C++ and the CLI…

So, a first approximation of an answer to what is C++/CLI is that it is a binding of the static C++ object model to the dynamic component object model of the CLI. In short, it is how you do .NET programming using C++ rather than C# or Visual Basic. Like C# and the CLI itself, C++/CLI is undergoing standardization under the European Computer Manufacturers Association (ECMA) and eventually under ISO.

The common language runtime (CLR) is the Microsoft version of the CLI that is specific to the Windows operating system. Similarly, Visual C++ 2005 is the implementation of C++/CLI.

As a second approximation of an answer, …C++/CLI integrates the .NET programming model within C++ in the same way as, back at Bell Laboratories, we integrated generic programming using templates within the then existing C++. In both of these cases your investments in an existing C++ codebase and in your existing C++ expertise are preserved. This was an essential baseline requirement of the design of C++/CLI.

Over the course of this book, I will simply refer to Microsoft implementation of C++/CLI as Visual C++.NET. For Mr. Lippman's full article, go to http://msdn.microsoft.com/msdnmag/issues/06/00/PureC/default.aspx.

2.3.   Why Visual C++.NET?

So why Visual C++.NET? What are the benefits of "managed" or .NET C++ applications? Simply put and in the words of a vice president of a major trading software vendor here in Chicago, "NET is the future." Most importantly, the .NET Framework contains many, many classes that aid in development of trading systems, as we will see. Furthermore, relative to the other .NET languages, VC++ contains much greater support for interoperability between managed and unmanaged code. In addition, in financial markets, interoperability is key. In VC++.NET, we have precise control over managed and unmanaged heap and stack memory allocation and managed and unmanaged code and all can exist seamlessly in the same project. This permits us to integrate our existing C++ applications, functionality, and objects quickly and easily into new .NET applications. This is especially true for COM applications, which are used heavily in the financial industry and are "unmanaged."

Further, if you have libraries of objects or financial functions written in native C++, VC++.NET with its extensive managed/unmanaged interop support will give you tremendous control. Alternatively, if you have existing C++ applications that you wish to convert to .NET, again VC++.NET will provide you with the tools the other .NET languages can't and don't. Finally, while the 2005 version of the STL (known as STL.NET) is not available quite yet, it will be soon and converting native STL-dependent code will be a breeze.

2.4. The VC++.NET Compiler

Here are a few things to remember about the VC++.NET compiler. The VC++.NET compiler, Cl.exe, uses the .c extension for C-only compiling and .cpp for C and C++. Also, the standard headers do not require the .h extension, as Microsoft has included its own versions of these files in the std namespace.

Further, a project's properties window displays all of the compiler settings for C/C++, including the linker and build events. Microsoft's Cl.exe compiler implements ANSI C and ISO C++ standards and is 98% C++ compliant according to Microsoft. The compiler offers Solution Configurations for Debug builds and Release builds. With a Debug build, we can interact with our code during runtime. This is a big help. However, no optimizations are made and for that we use the Release build, which will generate faster, optimized code.

The compiler allows us to incorporate native C++ code in our projects and first compiles into Microsoft Intermediate Language (MSIL). Then the MSIL is converted into native code by the Just In Time (JIT) compiler. With JIT some operations will be faster than native C++, whereas others will be slower. As a result, there are trade-offs between development speed and execution speed. However, there are things we can do to minimize the cost of certain operations. The VC++.NET compiler and JIT can be tuned to generate the fastest possible code using the available compiler options. If you are serious about speed, take some time to investigate further Microsoft's VC++.NET compiler.

2.5. What About Speed?

Speed is important, of course. For an in-depth discussion of speed considerations in managed code, I will refer you to a few excellent articles in the MSDN Library (msdn.Microsoft.com/library):

- "A Baker's Dozen: Thirteen Things You Should Know Before Porting Your Visual C++ .NET Programs to Visual Studio 2005" by Stanley Lippman.
- "Best Practices for Writing Efficient and Reliable Code with C++/CLI" by Kenny Kerr.
- "C++: The Most Powerful Language for .NET Framework Programming" by Kenny Kerr.
- "Writing Faster Managed Code: Know What Things Cost" by Jan Gray.
- "Writing High-Performance Managed Applications: A Primer" by Gregor Noriskin (includes an overview of the CLR Profiler).
- "Tips for Improving Time-Critical Code".
- "Optimization Best Practices" in the Visual C++ section.

2.6. The .NET Framework

When we create managed Visual C++.NET applications, our programs are developed, compiled, and executed within the .NET Framework. The .NET Framework consists of three parts:

1. Common Language Runtime (CLR).
2. .NET Class Libraries.
3. ASP.NET.

ASP.NET is Microsoft's web development platform for building enterprise web applications, which run too slow for real-time, financial markets application, and so we will spend no time examining it. Rather we will spend our time learning about the common language runtime and the .NET class libraries and how we can use them to build financial applications that can potentially run on multiple operating systems, not just Windows, including Unix, Linux, and Mac.

2.6.1. Common Language Runtime

The CLR drives code execution within the .NET Framework and provides .NET-based programs with cross language integration, security, dynamic memory management, and debugging services. Further, the CLR controls what we call managed code, which is executed within the managed heap. That is to say, the managed heap is controlled by the .NET Framework rather than the operating system. Unmanaged code (or non-.NET code), however, is controlled by the operating system.

The CLR also provides for dynamic memory management by using a garbage collector to manage the allocation and deallocation of memory space, eliminating the common memory leak problems that often occur in software. The CLR's allocation of memory on the managed heap is, it turns out, actually faster than unmanaged heap allocation and nearly as fast as stack memory allocation because it allocates contiguous memory locations by simply incrementing a pointer.

In .NET, the compiler compiles managed source code first into MSIL. Before code is run, MSIL is converted by a just-in-time (JIT) compiler specific to your computer architecture. JIT converts MSIL into machine language, or native code, at runtime.

2.6.2. Garbage Collection

The .NET garbage collector determines the best time to perform a collection of unreferenced objects. The garbage collector releases the memory space allocated to objects that are no longer being referenced (or, pointed to) within the application.

The .NET Framework keeps a list of active references that the JIT compiler and the CLR maintain. The garbage collector uses this list to examine all of an application's references. Objects that are not on the list are considered unreachable and the memory space will be released. As a result, the garbage collector examines the managed heap and finds blocks of space occupied by unreferenced objects. At the same time, referenced memory locations are compacted and moved and the necessary updates to the pointer references are made. It's important to note then that the garbage collector will be moving objects around in memory without our knowledge. This has important implications later on.

2.6.3. Assemblies

Assemblies form the fundamental building blocks for the .NET Framework and any application developed within it. Assemblies most often exist as executable files or dynamic link library files and contain groups of classes that form a logical functional unit.

Assemblies contain information about content, versioning, and dependencies; as a result the applications we create with Visual C++.NET do not need to rely on registry values to work properly. Since registry is not required, we can generally install Visual C++.NET applications by simply copying the executable's directory onto the target computer.

2.6.4. Namespaces

Namespaces organize the thousands of classes in the .NET libraries, prevent ambiguity, and simplify references, as we will see. (VC++.NET programs that we write will often contain or "use" multiple namespaces.) In .NET the System namespace is the root namespace and contains primitive data types and fundamental classes such as Object (from which all objects are derived), String, Exception, and the garbage collector class, GC.

The Visual Studio Documentation (the .NET Help Files) contains a .NET Framework Class Library Reference page that provides a comprehensive list of the .NET namespaces with descriptions. Since all programming in .NET depends on the objects contained in these namespaces, you may want to spend some time familiarizing yourself with the different namespaces and the types of objects they contain.

2.6.4.1 Fully Qualified Names

When using libraries, we can instantiate objects defined in external locations, as long as we add a reference to the assembly and then use the fully qualified name for the class in our code. A fully qualified name is a class reference that is prefixed with its namespace name. Here is an example of how to create an object using the fully qualified class name for a class in another namespace:

```
System::Windows::Forms::MessageBox::Show("Hello, world!");
```

Fully qualified names prevent naming conflicts because the compiler can always determine which class is being used. However, the names themselves can get long and cumbersome. As a way around this, we can use the "using namespace" statement. The following code uses this shortcut:

```
using namespace System::Windows::Forms;
MessageBox::Show("Hello, world!");
```

As you will see, within our own user-defined namespaces, we can define modules, interfaces, classes, delegates, enumerations, structures, and even other namespaces.

2.7. Sample Code: MessageBox_Example

Let's create a new Visual C++.NET program that will illustrate the use of namespaces.

Step 1. Start Visual Studio 2005.
Step 2. In the File menu item, click on New and Project... The New Project window will appear (Figure 2-1).
Step 3. Highlight Visual C++ Projects in the Projects Types pane and CLR Console Application in the templates pane. Also, be sure to give your project a name and a location. Click OK.

When your solution is ready, you should see the Solution Explorer window on the right-hand side of your screen . If not, click on the icon as shown. The Solution Explorer will allow you to navigate through the files that comprise your solution (Figure 2-2).

Because our Console Application does not by default allow for a user interface, we need to add a reference to the System::Windows::Forms namespace. The Forms namespace contains the class definitions for Windows forms.

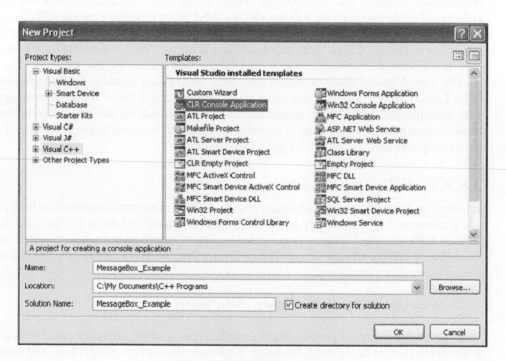

FIGURE 2-1

FIGURE 2-2

Step 4. In the Solution Explorer window, right click on the project name and select References... The MessageBox_Example Property Pages window will appear. Click on the Add New Reference icon. In the .NET list of components, navigate down to System::Windows::Forms. Click Select and then click OK. The References directory in the Property Pages window should now list System:: Windows::Forms.

Step 5. In the MessageBox_Example.cpp code window, type the following:

```
// MessageBox_Example.cpp : main project file.

#include "stdafx.h"

using namespace System;
using namespace System::Windows::Forms;

int main(array<System::String^>^args)
{
    Console::WriteLine(L"Hello, World");
    MessageBox::Show("Hello, World!");

    return 0;
}
```

Step 6. Compile the program by clicking the Build menu item and Build MessageBox_Example. Run the program by clicking the Debug menu item and Start Without Debugging.

Notice again that the MessageBox class definition is located within the System:: Windows::Forms namespace. (Using the optional L before a string constant designates the native, wide character type wchar_t.)

2.8. Sample Code: StringConcat_Example

Concatenating strings for display can be done in many ways as can formatting numbers for display using the String class or the ToString method as shown. The StringBuilder class also comes in handy. In order to use the StringBuilder class, use the System::Text namespace as shown.

```
#include "stdafx.h"

using namespace System;
using namespace System::Text;

int main(array<System::String^> ^args)
{
    String ^m_Lang = "C++";
    int m_Y = 2005;
```

```
Console::WriteLine("This is Visual {0} {1}," m_Lang, m_Y);
Console::WriteLine(String::Concat("This is Visual ," m_Lang, " ," m_Y));
Console::WriteLine("This is Visual"+m_Lang+" "+m_Y);

// Notice the formatting possible using the ToString method.
Console::WriteLine(Math::PI.ToString("#.###"));

StringBuilder ^m_Builder=gcnew StringBuilder("This is Visual C++ ");
m_Builder->Append(m_Y);
Console::WriteLine(m_Builder);

return 0;
}
```

2.9.   Sample Code: Debug_Example

Here is another example that illustrates the use of the Debug class and the Output Window.

Step 1.   Start Visual Studio 2005 as before. This time highlight Visual C++ Projects in the Projects Types pane and Windows Forms Application in the templates pane. Again, be sure to give your project a name and a location.

Step 2.   The Form1.h [Design] Window should appear. Double click on your Form1 and Visual Studio will automatically generate an event handler for the Form1 load event. This function will run when Form1 loads. Add the following code to the method:

```
private: System::Void Form1_Load(System::Object^ sender, System::EventArgs^ e)
{
    Debug::WriteLine("Hello, World!");
}
```

The output of this program does not show a message box, but rather will print the output through the Debug class, which is defined in the System::Diagnostics namespace, which we will need to add.

Step 3.   In the Form1.h code window, be sure to add:

```
using namespace System::Diagnostics;
```

Here is what the completed, Form1 code window should look like.

```
#pragma once

namespace Debug_Example
{

    using namespace System;
    using namespace System::ComponentModel;
    using namespace System::Collections;
```

```
using namespace System::Windows::Forms;
using namespace System::Data;
using namespace System::Drawing;
using namespace System::Diagnostics;

public ref class Form1 : public System::Windows::Forms::Form
{
public:
    Form1(void)
    {
        InitializeComponent();
    }
protected:
    ~Form1()
    {
        if (components)
        {
            delete components;
        }
    }
private:
    System::ComponentModel::Container ^components;

//Windows Forms Designer generate code

private: System::Void Form1_Load(System::Object^ sender, System::EventArgs^ e)
    {
        Debug::WriteLine("Hello, World!");
    }
    };
}
```

Step 4.   Build your application and then run it using the blue "Start" icon on your task bar.

To view the output, view the aptly named Output window (Figure 2-3). If you cannot find it, click on the Other Windows icon.

We often use the static methods of the Debug class to print program information and to check program logic. Use of the Debug class does not impact the performance of the application.

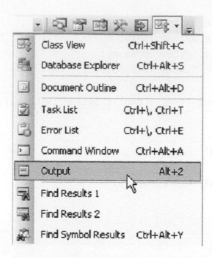

FIGURE 2-3

2.10. Versioning

The .NET Framework provides help with project versioning. In a project's AssemblyInfo.cpp file, we can set the version number easily.

```
// Version information for an assembly consists of the following four values:
//
//      Major Version
//      Minor Version
//      Build Number
//      Revision
//
// You can specify all the value or you can default the Revision and
// Build Numbers by using the '*' as shown next:
[assembly:AssemblyVersionAttribute("1.0.*")];
```

2.11. Summary

This chapter reviewed the VC++ solution structure, how assemblies and namespaces are organized, how the CLR controls managed memory, and the garbage collector. Also, we developed some simple solutions to illustrate use of message boxes, the debug window, the console window, and string concatenation. Finally, we looked at some of the reasons why VC++.NET is such a great language for developing automated trading systems.

CHAPTER • 3

Tracking References

Because a referenced type may be moved around at runtime by the common language runtime (CLR), the native C++ "&" cannot be used to reference an object on the garbage collected heap. In VC++.NET the CLR will update the new tracking reference "%" with the new location. A .NET tracking reference can refer to a managed or native object, a data member, or a storage location, but cannot be a member of a class. Also, by using a tracking reference in a template function, we can ensure that the function can be called with native, value, or reference types.

3.1. Sample Code: TrackingReference_Example

This example shows that the % tracking reference replaces the native C++ & reference. As you will see, however, we will still use the native & on occasion.

```
#include "stdafx.h"

using namespace System;

int main(array<System::String ^> ^args)
{
    int x=3;
    int &a=x;
    int %b=x;
    Console::WriteLine(x);
    Console::WriteLine(a);
    Console::WriteLine(b);
    return 0;
}
```

3.2.   Sample Code: TemplateFunction_Example

For now, do not worry about the distinction between a ref class, a native class, and a value class. This is not a fully working code example as the class definitions are left out. Here, simply note the use of the % tracking reference operator in the template function.

```
#include "stdafx.h"
#include "MyRefClass.h"
#include "MyNativeClass.h"
 #include "MyValueClass.h"

using namespace System;

template<typename T>
void function_1(T%);

int main(array<System::String ^> ^args)
{
    MyRefClass m_RefObj(3);              //Managed Heap
    MyNativeClass m_NativeObj(4);        //Stack
    MyValueClass m_ValueObj(5);          //Stack

    function_1(m_RefObj);
    function_1(m_NativeObj);
    function_1(m_ValueObj);

    return 0;
}

template< typename T >
void function_1(T% m_AnyObj)
{
    Console::WriteLine(m_AnyObj.get_Value());
}
```

VC++ supports templates and also things called generics, which we will look at in a later chapter.

3.3.   ^Managed Handle

Because a referenced object may be moved around at runtime by the common language runtime, the native C++ "*" cannot be used to point on an object on the garbage collected, or "managed," heap. In VC++.NET, ^ replaces * to declare a handle to an object on the managed heap and then uses gcnew rather than the traditional new keyword to create instances. Object member selection through this handle uses the arrow notation.

3.4. Sample Code: RefType_Example

This example will be explained in more detail in a later chapter. For now, just take note of the new ^ notation, which declares a handle to a managed object. A handle, for our purposes, operates in a fashion logically equivalent to a C++ pointer.

```
#include "stdafx.h"
#include "MyClass.h"
using namespace System;

int main(array<System::String ^> ^args)
{
    MyClass ^m_Obj=gcnew MyClass(2);
    Console::WriteLine(m_Obj->get_Value());

    return 0;
}
```

3.5. Summary

This chapter looked at the new syntax for managed references, %, and managed pointers, ^. We will be using managed references thoughout the book, so be sure you are comfortable with them before you proceed.

CHAPTER • 4

Classes and Objects

This book uses objects and object-oriented programming (OOP) to control program flow. OOP enables us to organize large programs logically and allows us to perform very large and complex tasks with fewer lines of code. Before we begin, let's review classes and objects.

An object is an instance of a class and, in addition to our own classes, Microsoft's .NET Framework gives us hundreds of ready-made classes in the .NET namespaces. We can create instances of these classes as reference types and as such they will be managed by the common language runtime (CLR).

Visual C++.NET is an object-oriented programming language. As such we will make use of classes, which have data and functionality together in their respective definitions. Classes have "member variables" or "data members" that store data and functionalities, or behaviors, held in procedures known as "methods" or "member functions." As we will see, classes may also have events associated with them. The button click is an example of an event. In a working program, different objects work together, or talk to each other, through their respective public interfaces—the collection of public methods exposed by an individual object. That is to say, private data within an object, which is not accessible from the outside world, is available to the outside programming environment only via the object's public interface. A major benefit of OOP is that because the data and methods encapsulated in classes are so closely tied together, we do not need to pass member variables back and forth as inputs to the member functions. Rather, member functions can access member variables directly within their definitions.

If you are not overly familiar with classes, Table 4-1 shows elements that make up a class. In Visual C++.NET, we can create our own user-defined classes and create objects based on them. For example, we could create a class called Instrument. In a program, a real-life, tradable instrument would be an object, i.e., an instance of the Instrument class.

Let's briefly review the four main concepts of object-oriented programming: abstraction, encapsulation, inheritance, and polymorphism.

4.1. Abstraction

Abstraction is the process of creating an abstract model of a real-world object or thing. The process consists of taking the attributes, or properties, and functionalities, or methods, of a thing and turning them into logical pieces of data and functionality.

TABLE 4-1

Member Variables	Description
Variables	Simple, primitive data.
Objects	Other types—classes, structures, interfaces, enums, etc.

Properties	Description
Property	Values of member variables can be defined and retrieved through public get and set methods using the "=" sign.

Member Functions	Description
Methods	Member functions that allow the object to do things.
Constructor	Method that runs when an instance of class is created.
Finalization	Method that runs when an object is destroyed.

Events	Description
Event	Message sent from an event source object to another object(s), called the event receiver(s).

Let's look at our Instrument class. To turn a tradable instrument into a class in Visual C++, we need to think about the properties of an instrument, i.e., what are the nouns associated with it, such as the symbol and price, as well as the verbs, or functionalities, or behaviours, of an instrument, such as setting and returning the price or entering an order. When we come up with a list of nouns, the "what it is" of an object, and verbs, the "what it does," we say that the object has been abstracted. Let's assume that we have fully abstracted our Instrument class into the nouns and verbs shown in Table 4-2.

TABLE 4-2

Nouns	Description
Symbol	The ticker symbol (unique identifier) of the instrument.
Bid	The highest bid price.
Ask	The lowest ask price.
Last Trade Price	The price at which the last trade was executed.
Last Trade Qty	The quantity of the last trade.
Bid Qty	The volume on the bid price in the exchange order book.
Ask Qty	The volume on the ask price in the exchange order book.
Expiration	The date of the expiration of the instrument, if any.

Verbs	Description
Enter Order	Sends an order to the exchange.
Cancel Order(s)	Sends a request to the exchange to cancel an order or orders.

4.2. Encapsulation

Encapsulation is the process of containing abstracted data and functionalities into a class, exposing to the outside world only those methods that absolutely must be exposed, which are then known collectively as the class' public interface. So, classes hide the implementation of their properties and methods and communicate with the external programming environment through the public interface. In this way, encapsulation protects the object from being tampered with and frees the programmer from having to know the details of the object's implementation.

In our Instrument class example, because the outside programming environment does not need to be exposed to the method of retrieving the real-time bid or ask price, this functionality is encapsulated and made invisible to the outside world.

4.3. Inheritance

Within an automated trading system, we need to represent tradable instruments in code. A futures contract is a tradable instrument, as is a stock or an option. All of these could become objects in our program so we will need to create classes for these. However, all of these are also instances of the Instrument class as we have abstracted it. The Instrument class contains only those properties and methods that are common to all tradable instruments.

In order to represent a futures contract in our program, we could create a new Futures class that inherits from the Instrument class. As such, the Futures class would inherit all the properties and methods from the base, or parent, Instrument class. The Futures class then may have some added properties or functionalities that are unique to futures contracts. Likewise, we could create an Option class that inherits from the Instrument class and has its own specific functionalities added on.

A derived class can add functionality beyond that of the base class and it can also override methods of its base class, i.e., a derived class may replace a member function definition of the base class with its own new definition.

It is important to note that Visual C++.NET provides for three types of classes—references types, value types, and unmanged types—and the abilities and intricasies of inheritance differ among the three types. As you will see, .NET's common type system dictates that all reference types inherit from the base Object class.

4.4. Polymorphism

Briefly, polymorphism allows us to have one method name, or function name, used in different derived classes, but yet have different implementations, or functionalities, associated with that name depending on the class. In a CallOption class and a PutOption class, for example, we may have inherited a BlackScholesPrice() method from the parent Option class, but yet each of the derived classes has their own method for calculation, as the equations for Black Scholes call and put pricing are different.

4.5. Memory Management in .NET

In .NET, there are four memory spaces—managed and unmanaged stacks and managed and unmanaged heaps.

4.5.1.   Managed and Unmanaged Stacks

The stack is used to store variable data of fixed length, such as integers, doubles, and booleans, but also structures and objects. There are both a managed stack and an unmanaged stack, the difference being that the managed stack is controlled by the CLR.

4.5.2.   Managed Heap

When you run a program, the CLR sets aside a contiguous region of space in memory, known as the managed heap. The managed heap always keeps a pointer to the next memory address where it will allocate the next reference type object. Because the CLR allocates and accesses memory on the managed heap by incrementing a pointer, it is faster than unmanaged heap memory allocation. In fact, it is almost as fast as stack memory allocation. The managed heap is the portion of memory controlled by the .NET Framework, which uses a garbage collector to manage the allocation and deallocation of memory space.

The heap is used to store data that has a size that can only be determined at runtime and is subject to change. The pointer to the heap address is stored on the stack.

4.5.3.   Unmanaged Heap

Unmanaged objects are allocated on the unmanaged heap, which is the standard C++ heap.

4.6.   .NET Types
4.6.1.   Value Types

A value type is any type that is represented by its actual value. Variables, structures, and enumerations are by default value types. Also, as you will see, we can create value type objects. Value type memory is allocated on the runtime stack, and deallocation occurs according to the traditional C++ scope rules. Relative to the memory spaces we have discussed:

- You can build a value type on the managed stack.
- You can build a value type on the managed heap.
- You can build a value type on the unmanaged heap as long as it contains no managed reference types.

4.6.2.   References Types

In .NET, reference (ref) types are instantiated using gcnew on the managed heap. In order for garbage collection to work properly, the CLR uses a managed reference, ^, to track the locations of all ref types on the managed heap. A managed reference is essentially a pointer whose value is known to the CLR; if the CLR moves the managed type around in memory, this value will automatically be updated. Unreferenced ref types are then subject to garbage collection. All classes in the .NET Framework libraries are reference type classes unless otherwise noted.

Furthermore, all reference type classes, whether provided by the .NET Framework or ones that we ourselves create, inherit from the Object class implicitly. Because all reference type classes in the .NET Framework are derived from Object, every method defined in the Object class is available in all objects. Relative to the memory spaces we have discussed:

- You can build a managed, reference type on the managed heap.
- You cannot build a managed, reference type on the unmanaged heap.
- You can build a managed, reference type using the native type stack notation, although the compiler actually creates the object on the managed heap anyway.

4.7. Unmanaged Types

Visual C++.NET gives you the ability to create objects outside of managed space. We call these unmanaged or native types. Using the traditional C++ syntax, we can create unmanaged, stack-based objects and heap-based objects. Relative to the memory spaces we have discussed:

- You can build a native type on the unmanaged stack.
- You can build a native type on the unmanaged heap.
- You cannot build a native type on the managed stack or heap.

4.8. Mixed Assemblies

We can, in fact, create applications in Visual C++.NET that contain both unmanaged and managed code. We call such an application a mixed assembly. Mixed assemblies allow us to take advantage of .NET components while allowing us to reuse existing unmanaged ones. As a result, migrating existing C++ applications to .NET is easy.

4.9. Summary

This chapter reviewed abstraction, encapsulation, inheritance, and polymorphism. Furthermore, we have examined four different memory locations used in VC++.NET applications. Finally, we took a brief look at value types, ref types, and unmanaged types, which will be reviewed in more depth in the coming chapters.

CHAPTER • 5

Reference Types

The ref prefix in a class or structure definition causes the lifetimes of the objects to be "managed" by the common language runtime (CLR), i.e., objects will be garbage collected automatically and you will not need to explicitly delete them unless you need to. Here are several important points to remember about managed types:

- A ref, i.e., managed, type can be instantiated on the managed heap using the gcnew operator.
- A ref class can be abstract or sealed.
- Ref types can contain pointers to unmanaged types, as we will see later.
- Ref classes can implement multiple managed interfaces.
- A ref class cannot inherit from an unmanaged one.
- An unmanaged class cannot inherit from a managed, ref one.
- A ref class cannot inherit from more than one ref class.
- Friend classes and functions are not allowed in ref types.
- A ref class cannot have const or volitile methods.
- The managed System::Object class is the ultimate base class of all ref classes.
- Calling delete on a ref type will cause the destructor (Dispose) to run, but will not deallocate it from memory and will suppress a call to a finalizer.
- Forcing garbage collection on an unreferenced ref-type object will cause its finalizer to run, assuming it has not been deleted explicitly.

A reference type can be created using the handle (or managed pointer) construct, ^, and the gcnew operator. If we assign a new instance of a class to a handle, we can reference the object's members through the arrow notation. Reference types can include classes, interfaces, delegates, and even value types.

Creating a managed reference type out of a class is a two-stage process. First, we declare the handle, which will then be a stack-based variable that holds a reference to the location of the object on the managed heap. Second, we create an instance of the class using the gcnew keyword. This is when the constructor method runs. Here is an example of showing the two-stage process:

```
Instrument ^myInstrument;
myInstrument = gcnew Instrument("ES");
```

Alternatively, we can accomplish the process using one line of code:

```
Instrument ^myInstrument = gcnew Instrument("ES");
```

In different situations it will be advantageous to use one of these two methods. As with variables, it is important to pay close attention to the scope of your reference types, which will dictate in many cases the method of instantiation.

5.1. Sample Code: RefType_Example

Now let's create a simple ref type class in Visual C++.NET.

Step 1. Open a new CLR Console Application named RefType_Example.

Step 2. Create a new managed class called MyClass with the usual .h and .cpp files. Using the class wizard helps. Select Project and then Add Class. Then select C++ and C++ class.

Step 3. Add the following code to MyClass. Be sure the "ref" keyword is before the class name declaration; this is what makes a ref type object "managed."

```
MyClass.h

#pragma once

using namespace System;

ref class MyClass
{
private:
    int m_Value;
public:
    MyClass(int);
    ~MyClass();
    int get_Value();
};
```

```
MyClass.cpp

#include "stdafx.h"
#include "MyClass.h"
```

```
MyClass::MyClass(int x)
{
    m_Value=x;
}

MyClass::~MyClass()
{
    Console::WriteLine("I'm dying!");
}
int MyClass::get_Value()
{
    return m_Value;
}
```

Step 4. Add the following code to the RefType_Example.cpp file. Be sure to #include the MyClass.h file.

```
RefType_Example.cpp

#include "stdafx.h"
#include "MyClass.h"
using namespace System;

int main(array<System::String ^> ^args)
{
    MyClass ^m_Obj=gcnew MyClass(2);
    Console::WriteLine(m_Obj->get_Value());
    delete m_Obj;

    return 0;
}
```

Any time an object is instantiated, or created, the object's constructor method executes. In this case the public constructor method accepts an integer and sets the value of m_Value, our private member variable, equal to it. By requiring that a symbol be passed to the constructor method, we prevent ourselves, or any other programmer using this class, from creating a new instance of MyClass object without an integer value.

Notice the use of the delete keyword to call what appears to be the object's destructor. In fact, ~MyClass is not a destructor at all, but rather the object's Dispose method.

5.2. Delete and Dispose

The ~MyClass implements and overrides the IDisposable::Dispose method inherited from Object, the base class of all ref type. We often use a dispose method in order to have some code execute at the end of an object's lifetime and very often this includes freeing the object's contained resources. In VC++.NET the dispose method would appear to be the logical equivalent of a destructor for a reference type. However, there are important differences.

```
ref class MyClass
{
    ~Derived()
    {
        // We free managed and unmanaged resources in the Dispose method.
    }
}
```

When we delete a reference type in .NET, the object's dispose (~MyClass) method executes. Deleting does not destroy the object. Object destruction occurs only when an unreferenced object is garbage collected at the whim of the CLR. We can also force garbage collection, as we will see. When we compile a VC++ solution, the compiler will implement the IDisposable::Dispose method and suppress any call to the Finalize method of the object after delete is called.

5.3.   Finalize

We can also create a Finalize method. A Finalize method overrides the Object::Finalize method and is called automatically anytime a reference type is destroyed during garbage collection unless it has been suppressed by a previous call to the Dispose method and is therefore exempt from finalization. Of course, there is no need to free managed resources in the Finalize method, as any reference type objects contained within the class will either be subject to garbage collection themselves or not if the other objects contain reference handles to them.

```
ref class MyClass
{
    !Derived()
    {
        // We free unmanaged resources only in the Finalize method.
    }
}
```

Calling a finalizer, though, has limitations. For example, the exact time that the finalizer will execute during garbage collection is not defined because the CLR has a special thread that is dedicated to Finalize method execution. As a result, we can never say for sure when and in what order the Finalize methods for multiple unreferenced objects will run. Furthermore, finalizers can hurt performance significantly, especially if there is synchronization, exception handling, or blocking involved. Although it is not always possible, it is preferable to avoid using a Finalize method and instead let a Dispose method and the garbage collector do their work.

This may not always be possible, however, especially when mission critical objects need to be destroyed absolutely. If, for example, some object that contains trading logic and trade execution code needs to destroyed, we should always use finalization. We don't want objects that we can't reference sending orders into the market until the CLR decides to clean it up!

5.4. Sample Code: Finalize_Example

Let's take another look at the previous example, this time using the Finalize method !MyClass() instead of the Dispose method.

```
MyClass.h

#pragma once

using namespace System;

ref class MyClass
{
private:
    int m_Value;
public:
    MyClass(int);
    !MyClass();
    int get_Value();
};
```

```
MyClass.cpp

#include "stdafx.h"
#include "MyClass.h"
MyClass::MyClass(int x)
{
    m_Value=x;
}

MyClass::!MyClass()
{
    Console::WriteLine("I'm dying!");
}

int MyClass::get_Value()
{
    return m_Value;
}
```

```
RefType_2_Example.cpp

#include "stdafx.h"
#include "MyClass.h"
using namespace System;
```

```
int main(array<System::String ^> ^args)
{
    MyClass ^m_Obj = gcnew MyClass(4);
    Console::WriteLine(m_Obj->get_Value());

    m_Obj = nullptr;
    GC::Collect();

    Console::WriteLine("All done!");

    return 0;

}
```

5.5. Stack Semantics for Ref Types

VC++ 2005 permits us to also use the traditional stack semantics with reference type objects, i.e., no gcnew. Objects instantiated in this way will nevertheless be allocated on the managed heap thanks to the compiler. When an object created in this way goes out of scope, there is no need to call delete; its Dispose method will automatically be called and the object will then be subject to garbage collection. Extra care should be taken when passing these types of objects to functions and should probably not be used at all when creating class libraries that will be used with other .NET languages. Let's look at creating an instance of MyClass in this way.

```
#include "stdafx.h"
#include "MyClass.h"
using namespace System;

int main(array<System::String ^> ^args)
{
    MyClass m_Obj(3);
    Console::WriteLine(m_Obj.get_Value());

    return 0;
}
```

5.6. Nullptr Reference

Notice that at the end of the program we set the object handles equal to nullptr. Since a handle to an object is really a variable holding a reference to the object in managed memory, we can assign it a value of nullptr (as opposed to NULL or 0 in traditional C++), thereby removing the reference. Unreferenced, managed objects are then subject to garbage collection. The object will be destroyed, but, of course, the handle lives on according to the scope with which is was declared.

5.7. This is Important

If a managed C++ object contains a method that never uses the "this" pointer (or instance data member), the method will act as if it is a static member function, i.e., the method will run even after the object has been destroyed. When the "this" pointer is used in the method definition, the runtime will detect that the "this" pointer is null and throw the appropriate exception. In C++ the difference between a static member function and an instance member function is that the instance member function has an extra, hidden parameter that is a pointer to the instance of the object on which this member function is currently operating. If the "this"pointer is never referenced, then you could make the instance member function static with no noticeable change in your program.

This is different than C#. In C# all instance member functions are called virtually even if they are nonvirtual. This forces the CLR to check that the "this" pointer is not null. In C# you cannot call an instance method with a null "this" pointer.

5.8. Summary

Over the course of this chapter, we have investigated in some detail the creation and destruction of managed, reference types in VC++.NET and the differences relative to traditional C++. While this is foundation level information, it is nevertheless extremely important to have a firm grasp of these topics before proceeding. The sample trading systems developed in later chapters use object-oriented programming, and because real money is involved in the use of actual trading systems, should you decide to build one, there is no room for error.

CHAPTER • 6

Value Types

A value type is any type that is represented by its actual value, which in some cases may be preferable for simple or short-lived objects. Value type memory is allocated on the runtime stack and not in the managed heap, and deallocation occurs according to the traditional C++ scope rules. This increases performance by removing the overhead of garbage collection for every object that is allocated and deallocated. Here are several important points to remember about value types:

- Value type declarations use the value keyword.
- Value types can contain pointers to unmanaged types.
- Value types can implement multiple ref type interfaces.
- Value types can be sealed.
- Value types can be instantiated as reference types using the gcnew keyword. As a result, they will be managed heap-based objects. Also, value types can exist on the managed heap by embedding them in ref type objects.
- Value types can be instantiated as reference types using the new keyword as long as it contains no ref types. In this case, allocation of memory will occur on the native C++ heap and not on the managed heap.
- Value types cannot inherit from an unmanaged class.
- Unmanaged classes cannot inherit from value types.
- Value types do not support inheritance, nor do they inherit from System::Object.
- Value types cannot have friend classes or functions.
- Value types cannot have const or volatile methods.

6.1.   Sample Code: ValueTypes_Example

```
MyClass.h

#pragma once

value class MyClass
{
private:
    int m_Value;
public:
    MyClass(int);
    int get_Value();
    void set_Value(int);
};
```

```
MyClass.cpp

#include "stdafx.h"
#include "./myclass.h"

MyClass::MyClass(int x)
{
    m_Value=x;
}

int MyClass::get_Value()
{
    return m_Value;
}

void MyClass::set_Value(int x)
{
    m_Value=x;
}
```

```
ValueTypes_Example.cpp
On the Stack

#include "stdafx.h"
#include "MyClass.h"
using namespace System;
```

```
int main(array<System::String ^> ^args)
{
    MyClass m_Obj(2);
    Console::WriteLine(m_Obj.get_Value());
    return 0;
}
```

```
On the Managed Heap

#include "stdafx.h"
#include "MyClass.h"
using namespace System;

int main(array<System::String ^> ^args)
{
    MyClass ^m_Obj = gcnew MyClass(2);
    Console::WriteLine(m_Obj->get_Value());
    return 0;
}
```

```
On the Unmanaged Heap

#include "stdafx.h"
#include "MyClass.h"
using namespace System;

int main(array<System::String ^> ^args)
{
    MyClass *m_Obj = new MyClass(2);
    Console::WriteLine(m_Obj->get_Value());
    return 0;
}
```

6.2. Sample Code: PassingValueTypes_Example

If we need to pass a value type object, or actually a reference to the object, back and forth, to and from a function, we can use the managed reference % syntax. Here is a short program that illustrates passing a reference to a value type back and forth to a function.

```
#include "stdafx.h"
#include "MyClass.h"
using namespace System;

MyClass %ChangeValue(MyClass %);

int main(array<System::String ^> ^args)
{
    MyClass m_Obj_1(2);
    MyClass m_Obj_2=ChangeValue(m_Obj_1);

    Console::WriteLine(m_Obj_1.get_Value());
    Console::WriteLine(m_Obj_2.get_Value());
    return 0;
}

MyClass %ChangeValue(MyClass %m_Temp)
{
    m_Temp.set_Value(3);
    return m_Temp;
}
```

6.3. Summary

This brief chapter reviewed the use of value types. Value type-ness is part of the class definition and not the method of instantiation as in traditional C++. Using value types and reference types instantiated using value type notation in the same program can cause confusion. Be aware.

CHAPTER ◆ 7

Unmanaged Objects

As discussed in previous chapters, the common language runtime controls managed code and the objects created on the managed heap and managed stack. The operating system controls unmanaged code and unmanaged memory. A complexity in VC++ comes when we have managed and unmanaged objects in the same program with pointers pointing from the managed heap into the unmanaged heap and vice versa. Here are several important points to remember about unmanaged types:

- Unmanaged types declarations are made using no prefix whatsoever.
- Unmanaged types can be instantiated on the stack.
- Unmanaged types can be instantiated on the unmanaged heap using the new operator.
- Unmanaged types can contain pointers to managed types using gcroot.
- Unmanaged classes cannot implement managed interfaces, nor can they inherit from managed classes.
- Unmanaged classes follow the traditional, native C++ syntax and functionality.

7.1. Sample Code: UnmanagedObject_Example

Here is a simple program to illustrate the creation of unmanaged types on the stack and the unmanaged heap.

```
MyClass.h

#pragma once
using namespace System;

class MyClass
{
private:
      int m_Value;
```

```
public:
    MyClass(int);
    ~MyClass();
    int get_Value();
    void set_Value(int);
};
```

MyClass.cpp

```cpp
#include "stdafx.h"
#include "./myclass.h"

MyClass::MyClass(int x)
{
    m_Value=x;
}

MyClass::~MyClass()
{
    Console::WriteLine("I'm dying!");
}

int MyClass::get_Value()
{
    return m_Value;
}

void MyClass::set_Value(int x)
{
    m_Value=x;
}
```

ManagedObject_Example.cpp
On the Stack

```cpp
#include "stdafx.h"
#include "MyClass.h"
using namespace System;

int main(array<System::String ^> ^args)
{
    MyClass m_Obj(2);
    Console::WriteLine(m_Obj.get_Value());
    return 0;
}
```

```
On the Unmanaged Heap

#include "stdafx.h"
#include "MyClass.h"
using namespace System;

int main(array<System::String ^> ^args)
{
    MyClass *m_Obj = new MyClass(2);
    Console::WriteLine(m_Obj->get_Value());
    delete m_Obj;

    return 0;
}
```

7.2. Summary

Unmanaged types are simply traditional C++ types. In VC++ we can mix managed types and unmanaged types in the same program. The reasons for doing this are determined by the nature of your project.

CHAPTER • 8

Composition

Very often, objects will have other objects as members—a relationship referred to as composition or containment. Conceptually, this can be somewhat difficult to grasp for those who are unfamiliar with object-oriented programming. Over this and the next few chapters, I will illustrate several variations on the composition theme. Remember,

- Managed types can contain pointers to unmanaged types, as shown later.
- Value types can contain pointers to unmanaged types.
- Unmanaged types can contain pointers to managed types using gcroot.

Also, it is imperative that you understand the creation and destruction of objects in your programs, which can be more difficult to conceptualize when managed objects contain reference handles to other managed objects or pointers to unmanaged ones. In these examples, pay close attention to allocation and deallocation on the managed heap.

8.1. Sample Code: Composition_Example

Here is a simple program that illustrates one object, the SystemManager object, having a member an instance of the Instrument class.

```
Instrument.h

#pragma once
using namespace System;

ref class Instrument
{
private:
    String ^mySymbol;
```

```
public:
      Instrument(String ^);
      ~Instrument(void);
      !Instrument(void);
};
```

Instrument.cpp

```
#include "StdAfx.h"
#include ".\instrument.h"

Instrument::Instrument(String ^mySym)
{
      mySymbol=mySym;
      Console::WriteLine(String::Concat(mySymbol, "created."));
}

Instrument::~Instrument(void)
{
      Console::WriteLine("Instrument dispose executing.");
}

Instrument::!Instrument(void)
{
      Console::WriteLine("Instrument dying!");
}
```

SystemManager.h

```
#pragma once
#include "Instrument.h"

ref class SystemManager
{
private:
      Instrument ^m_Instr;

public:
      SystemManager(void);
      ~SystemManager(void);
      !SystemManager(void);

      void CreateInstrument(String ^);
};
```

SystemManager.cpp

```
#include "StdAfx.h"
```

```
#include ".\systemmanager.h"

SystemManager::SystemManager(void)
{
}


SystemManager::~SystemManager(void)
{
      delete m_Instr;
      Console::WriteLine("SystemManager dispose executing.");
}

SystemManager::!SystemManager(void)
{
      Console::WriteLine("SystemManager dying!");
}

void SystemManager::CreateInstrument(String ^m_S)
{
      m_Instr=gcnew Instrument(m_S);
}
```

In the main function, notice that the delete call is commented out. Calling delete would automatically suppress any call to the objects' finalizers. Causing the finalizers to run by setting the reference handle equal to nullptr and forcing garbage collection gives us better control over managed memory, although at the expense of performance.

```
Composition_Example.cpp

#include "stdafx.h"
#include "SystemManager.h"
using namespace System;

int main(array<System::String ^> ^args)
{
      SystemManager ^m_Manager=gcnew SystemManager;
      m_Manager->CreateInstrument("IBM");

      Console::WriteLine("Deleting objects:");
      //delete m_Manager;

      Console::WriteLine("Collecting objects:");
      m_Manager=nullptr;
      GC::Collect();
      Console::WriteLine("All done!");

      return 0;
}
```

There is no need to free managed resources in the Finalize method of SystemManager, as the reference type object, m_Instr, contained within the class is unreferenced as well and therefore subject to garbage collection itself or else may also persist if any other living, referenced object contains a reference handle to it.

8.2. Sample Code: UnmanagedComposition_Example

Here is a program where a managed object, an instance of ManagedClass, has as one of its members an unmanaged object, an instance of UnmanagedClass. In this case a pointer in managed memory is pointing to a memory location in the unmanaged heap.

```
ManagedClass.h

#pragma once
#include "UnmanagedClass.h"

ref class ManagedClass
{
private:
    UnmanagedClass *m_Unmanaged;
public:
    ManagedClass();
    ~ManagedClass(void);
    !ManagedClass(void);
    char *get_UnmanagedName();
};
```

```
ManagedClass.cpp

#include "StdAfx.h"
#include ".\managedclass.h"

ManagedClass::ManagedClass()
{
    m_Unmanaged = new UnmanagedClass("Hello");
}

ManagedClass::~ManagedClass(void)
{
    delete m_Unmanaged;
    Console::WriteLine("Managed object deleted.");
}

ManagedClass::!ManagedClass(void)
{
    delete m_Unmanaged;
    Console::WriteLine("Managed object destroyed");
}
```

```
char *ManagedClass::get_UnmanagedName()
{
        return m_Unmanaged->get_Name();
}
```

UnmanagedClass.h

```
#pragma once
using namespace System;

class UnmanagedClass
{
private:
      char *myName;
public:
      UnmanagedClass(char *);
      ~UnmanagedClass(void);
      char *get_Name();
};
```

UnmanagedClass.cpp

```
#include "StdAfx.h"
#include ".\unmanagedclass.h"

UnmanagedClass::UnmanagedClass(char *myS)
{
      myName=myS;
}

UnmanagedClass::~UnmanagedClass(void)
{
      Console::WriteLine("Unmanaged object destroyed.");
}
char *UnmanagedClass::get_Name()
{
      return myName;
}
```

UnmanagedComposition_Example.cpp

```
#include "stdafx.h"
#include "ManagedClass.h"

using namespace System;
```

```
int main(array<System::String ^> ^args)
{
    ManagedClass ^m_Managed = gcnew ManagedClass;

    // Convert char * to String first, then write line.
    Console::WriteLine(gcnew String(m_Managed->get_UnmanagedName()));

    //delete m_Managed;
    m_Managed = nullptr;
    GC::Collect();

    Console::WriteLine("All done!");
    return 0;
}
```

Finally, let's take a look at the case where an unmanaged object contains a managed object. In this instance, we are attempting to have a pointer in unmanaged memory point to a memory location in the managed heap. This, however, is not valid.

8.3. Sample Code: ManagedComposition_Example

In order to make this possible, we need to use gcroot, a type-stage template wrapper, which is found in the header file vcclr.h. Note that gcroot uses the System::Runtime:: InteropServies::GCHandle namespace, which provides a handle into the managed heap. The CLR will maintain the managed, reference handle. If the CLR moves the managed object during compaction, the location of the managed object will not be lost. As shown in a later chapter, we do not need to "pin" a managed object before we use gcroot.

```
UnmanagedClass.h

#pragma once

#include "ManagedClass.h"
#include <vcclr.h>

using namespace System;

class UnmanagedClass
{
private:
    gcroot < ManagedClass ^ > m_Managed;

public:
    UnmanagedClass();
    ~UnmanagedClass(void);
    String ^get_ManagedName();
};
```

```
UnmanagedClass.cpp

#include "StdAfx.h"
#include ".\unmanagedclass.h"

UnmanagedClass::UnmanagedClass()
{
    m_Managed = gcnew ManagedClass("Hello");
}

UnmanagedClass::~UnmanagedClass(void)
{
    //delete m_Managed;
    Console::WriteLine("Unamanged object destroyed.");
}

String ^UnmanagedClass::get_ManagedName()
{
    return m_Managed->get_Name();
}
```

```
ManagedClass.h

#pragma once
using namespace System;

ref class ManagedClass
{
private:
    String ^m_Name;

public:
    ManagedClass(String ^);
    ~ManagedClass(void);
    !ManagedClass(void);
    String ^get_Name();
};
```

```
ManagedClass.cpp

#include "StdAfx.h"
#include ".\managedclass.h"

ManagedClass::ManagedClass(String ^m_S)
{
    m_Name = m_S;
}
```

```
ManagedClass::~ManagedClass(void)
{
    Console::WriteLine("Managed object deleted.");
}
ManagedClass::!ManagedClass(void)
{
    Console::WriteLine("Managed object destroyed.");
}
String ^ManagedClass::get_Name()
{
    return m_Name;
}
```

```
ManagedComposition_Example.cpp

#include "stdafx.h"
#include "UnmanagedClass.h"
using namespace System;

int main(array<System::String ^> ^args)
{
    UnmanagedClass *m_Unmanaged = new UnmanagedClass;
    Console::WriteLine(m_Unmanaged->get_ManagedName());

    delete m_Unmanaged;
    GC::Collect();

    Console::WriteLine("All done!");
    return 0;
}
```

Notice in this example that when the unmanaged object is deleted, the contained managed object becomes unreferenced and is therefore then subject to garbage collection, which causes the managed object's Finalize method to run, albeit on a different thread than that of the destructor of the unmanaged object, which may be observable when you execute the program.

8.4.   Summary

This chapter investigated some important topics related to objects containing other objects. Object-oriented programs often pass references to objects back and forth, and gaining intuition on object-oriented architecture is not always easy. It would certainly be beneficial at this point to create some additional programs that make use of object containment to familiarize yourself with basic object-oriented design concepts.

CHAPTER • 9

Properties

In Visual C++.NET the property keyword allows us to define the get and set methods around a private data member and to access it using the equals sign.

9.1.   Sample Code: Properties_Example

In this example, we can get and set the value of m_Qty property via the Qty property.

```
SystemManager.h

#pragma once

ref class SystemManager
{
private:
    int m_Qty;

public:
    SystemManager(void) {}
    ~SystemManager(void) {}

    property int Qty
    {
        int get()
        {
            return m_Qty;
        }
        void set(int value)
        {
            m_Qty=value;
        }
    }
};
```

```
Properties_Example.cpp

#include "stdafx.h"
#include "SystemManager.h"
using namespace System;

int main(array<System::String ^> ^args)
{
      SystemManager ^m_Manager = gcnew SystemManager;
      m_Manager->Qty = 100;

      Console::WriteLine(m_Manager->Qty);
      return 0;
}
```

9.2.   Summary

This very brief chapter reviewed the VC++.NET syntax for properties.

CHAPTER ◆ 10

Structures and Enumerations

In .NET, structures can be value types or reference types. Value type structures will be stored on the stack. Managed, ref, structures will be reference types and thus stored on the managed heap. We use value type structures when we need a type to act like a primitive data type.

10.1. Sample Code: ValueStructure_Example

In this example, we can get and set the public elements of the structure directly.

```
Tick.h

#pragma once
using namespace System;

value struct Tick
{
    double Price;
    int Volume;
    DateTime Time;
};
```

```
ValueStructure_Example.cpp

#include "stdafx.h"
#include "Tick.h"
using namespace System;

int main(array<System::String ^> ^args)
{
    Tick m_Tick;
    m_Tick.Price=105.25;
```

```
    m_Tick.Volume = 100;
    m_Tick.Time = DateTime::Now;

    Console::WriteLine(m_Tick.Price);

    return 0;
}
```

10.2.   Sample Code: ReferenceStructure_Example

In this example, we can get and set the public elements of the structure directly through the pointer.

```
Bar.h

#pragma once

ref struct Bar
{
    double Open;
    double High;
    double Low;
    double Close;
    double Volume;
};
```

```
ReferenceStructure_Example.cpp

#include "stdafx.h"
#include "Bar.h"
using namespace System;

int main(array<System::String ^> ^args)
{
    Bar ^m_Bar = gcnew Bar;

    m_Bar->Open = 100.00;
    m_Bar->High = 101.50;
    m_Bar->Low = 99.78;
    m_Bar->Close = 99.80;
    m_Bar->Volume = 150000;

    Console::WriteLine(m_Bar->Close);

    return 0;
}
```

10.3. Sample Code: Enums_Example

An enumeration, or an enum, is a special kind of user-defined value type. An enum allows us to provide alternate names for the values of integers. However, we cannot define methods within an enum, nor can we add properties or events.

```
Enums.h

#pragma once

enum class MarketClass
{
    TRENDING, SIDEWAYS
};

enum class Position
{
    FLAT, LONG, SHORT
};
```

```
Enums_Example.cpp

#include "stdafx.h"
#include "Enums.h"
using namespace System;

int main(array<System::String ^> ^args)
{
    MarketClass myMarket=MarketClass::TRENDING;
    Position myPosition=Position::LONG;

    if (myPosition==Position::LONG && myMarket==MarketClass::TRENDING)
    {
        Console::WriteLine("We are long and the market is trending.");
    }
    return 0;
}
```

10.4. Summary

This brief chapter looked at the VC++.NET syntax for structures and enums. Using enumerations can make complicated trading system logic more readable.

CHAPTER ◆ 11

Inheritance

The rules for inheritance in VC++ 2005 are different from those of ISO C++. Here they are:

- Managed classes can implement multiple managed interfaces.
- A ref class cannot inherit from an unmanaged one.
- An unmanaged class cannot inherit from a managed one.
- A managed class cannot inherit from more than one managed class.
- The managed System::Object class is the ultimate base class of all managed classes.
- Value types cannot inherit from an unmanaged class.
- Unmanaged classes cannot inherit from value types.
- Value types do not support inheritance, nor do they inherit from System::Object.

11.1. Access Modifiers

To briefly review, Table 11-1 shows the available access modifiers that have important implications for inheritance of member variables and methods.

TABLE 11-1

Access Modifier	Scope
Public	Accessible anywhere.
Private	Accessible only by methods of the class. Derived class methods cannot access Private properties or methods.
Protected	Accessible by base class and derived class methods.

11.2. Object Class

As mentioned previously, all ref type classes .NET, whether provided by the .NET Framework or ones that we ourselves create, inherit from the Object class implicitly. As a result, while we do not explicitly declare inheritance from the Object class, all classes inherit its methods (Table 11-2).

TABLE 11-2

Object Class Method	Description
Equals	Used for comparison between objects.
Finalize	Protected method that runs prior to garbage collection.
GetHashCode	Used when employing hash tables.
GetType	Returns the type of the object.
ReferenceEquals	Used to determine if two objects are the same.
ToString	Used for a string representation of an object.

11.3. Abstract and Sealed Classes

To create abstract class in .NET, we postfix the class declaration with an abstract. Thus, we will not be able to create an instance of the class. To use an abstract class, we must create an instance of a class that inherits from the abstract class.

```
ref class MyClass abstract
```

To create a class that cannot be inherited from or to create a class method that cannot be overridden, we postfix the class or method declaration with sealed. Thus, we are not able to use the sealed class as a base class or, in the case of a sealed method, override its base class definition.

```
ref class MyClass sealed
```

11.4. Sample Code: Inheritance_Example

Here is a simple example illustrating inheritance with managed classes.

MyParent.h

```
#pragma once

ref class MyParent
{
protected:
      int m_Value;
public:
      MyParent(int);
      int Increase_Value(int);
};
```

MyParent.cpp

```
#include "StdAfx.h"
#include ".\myparent.h"

MyParent::MyParent(int m_V)
{
      m_Value=m_V;
}

int MyParent::Increase_Value(int m_V)
{
      m_Value += m_V;
      return m_Value;
}
```

MyChild.h

```
#pragma once
#include "MyParent.h"

ref class MyChild : public MyParent
{
public:
      MyChild(int);
      int Decrease_Value(int);
};
```

```
MyChild.cpp

#include "StdAfx.h"
#include ".\mychild.h"

MyChild::MyChild(int m_V) : MyParent(m_V)
{
}

int MyChild::Decrease_Value(int m_V)
{
    m_Value-=m_V;
    return m_Value;
}
```

```
Inheritance_Example.cpp

#include "stdafx.h"
#include "MyChild.h"

using namespace System;

int main(array<System::String ^> ^args)
{
    MyChild ^m_Obj=gcnew MyChild(5);

    Console::WriteLine(m_Obj->Increase_Value(3));
    Console::WriteLine(m_Obj->Decrease_Value(6));

    return 0;
}
```

11.5. Interfaces

While interfaces cannot contain data or class members or any static members, they can, much like a class, contain methods, properties, and events, with one important difference. An interface does not supply definitions for its methods; it simply declares the public members that comprise it. The classes that implement the interface must supply the definitions. In general though, base class inheritance is preferred to interface implementation because new functionality is added more easily with classes. Adding a method to an interface will cause any implementing class to break, as it will not provide a definition. Using inheritance, derived classes will simply inherit the base class definition throughout the entire program structure.

Also, as with class inheritance, only managed classes can implement managed interfaces. As a result, in a sense a managed interface is essentially an abstract base class, whose methods are purely virtual ones implicitly.

11.6. Sample Code: Interface_Example

Here is a simple example illustrating the implementation of an interface named ITradable.

```
ITradable.h

#pragma once
using namespace System;

interface class ITradable
{
public:
    String ^EnterOrder(String ^, double, double, String ^);
    bool CancelOrder(String ^);
};
```

```
Instrument.h

#pragma once
#include "ITradable.h"

using namespace System;

ref class Instrument : public ITradable
{
public:
    Instrument(void);
    ~Instrument(void);

    virtual String ^EnterOrder(String ^, double, double, String ^);
    virtual bool CancelOrder(String ^);
};
```

```
Instrument.cpp

#include "StdAfx.h"
#include ".\instrument.h"

Instrument::Instrument(void)
{
}

Instrument::~Instrument(void)
{
}
```

```
String ^Instrument::EnterOrder(String ^m_BuySell, double m_Qty, double m_Price, String
                                               ^m_Text)
{
    return "12345";
}
bool Instrument::Cancelorder(String ^m_OrderID)
{
    return true;
}
```

```
Interface_Example.cpp

#include "stdafx.h"
#include "Instrument.h"
using namespace System;

int main(array<System::String ^> ^args)
{
    Instrument ^m_Instr=gcnew Instrument();
    Console::WriteLine(m_Instr->Enterorder("BUY", 10, 52.50, "ATS"));
    return 0;
}
```

11.7.   Runtime Callable Wrapper

While managed objects cannot inherit from unmanaged objects, the .NET Framework does provide for inheritance from COM coclasses by way of the runtime callable wrapper. As a result, a managed class can expose all of the methods from an unmanaged COM object. We will look at this topic in more depth in a later chapter.

11.8.   Summary

This chapter reviewed some of the idiosyncrasies of inheritance in VC++.NET, which differs from both traditional C++ and other .NET languages due to the inclusion on unmanaged types. Furthermore, we looked at the Object class, which is the ultimate base class for all managed classes. Finally, we reviewed interfaces, which are essentially pure abstract classes.

CHAPTER • 12

Converting and Casting

12.1. Converting

The Convert class contains methods that convert primitive data types to other types. The supported types are Boolean, Char, SByte, Byte, Int16, Int32, Int64, UInt16, UInt32, UInt64, Single, Double, Decimal, DateTime, and String ^, and a method exists to convert every type to every other type. Although invalid conversions will throw exceptions, those that result in a loss of precision will not, e.g., converting a double to a single will not throw an exception.

12.2. Sample Code: Convert_Example

Because most of the types supported by the Convert class also implement the IConvertible interface, Convert class method calls can usually be invoked from the type instance itself, as shown in this example.

```
#include "stdafx.h"

using namespace System;

int main(array<System::String ^> ^args)
{
    double m_Double=2.71828;
    String ^m_String=Convert::ToString(m_Double);

    Console::WriteLine(m_String);
    Console::WriteLine(m_Double.ToString());

    // This also works in 2005.
    Console::WriteLine(m_Double);

    return 0;
}
```

12.3.   Static Casting

We use static casting when we want to convert a numeric data type from one type to another, e.g., if we wanted to convert a double to an int. The danger with a static cast is that because no runtime check is performed, we are left to our own devices to make sure no data are lost in the conversion.

12.4.   Sample Code: StaticCast_Example

```
#include "stdafx.h"

using namespace System;

int main(array<System::String ^> ^args)
{
    int i = 1;
    double d;

    d = static_cast< double >(i);
    Console::WriteLine(d);

    return 0;
}
```

12.5.   Dynamic Casting

We use dynamic casts to convert a pointer to an object to a pointer to an object of a different class. Dynamic casts only work on pointers and, relative to static casts, are safer because a runtime check is performed. This, however, adds overhead to the operation.

We will make use of dynamic casts often, especially because many operations within the .NET Framework's class libraries return a pointer to an instance of the Object class, which will then be converted to a pointer to an object of a specific, derived class in order to access a public member.

12.6.   Sample Code: DynamicCast_Example

```
MyParent.h

#pragma once

ref class MyParent
{
public:
    MyParent(void);
    double Square(double);
};
```

MyParent.cpp

```cpp
#include "StdAfx.h"
#include ".\myparent.h"

MyParent::MyParent(void)
{
}

double MyParent::Square(double x)
{
      return x * x;
}
```

MyChild.h

```cpp
#pragma once
#include "MyParent.h"

ref class MyChild:
      public MyParent
{
public:
      MyChild(void);
      double Cube(double);
};
```

MyChild.cpp

```cpp
#include "StdAfx.h"
#include ".\mychild.h"

MyChild::MyChild(void)
{
}

double MyChild::Cube(double d)
{
      return d * d * d;
}
```

```
DynamicCast_Example.cpp

#include "stdafx.h"
#include "MyParent.h"
#include "MyChild.h"
using namespace System;

int main(array<System::String ^> ^args)
{
     MyChild ^m_Child=gcnew MyChild;
     MyParent ^m_Parent=m_Child;
     Console::WriteLine(dynamic_cast< MyChild ^ >(m_Parent)->Cube(3));

     return 0;
}
```

12.7.   Safe Casting

The safe cast method, which functions similar to dynamic cast, will automatically throw an exception of type System::InvalidCastException if a casting operation fails.

12.8.   Sample Code: SafeCast_Example

```
#include "stdafx.h"
#include "MyParent.h"
#include "MyChild.h"
using namespace System;

int main(array<System::String ^> ^args)
{
    MyParent ^m_Parent=gcnew MyParent;

    try
    {
       MyChild ^m_Child=safe_cast< MyChild ^ >(m_Parent);
    }
    catch(System::InvalidCastException ^e)
    {
       Console::WriteLine(e->Message);
    }

     return 0;
}
```

12.9. Summary

This chapter discussed the Convert class and the IConvertible interface. Furthermore, it looked at static and dynamic casting and the new safe cast that is part of the .NET Framewok.

CHAPTER • 13

Operator Overloading

Overloading operators in managed, Visual C++.NET are the same as in ISO C++. For VC++, Table 13-1 shows a list of operators.

The operator keyword declares a function that defines what the particular operator means when applied to an instance of the class. This of course gives the operator multiple meanings, i.e., it is overloaded and the VC++ compiler deciphers the particular usage. We can redefine most operators on a class-by-class basis.

13.1. Sample Code: OpOverload_Example

This example illustrates the use of VC++.NET operator overloading for a managed reference type.

```
MyClass.h

#pragma once

ref class MyClass
{
private:
    int m_Value;

public:
    MyClass(int);
    int get_Value();
    MyClass ^operator+(MyClass ^);
    bool operator==(MyClass ^);
};
```

TABLE 13-1

Unary Operator	Description	Usage
--	op_Decrement	operator--
++	op_Increment	operator++
!	op_Negation	operator!
-	op_UnaryNegation	operator-
+	op_UnaryPlus	operator+

Binary Operator	Description	Usage
+	op_Addition	operator+
=	op_Assign	operator=
&	op_BitwiseAnd	operator&
|	op_BitwiseOr	operator|
/	op_Division	operator/
==	op_Equality	operator==
^	op_ExclusiveOr	operator^
>	op_GreaterThan	operator>
>=	op_GreaterThanOrEqual	operator>=
!=	op_Inequality	operator!=
<<	op_LeftShift	operator<<
<	op_LessThan	operator<
<=	op_LessThanOrEqual	operator<=
&&	op_LogicalAnd	operator&&
||	op_LogicalOr	operator||
%	op_Modulus	operator%
*	op_Multiply	operator*
>>	op_RightShift	operator>>
-	op_Subtraction	operator-

```
MyClass.cpp

#include "StdAfx.h"
#include ".\myclass.h"

MyClass::MyClass(int m_V)
{
     m_Value=m_V;
}

int MyClass::get_Value()
{
     return m_Value;
}
```

```
MyClass ^MyClass::operator+(MyClass ^m_Right)
{
        return gcnew MyClass(m_Value+m_Right->get_Value());
}
bool MyClass::operator==(MyClass ^m_Right)
{
        return m_Value==m_Right->get_Value();
}
```

```
ReferenceType_Example.cpp

#include "stdafx.h"
#include "MyClass.h"
using namespace System;

int main(array<System::String ^> ^args)
{
      MyClass ^m_Obj_1=gcnew MyClass(1);
      MyClass ^m_Obj_2=gcnew MyClass(2);

      Console::WriteLine(m_Obj_1==m_Obj_2);

      MyClass ^m_Obj_3=m_Obj_1+m_Obj_2;
      Console::WriteLine(m_Obj_3->get_Value());

      return 0;
}
```

13.2. Summary

This brief chapter showed that the VC++ syntax for operator overloading is essentially the same as the traditional C++ syntax.

CHAPTER • 14

Delegates and Events

Automated trading systems are event-driven applications (EDAs). Unlike traditional applications, which follow their own program flow, event-driven programs react to external events, in our case to events that occcur on electronic exchanges, namely changes in bid and ask prices and ladder volumes and trades. EDAs are programmed with event loops, to look repeatedly for new information and then execute a trigger function. As a result, programming a trading system is a matter of writing the trigger functions that gather the new information and make trading decisions. These trigger functions are called event handlers. The CLR controls a dispatcher, which will call the event handlers using a queue to hold unprocessed events.

14.1. Delegates

In .NET, a delegate is a managed reference type that is essentially a pointer to a static function or instance method. However, a delegate cannot just point to any function, it must point to a function with a specific signature according to the declaration of its type. We use the delegate's Invoke() method, inherited from the base System::Delegate class, to call the function(s) to which the delegate points; delegates can point to more than one function, called multicasting. As we will see, we can call a delegate's Combine() and Remove() methods to add and remove pointers to the list of functions to be invoked. We could even call them asynchronously if need be. Alternatively, a delegate could be single cast and point to only one function.

When we create a new delegate object, we must pass in to its constructor the name of the class and the fully qualified name of the method to which it will point. For static methods, the class name should be omitted. If the method to which the delegate points returns a value, then the delegate will return the value. In the case of multicasting, the delegate will return the value of the last function invoked. Also, be careful with multicasting; if an invoked function receives a reference type as a parameter and alters it, all subsequently invoked functions in the list will receive the altered object.

14.2.   Sample Code: Delegates_Example

Here is a simple example that shows the declaration of the delegate type MyDelegate Handler(). m_Del1 and m_Del2 are the actual delegate objects themselves and point to the MathOps::Square() method as a static class member and as an object method, respectively. In this case, use of the & operator in the delegate constructor is optional.

```
MathOps.h

#pragma once

ref class MathOps
{
public:
        MathOps(void);
        ~MathOps(void);

        static double Square(double);
        double Cube(double);
};
```

```
MathOps.cpp

#include "StdAfx.h"
#include ".\mathops.h"

MathOps::MathOps(void)
{
}

MathOps::~MathOps(void)
{
}

double MathOps::Square(double d)
{
    return d * d;
}

double MathOps::Cube(double d)
{
    return d * d * d;
}
```

```
Delegates.h

#pragma once

delegate double MyDelegateHandler(double);
```

```
Delegates_Example.cpp

#include "stdafx.h"
#include "Delegates.h"
#include "MathOps.h"

using namespace System;

int main(array<System::String ^> ^args)
{
    // Create a delegate of type MyEventHandler that points to static
    // MathOps class member square.
    MyDelegateHandler ^m_Del1=gcnew MyDelegateHandler(&MathOps::Square);

    Console::WriteLine(m_Del1->Invoke(3.0));

    // Create an instance of MathOps object myOps.
    MathOps ^m_Ops=gcnew MathOps();

    // Create a new delegate of type MyEventHandler that points
    // to instance member square.
    MyDelegateHandler ^m_Del2=gcnew MyDelegateHandler(m_Ops, &MathOps::Cube);

    Console::WriteLine(m_Del2->Invoke(4.0));

    return 0;
}
```

14.3. Multicasting

By default, delegates are multicastable and can call several functions when invoked. When a multicast delegate is invoked, the functions in the invocation list are called synchronously.

14.4. Sample Code: Multicast_Example

In this program, there are two class, MyClass_1 and MyClass_2, each with a static method named Update(). Using the MyDelegateHandler type declaration, we create several delegates and Combine() and Remove() to demonstrate multicasting.

Delegates.h

```
#pragma once

delegate void MyDelegateHandler(double);
```

Multicast_Example.cpp

```cpp
#include "stdafx.h"
#include "Delegates.h"
using namespace System;

ref class MyClass_1
{
public:
    static void Update(double d)
    {
        Console::WriteLine("Class_1 received: " +d);
    }
};

ref class MyClass_2
{
public:
    static void Update(double d)
    {
        Console::WriteLine("Class_2 received: " +d);
    }
};

int main(array<System::String ^> ^args)
{
    MyDelegateHandler ^myH_1=gcnew MyDelegateHandler(&MyClass_1::Update);
    MyDelegateHandler ^myH_2=gcnew MyDelegateHandler(&MyClass_2::Update);

    MyDelegateHandler ^myH_3=dynamic_cast< MyDelegateHandler ^ >
                                (Delegate::Combine(myH_1, myH_2));

    myH_3->Invoke(3.0);

    MyDelegateHandler ^myH_4=dynamic_cast< MyDelegateHandler ^ >
                                (Delegate::Combine(myH_3, myH_3));

    myH_4->Invoke(4.0);

    MyDelegateHandler ^myH_5=dynamic_cast< MyDelegateHandler ^ >
                                (Delegate::Remove(myH_3, myH_1));

    myH_5->Invoke(5.0);

    return 0;
}
```

When myH_3 is invoked, both delegate myH_1 and myH_2 are invoked in order, as they are part of the invocation list of myH_3. When myH_4 is invoked, myH_3 is invoked twice, which subsequently invokes myH_1 and myH_2 each twice. When delegate myH_5 is created, myH_3 is added to the list, but myH_1 is removed from myH_3. As a result, when myH_5 is invoked, only myH_2 runs. Here is what the output should be:

Class_1 received: 3

Class_2 received: 3

Class_1 received: 4

Class_2 received: 4

Class_1 received: 4

Class_2 received: 4

Class_2 received: 5

14.5. Events

There are times when an object will need to notify other parts of our program that something has happened, that an event has occurred. Say, for example, the bid and ask price of the E-Mini S&P 500 futures contract changes. Our program has to have a way to communicate the occurrence of that event to other objects. We accomplish this through the use of delegates to communicate from the object that raises, or sends or fires or triggers, the event to the object that receives it.

The .NET can raise events using delegates. When the event is raised, an event handler method will execute. Microsoft provides a predefined delegate, EventHandler, generally for events that do not pass in data. For events in this text, which usually will pass in data, we will, for simplicity, pass in the data directly (as int or double or String ^) as opposed to creating a class to hold the event data. Nonetheless, the standard signature of an event handler is a void return type and two input parameters—a pointer to the object that raised the event and an object that holds the event data, which is normally derived from the EventArgs class.

In order to subscribe to an event, i.e., to associate an event handler with an event, we add a new instance of the delegate. The following program illustrates this process. As in the previous two programs, the MyEventHandler delegate declaration is made and MyClass contains an event object, OnUpdate, that is an instance of this delegate. In the Button1_Click method, a new SystemManager object is created. Next, we subscribe to the OnUpdate event, i.e., we associate a method in Form1, OnUpdate_Handler, with the event. This method will handle the event from the SystemManager object. Like this:

```
m_Obj->OnUpdate += gcnew MyEventHandler(this, &Form1::OnUpdate_Handler);
```

When the OnUpdate event is raised, program control will transfer to the associated function.

14.6.   Sample Code: Event_Example

Create the GUI as shown and add the appropriate code (see Figure 14-1).

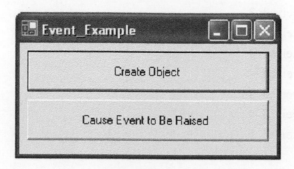

FIGURE 14-1

```
MyClass.h

#pragma once
#include "Delegates.h"

ref class MyClass
{
private:
      double m_Value;

public:
      MyClass(void);

      event MyEventHandler ^OnUpdate;
      void CauseEvent();
};
```

```
MyClass.cpp

#include "StdAfx.h"
#include ".myclass.h"

MyClass::MyClass(void)
{
      m_Value=25;
}
```

```
void MyClass::CauseEvent()
{
        OnUpdate(m_Value);
}
```

Delegates.h
```
#pragma once

delegate void MyEventHandler(double);
```

Form1.h
```
#pragma once
#include "Delegates.h"
#include "MyClass.h"

namespace Event_Example
{
   using namespace System;
   using namespace System::ComponentModel;
   using namespace System::Collections;
   using namespace System::Windows::Forms;
   using namespace System::Data;
   using namespace System::Drawing;

public ref class Form1 : public System::Windows::Forms::Form
{
// Windows generated code here.

private: MyClass ^m_Obj;

private: System::Void button1_Click(…)
{
   m_Obj = gcnew MyClass;
   m_Obj->OnUpdate += gcnew MyEventHandler(this, &Form1::OnUpdate_Handler);
}
private: System::Void button2_Click(…)
{
   m_Obj->CauseEvent();
}

private: void OnUpdate_Handler(double x)
{
   MessageBox::Show("Event raised: "+x);
}

};
}
```

At times it will be necessary to disassociate the delegate. Because delegates are pointers, objects that are unreferenced but contain active delegates will not be garbage collected. Disassociation is done thusly:

```
m_Obj->OnUpdate -= gcnew MyEventHandler(this, &Form1::OnUpdate_Handler);
```

14.7.   Wrappers

As shown in previous chapters, we cannot have pointers in unmanaged objects pointing to locations in managed memory. By using the gcroot, we can contain a pointer to a managed object in an unmanaged object. As a result, in this example, Form1 contains a pointer to MyClass, an unmanaged class, and MyClass contains a pointer to Form1. In this case then, when we need to raise an event, we can simply call the appropriate method in Form1. Notice in the program that Form1 implements the Icallback interface.

14.8.   Sample Code: Wrapper_Example

Create the GUI and add the code shown in Figure 14–2.

```
MyClass.h

#pragma once
#include "Icallback.h"
#include <vcclr.h>

class MyClass
{
private:
     gcroot < Icallback ^ > m_Form;

public:
     MyClass(Icallback ^);
     void Square(double a);
};
```

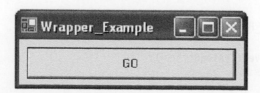

FIGURE 14-2

```
MyClass.cpp

#include "StdAfx.h"
#include ".\myclass.h"

MyClass::MyClass(Icallback ^m_Form1)
{
      m_Form=m_Form1;
}

void MyClass::Square(double a)
{
      m_Form->UpdateForm((a*a).ToString());
}
```

```
Icallback.h

#pragma once

interface class Icallback
{
      public:
            System::Void UpdateForm(System::String ^m_Value);
};
```

```
Form1.h

#pragma once
#include "Icallback.h"
#include "MyClass.h"

namespace Wrapper_Example
{
   using namespace System;
   using namespace System::ComponentModel;
   using namespace System::Collections;
   using namespace System::Windows::Forms;
   using namespace System::Data;
   using namespace System::Drawing;

public ref class Form1 : public System::Windows::Forms::Form, public Icallback
{
// Windows generated code here.

private: MyClass *m_Obj;
```

```
private: System::Void button1_Click(…)
{
    m_Obj=new MyClass(this);
    m_Obj->Square(3.5);
}

public: virtual void UpdateForm(String ^m_Value)
{
    button1->Text=m_Value;
}
};
}
```

14.9.   Asynchronous Method Calls

Using objects in the System::Threading namespace, we can call, or invoke, methods and have them run on separate threads. In this simple example, we see how to call methods asynchronously.

14.10.   Sample Code: AsynchEvent_Example

In this CLR Console Application, we will first need to add that we are using namespace System::Threading. (Later chapters will look at threading in more detail.)

```
#include "stdafx.h"
using namespace System;
using namespace System::Threading;
```

Now let's add a class with a single method, Add. We will sleep the thread that is running the method to simulate some long running process.

```
MyClass.h
ref class MyClass : public ContextBoundObject
{
public:
    int Add(int a, int b)
    {
        // Simulate some work being done by putting this thread to sleep.
        Thread::Sleep(1000);
        // We're not on the Main thread anymore!
        Console::WriteLine("Thread: "+Thread::CurrentThread->Name);
        return a+b;
    }
};
```

We can run methods asynchronously, i.e., on separate threads, using the IAsyncResult design pattern and delegate methods BeginInvoke() and EndInvoke(). In this example, after calling BeginInvoke on a delegate, our main function will continue executing on the Main thread, while the method MyClass::Add runs on a different thread, which has no name. We then call EndInvoke() to get the return value.

Let's create a delegate that will point to MyClass::Add.

```
delegate int MyDelegate(int, int);
```

The MyDelegate::BeginInvoke() method accepts the input parameters of the method its delegate points to, an AsyncCallback delegate that points to a separate method to be called when the asynchronously called method completes, and a state object. For simplicity, we have set these last two parameters to nullptr.

The return value of the MyDelegate::EndInvoke() method is the same type returned by the MyClass::Add method that the delegate points to. The EndInvoke has a parameter the IAsyncResult returned by the previous and corresponding BeginInvoke call. If the asynchronously called operation has not yet completed when EndInvoke is called, EndInvoke will block the calling thread until the method completes its work. In this example, we cause the MyClass::Add method to pause for 5 seconds. Notice that after BeginInvoke, the main function does not wait for the MyClass::Add method to finish executing before it continues. Then, the main function, running on the main thread, will wait at EndInvoke() until MyClass::Add is finished.

```
AsynchEvent_Example.cpp

int main(array<System::String ^> ^args)
{
    // Name the current thread.
    Thread::CurrentThread->Name = "Main";
    MyClass ^m_Obj = gcnew MyClass;

    // Call the Add method asynchronously, passing in 2 and 3.
    MyDelegate ^m_Delegate = gcnew MyDelegate(m_Obj, &MyClass::Add);
    IAsyncResult ^m_Result = m_Delegate->BeginInvoke(2, 3, nullptr, nullptr);

    // Main thread does not wait for operation to complete.
    Console::WriteLine(Thread::CurrentThread->Name + " is waiting.");

    // We could explicitly block the Main thread until the method call to
    // complete.
    // m_Result->AsyncWaitHandle->WaitOne();
    // We could check to see if the method is complete.
    // if (m_Result->IsCompleted)

    int m_Value = m_Delegate->EndInvoke(m_Result);
    Console::WriteLine("Return value: " + m_Value);
    return 0;
}
```

14.11. Summary

Because automated trading systems are event-driven applications, it is absolutely imperative to understand the delegate/event structures in .NET. This chapter covered the basics, enough to get started, but additional time researching more advanced topics would be well worth the effort. Further, we briefly investigated the asynchronous pattern for calling methods. The Event-based Asynchronous Pattern, for use in multithreaded applications, and the BackgroundWorker class in the Visual Studio Documentation help files are worthy topics for additional research. Again, we will review multithreading in .NET more in later chapters.

CHAPTER ◆ 15

Arrays

Here is a simple program used to illustrate the use of .NET's managed arrays. Notice that because arrays are reference types in .NET, there are several member functions that we can take advantage of, most notably the GetUpperBound() method; managed arrays are self-aware and know their own size.

15.1. Sample Code: ManagedArray_Example

```
#include "stdafx.h"

using namespace System;

int main(array<System::String ^> ^args)
{
    // One dimensional managed array.

    int m_Sum=0;

    array< int > ^m_1DArray=gcnew array< int >(5);

    for (int x=0; x<=m_1DArray->GetUpperBound(0); x++)
    {
        m_1DArray[x]=x;
        m_Sum+=m_1DArray[x];
    }
    Console::WriteLine(m_Sum);

    // Sort the array
    Array::Sort(m_1DArray);

    // Two dimensional managed array.
```

```
    int m_2DSum=0;
    array< int, 2 > ^m_2DArray=gcnew array< int, 2 > (5, 5);
    for (int i=0; i<=m_2DArray->GetUpperBound(0); i++)
    {
        for (int j=0; j<=m_2DArray->GetUpperBound(1); j++)
        {
            m_2DArray[i, j]=i*j;
            m_2DSum+=m_2DArray[i, j];
        }
    }
    Console::WriteLine(m_2DSum);

    // Managed jagged array.

    int m_JaggedSum=0;
    array< array< int > ^ >^ m_JaggedArray=gcnew array< array< int > ^ >(5);
    for (int i=0; i<=m_JaggedArray->GetUpperBound(0); i++)
    {
        m_JaggedArray[i]=gcnew array< int >(5);
        for (int j=0; j<=m_JaggedArray[i]->GetUpperBound(0); j++)
        {
            m_JaggedArray[i][j]=i*j;
            m_JaggedSum+=m_JaggedArray[i][j];
        }
    }
    Console::WriteLine(m_JaggedSum);

    return 0;
}
```

15.2.   Sample Code: PassingArrays_Example

Here is a simple CLR console application program that illustrates passing managed arrays to and from a function.

```
#include "stdafx.h"

using namespace System;

// Prototype a function that accepts and returns a managed array.
array< int > ^DefineElements(array< int > ^m_InArray);

int main(array<System::String ^> ^args)
{
    array< int > ^m_Array_A=gcnew array< int >(5);
```

```
    array< int > ^m_Array_B=DefineElements(m_Array_A);

    Console::WriteLine(m_Array_B[4]);

    return 0;
}

array< int > ^DefineElements(array< int > ^m_InArray)
{
      int a=0;

      // Using for..each, when the identifier is a tracking reference,
      // we can modify the element.
      for each (int %x in m_InArray)
      {
          x=a++;
      }
      return m_InArray;
}
```

15.3. Summary

In VC++.NET we can make use of managed arrays that are reference types. The methods of the array class make using them much easier than native C++ arrays. Also, we saw that arrays can be passed to and from functions.

```
array<int>^ Array::DefineElements(array<int>^ Array )
{
    consta.extra[index:Array[id]];

    return 0;

    array<int>^ ^DefineElements(array<int>^ >^ m_Library)

        int x=0;

        // Using for, each, when the identifier is a pointer reference,
        //   we can modify the element.
        for each (int x in m_Library)
        {
            x;&&;

            centre m_library[];
        }
}
```

15.3. Summary

In VC++.NET we can make use of managed arrays that are reference types. The methods of the array class make using them much easier than native C++ arrays. Also, we saw that arrays can be passed to and from functions.

CHAPTER • 16

Generating Random Numbers

A System::Random object will generate uniform deviates, which are accessible through its NextDouble() method. Also, it will be necessary to seed the generator through the constructor, which we can accomplish using a time-dependent value.

16.1. Sample Code: Random_Example

This example demonstrates the generation of uniform, zero to one, deviates using the Random class.

```
#include "stdafx.h"

using namespace System;

int main(array<System::String ^> ^args)
{
    Random ^m_Random=gcnew Random(DateTime::Now.Millisecond);
    for (int x=0; x < 100; x++)
    {
        Console::WriteLine(m_Random->NextDouble().ToString());
    }
    return 0;
}
```

16.2. Sample Code: StdNormRandom_Example

In this example, the StdNormRandom class inherits from Random and provides the NextSNRnd() method to generate random numbers drawn from the standard normal distribution.

StdNormRandom.h

```
#pragma once

ref class StdNormRandom : public System::Random
{
public:
     StdNormRandom(int);
     ~StdNormRandom(void);
     double NextSNRnd();
};
```

StdNormRandom.cpp

```
#include "StdAfx.h"
#include ".\stdnormrandom.h"

StdNormRandom::StdNormRandom(int Seed) : Random(Seed)
{
}

StdNormRandom::~StdNormRandom(void)
{
}

double StdNormRandom::NextSNRnd()
{
     return Random::Sample()+Random::Sample()+Random::Sample()+
            Random::Sample()+Random::Sample()+Random::Sample()+
            Random::Sample()+Random::Sample()+Random::Sample()+
            Random::Sample()+Random::Sample()+Random::Sample()- 6.0;
}
```

StdNormRandom_Example.cpp

```
#include "stdafx.h"
#include "StdNormRandom.h"

using namespace System;

int main(array<System::String ^> ^args)
{
     StdNormRandom ^m_Random=gcnew StdNormRandom(DateTime::Now.Millisecond);
     for (int x=0; x < 100; x++)
```

```
    {
        Console::WriteLine(m_Random->NextSNRnd().ToString());
    }
    return 0;
}
```

16.3. Summary

This chapter showed how to use the Random class to generate uniform deviates. Furthermore, we inherited from Random to add a function that generates standard normal deviates.

CHAPTER • 17

Time and Timers

A millisecond is one thousandth of a second. A microsecond is one millionth of a second, or one thousandth of a millisecond. A nanosecond is one billionth of a second, or one thousandth of a microsecond, and is the unit of measure for logical operation on a digital circuit and within the .NET Framework. Time values in .NET are measured in 100-nanosecond increments, called ticks. The time value is represented by a 64-bit integer value type called a long long and is contained by the DateTime value type structure. Although DateTime has precision to the nanosecond, the accuracy is usually significantly less depending on the system.

Nonetheless, using the DateTime type, we can add, subtract, and compare times, and the TimeSpan structure can be used to represent an interval of time. On my desktop the precision of both of these types is to the eighth of a millisecond, which is demonstrated in the following code example. Here is an example of a date and time represented as a long long integer.

```
00:13:05.3593750 on Sunday, February 26, 2005
632450599853593750
```

17.1. Sample Code: Milliseconds_Example

```
#include "stdafx.h"

using namespace System;
using namespace System::Threading;

int main(array<System::String ^> ^args)
{
    // Set starting time.
    DateTime m_StartTime=DateTime::Now;
    Console::WriteLine(m_StartTime.ToString("HH:mm:ss.fffffff"));
```

```
    // Pause execution for one second.
    Thread::Sleep(1000);

    // Set ending time.
    DateTime m_EndTime=DateTime::Now;
    Console::WriteLine(m_EndTime.ToString("HH:mm:ss.fffffff"));

    // Show time span in milliseconds.
    TimeSpan m_TimeSpan=m_EndTime - m_StartTime;
    Console::WriteLine(m_TimeSpan.Ticks.ToString());

    // Add time.
    DateTime m_LaterTime=m_EndTime.Add(m_TimeSpan);
    Console::WriteLine(m_LaterTime.ToString("HH:mm:ss.fffffff"));

    // Show the end time in milliseconds as long long.
    long long m_LongEndTime=m_EndTime.Ticks;
    Console::WriteLine(m_LongEndTime.ToString());

    // Show time span in milliseconds as long long.
    long long m_LongTimeSpan=m_TimeSpan.Ticks;
    Console::WriteLine(m_LongTimeSpan.ToString());

    // Compare times.
    if (m_StartTime < m_EndTime)
    {
        Console::WriteLine("True");
    }
    else
    {
        Console::WriteLine("False");
    }

    return 0;
}
```

17.2. Stopwatch

A System::Diagnostics::Stopwatch object will track time in ticks—100-nanosecond increments. Depending on your computer and your version of Windows, however, an instance
of a Stopwatch in your program may or may not support high-resolution performance
counting. If not, a Stopwatch object will use the system timer instead. You can use the
IsHighResolution property to determine whether or not your system will support a high-
resolution counter.

17.3. Sample Code: Stopwatch_Example

```
#include "stdafx.h"

using namespace System;
using namespace System::Diagnostics;
using namespace System::Threading;

int main(array<System::String ^> ^args)
{
    Stopwatch ^m_Stopwatch = gcnew Stopwatch;

    Console::WriteLine("Starting: ");

    m_Stopwatch->Start();

    Thread::Sleep(1000);

    m_Stopwatch->Stop();

    Console::WriteLine(m_Stopwatch->ElapsedTicks);
    Console::WriteLine(m_Stopwatch->IsHighResolution);

    m_Stopwatch->Reset();

    return 0;
}
```

17.4. Timers

A timer is an object that raises event at regular intervals. The .NET Framework gives us three timer controls:

1. System::Windows::Forms::Timer
2. System::Threading::Timer
3. System::Timers::Timer

The System::Windows::Forms::Timer is designed for single-threaded threaded applications. While it is optimized to work with Windows, the accuracy of this timer is limited to 55 milliseconds.

17.5. Sample Code: FormsTimer_Example

For this program, open a new Windows Forms Application (NET) and place a single button on the form. The button1_Click should simply create an instance of the SystemManager class. When the Timer is enabled, it will print "Tick" to the Output window at 1-second intervals.

```
SystemManager.h

#pragma once
using namespace System::Diagnostics;
using namespace System::Windows::Forms;

ref class SystemManager
{
private:
    Timer ^m_Timer;
    void OnTimerTick(Object ^, System::EventArgs ^);

public:
    SystemManager(void);
};
```

```
SystemManager.cpp

#include "StdAfx.h"
#include ".\systemmanager.h"

SystemManager::SystemManager(void)
{
    m_Timer = gcnew Timer;
    m_Timer->Interval = 1000;
    m_Timer->Tick += gcnew System::EventHandler(this, &SystemManager::OnTimerTick);
    m_Timer->Enabled = true;
}

void SystemManager::OnTimerTick(Object ^Source, System::EventArgs ^e)
{
    Debug::WriteLine("Tick.");
}
```

```
Form1.h

SystemManager ^m_Manager;

private: System::Void button1_Click(…)
{
    m_Manager = gcnew SystemManager();
}
```

The System::Threading::Timer is a server-based timer and differs from the other two in that it uses callback methods rather than events and is served by threadpool threads.

17.6. Sample Code: ThreadingTimer_Example

```
MyClass.h

#pragma once
using namespace System;
using namespace System::Threading;

ref class MyClass
{
private:
     Timer ^m_Timer;
     AutoResetEvent ^m_Ready;
     int m_Counter;

public:
     MyClass(void);
     void OnTimerCallback(Object ^);
     AutoResetEvent ^get_AutoResetEvent();
};
```

```
MyClass.cpp

#include "StdAfx.h"
#include ".\myclass.h"

MyClass::MyClass(void)
{
   m_Ready=gcnew AutoResetEvent(false);
   m_Timer=gcnew Timer(gcnew TimerCallback(this, &MyClass::OnTimerCallback), nullptr, 0,
                                         1000);
}

AutoResetEvent ^MyClass::get_AutoResetEvent()
{
     return m_Ready;
}

void MyClass::OnTimerCallback(Object ^Source)
{
     Console::WriteLine((++m_Counter).ToString());
     if (m_Counter == 10)
     {
          m_Ready->Set();
     }
}
```

```
ThreadingTimer_Example.cpp

#include "stdafx.h"
#include "MyClass.h"
using namespace System;

int main(array<System::String ^> ^args)
{
        MyClass ^m_Obj=gcnew MyClass;
        m_Obj->get_AutoResetEvent()->WaitOne();

        Console::WriteLine("Finished counting.");
        return 0;
}
```

The System::Timers::Timer is a server-based timer and is designed to be used in a multithreaded environment. Because it is server based and because it can move among threads, this timer is much more accurate than the Windows.Forms-based timer.

17.7. Sample Code: TimersTimer_Example

```
MyClass.h

#pragma once
using namespace System;
using namespace System::Timers;
using namespace System::Threading;

ref class MyClass
{
private:
        System::Timers::Timer ^m_Timer;
        AutoResetEvent ^m_Ready;
        int m_Counter;

public:
        MyClass(void);
        ~MyClass(void);
        void OnTimerElapsed(Object ^, ElapsedEventArgs ^);
        AutoResetEvent ^get_Ready();
};
```

```
MyClass.cpp

#include "StdAfx.h"
#include ".\myclass.h"

MyClass::MyClass(void)
{
    m_Ready=gcnew AutoResetEvent(false);
    m_Timer=gcnew System::Timers::Timer(1000);
    m_Timer->Elapsed+=gcnew ElapsedEventHandler(this, &MyClass::OnTimerElapsed);
    m_Timer->Start();
}

MyClass::~MyClass(void)
{
}

AutoResetEvent ^MyClass::get_Ready()
{
    return m_Ready;
}

void MyClass::OnTimerElapsed(Object ^Source, ElapsedEventArgs ^e)
{
    Console::WriteLine((++m_Counter).ToString());
    if (m_Counter==10)
    {
        m_Timer->Stop();
        m_Ready->Set();
    }
}
```

```
TimersTimer_Example.cpp

#include "stdafx.h"
#include "MyClass.h"

using namespace System;

int main(array<System::String ^> ^args)
{
    MyClass ^m_Obj=gcnew MyClass;
    m_Obj->get_ Ready()->WaitOne();

    Console::WriteLine("Finished counting.");
    return 0;
}
```

17.8.   Summary

This chapter looked at the precision with which time can be measured in a computer. This precision will vary from machine type to machine type. Also, we looked at three different types of timers that the .NET Framework contains. For simple applications, the Forms timer is usually sufficient, but for larger, multithreaded applications that require more control and precision, one of the other two will be needed.

CHAPTER • 18

Input and Output Streams

The System::IO namespace contains (1) types that allow for reading and writing to files and data streams and (2) types that provide basic file and directory support. This chapter looks at a few of them.

18.1. FileStream Class

A FileStream object exposes a Stream that enables synchronous and asynchronous read and write operations on byte streams. We also use FileStreams to open and close files on a file.

The FileStream methods Read and Write allow for synchronous input and output, and the methods BeginRead, BeginWrite, EndRead, and EndWrite will actually work in either synchronous or asynchronous mode. Although FileStreams default to opening files for synchronous input and output, the overloaded constructor allows us to open them from asynchronous reading and writing.

18.2. StreamWriter Class

The StreamWriter class implements the abstract TextWriter class and enables us to write characters and Strings to a stream. The alternative writers and readers, such as the FileStream class, inherit from the Stream class and enable byte input and output.

18.3. File and Directory Classes

The File class contains static methods for creating, copying, deleting, moving, and opening files. In order to use the methods of the File class, we will need to supply the full pathname to the appropriate file.

The Directory class contains static methods for creating, moving, and enumerating through directories and subdirectories.

18.4.   Application Class

The abstract Application class provides static methods that enable us to manage an application. These methods include Run, which will run an application on the current thread, and Exit, which will stop the application. The StartUpPath property will return the pathname to the directory in which the program is located.

18.5.   FileMode Enumeration

FileMode is an enumeration that specifies how the operating system should open a particular file. The values are Append, Create, CreateNew, Open, OpenOrCreate, and Truncate.

18.6.   Sample Code: StreamWriter_Example

```cpp
#include "stdafx.h"

using namespace System;
using namespace System::IO;
using namespace System::Windows::Forms;

int main(array<System::String ^> ^args)
{
    FileStream ^m_FileStream;
    StreamWriter ^m_Writer;

    // Check to see if the file already exists.
    String ^m_Data=String::Concat(Application::StartupPath, "\\MyData.txt");
    if (File::Exists(m_Data))
    {
        m_FileStream=gcnew FileStream(m_Data, FileMode::Append);
        Console::WriteLine("File exists");
    }
    else
    {
        m_FileStream=gcnew FileStream(m_Data, FileMode::Create);
        Console::WriteLine("File created");
    }

    // Write data to the file.
    m_Writer=gcnew StreamWriter(m_FileStream);
    m_Writer->WriteLine("Hello, world!");
    m_Writer->Flush();

    // Close the file.
    m_FileStream->Close();
    return 0;
}
```

18.7. Sample Code: StreamReader_Example

```
#include "stdafx.h"
using namespace System;
using namespace System::IO;
int main(array<System::String ^> ^args)
{
    StreamReader ^m_Reader;

    // Check to see if the file already exists.
    String ^m_Data ="C:\\Temp\\MyData.txt";
    if (File::Exists(m_Data))
    {
        m_Reader=gcnew StreamReader(m_Data);
        Console::WriteLine("File exists.");
    }
    else
    {
        Console::WriteLine("File does not exist.");
        return 0;
    }

    // Read data from the file.
    String ^m_String;

    while((m_String=m_Reader->ReadLine())!=nullptr)
    {
        Console::WriteLine(m_String);
    }

    // Close the reader.
    m_Reader->Close();
    return 0;
}
```

18.8. Summary

The System::IO namespace contains many classes that aid in writing to and reading from files. This chapter focused on the FileStream and StreamWriter and StreamReader classes. Also, the Application and File classes contain static methods that allow us to navigate around the file hierarchy on the system.

CHAPTER • 19

Exception Handling

Exception handling is the process of catching and dealing with runtime errors as they occur. In code, an exception is actually an object. Exceptions occur (or are thrown at a "throw point") in procedures that are not able to handle them and they will propagate back out to the calling procedure. If that calling method is unable to handle it, it is then again transmitted back to the method calling it and so on. In this way, the CLR searches for an exception handler and will continue up the series of procedure calls until it finds one. If no handler is ever found, the CLR displays an error message and shuts the program down. We can build in to our programs exception handlers to catch exceptions before they become errors.

Within a Try..Catch block, the Try block will usually contain some code that may generate an error. For example, if we are trying to connect to some external piece of software, data feed, or database, a problem beyond our control may occur and create an error. When an exception occurs, code execution terminates immediately and the CLR searches the available Catch statements and executes the first one that is able to handle an exception of that type. Within a Try…Catch block there are one or more Catch statements, each specifying an optional exception parameter, which represents a unique exception type.

The optional Finally block can contain code that will always execute, regardless of whether an exception is thrown. Because it will always run immediately before the Try… Catch block loses scope, the Finally block is usually an excellent location to place a deallocation code to, for example, close files or connections or release objects.

19.1. Sample Code: Exceptions_Example

One way to correct logic errors in our programs before they create problems is to perform validation before using a value. For example, the .NET Framework's common language runtime allows division by zero. Division by zero will produce an infinity, and other mathematical errors will produce a NaN value, for "not a number." To account for these types of problems, we can validate numerical values using the methods of the Double structure—IsInfinity and IsNaN.

```
#include "stdafx.h"

using namespace System;
int main(array<System::String ^> ^args)
{
    double m_Value, m_Ratio;
    Console::WriteLine("Enter a Number: ");
    try
    {
        m_Value = Convert::ToDouble(Console::ReadLine());
        m_Ratio = 1 / m_Value;
        if ( Double::IsInfinity(m_Ratio ))
        {
            throw gcnew DivideByZeroException;
        }
        else
        {
            Console::WriteLine(m_Ratio);
        }
    }
    catch (DivideByZeroException ^e)
    {
        Console::WriteLine(String::Concat("Division Error: ", e->Message));
    }
    catch (Exception ^e)
    {
        Console::WriteLine(String::Concat("Data Error: ", e->Message));
    }
    finally
    {
        Console::WriteLine("Thanks for playing.");
    }
    return 0;
}
```

Notice the use of the two catch statements. Run the program once and enter 0 at the prompt. The Double::IsInfinity validation will evaluate to true and throw the managed DivideByZeroException. Try the program again and enter characters. This time the division itself will throw an Exception, which will be caught by the second catch block.

19.2. Catching Unmanaged C++ Types

When unmanaged C++ code throws an object, the CLR will wrap it with an object of type System::Runtime::InteropServices::SEHException. If the object is a native C++ type and a native type catch block containing a native type can handle it, the object will be unwrapped and handled in the normal way. If a catch block containing the managed type SEHException or any of its base classes is encountered first, the managed catch block will handle the exception. To handle any unmanaged exception, we can use catch (Object ^), which will catch any thrown type, including SEH exceptions.

When throwing or catching unmanaged C++ exceptions, either the /EHs or the /EHa C++ exception handling compiler options must be turned on, which should be the case by default.

19.3. Summary

The .NET Framework contains classes for exception handling in much the same way that traditional C++ does. Unmanaged exceptions can be caught, too.

CHAPTER ◆ 20

Collections

The .NET Framework gives us several collection classes in the System::Collections namespace. While classes in STL.NET (which is not available as of publication of this text) are preferred to these (especially for experienced programmers), it is worthwhile to be aware of these classes (Table 20-1).

In addition, the System::Collections namespace contains the IEnumerator and IDictionaryEnumerator, which support enumeration over list and dictionary collections, respectively.

TABLE 20-1

Class	Description
Array List	List collection that uses a dynamically sized array.
Hashtable	Dictionary collection that uses key and value pairs.
Queue	A first-in, first-out collection.
Sorted List	A sorted dictionary collection of key and value pairs.
Stack	A last-in, first-out collection.

20.1. Sample Code: Hashtable_Example

A Hashtable is a collection of key and value pairs. In this example, several Element objects will be added to the Hashtable. Notice the method for retrieving an item in the Hashtable using the bracket notation for the default item method.

```
Element.h

#pragma once

ref class Element
{
private:
    int m_Number;

public:
    Element(int x) : m_Number(x) {}
    property int Number
    {
       int get()
       {
           return m_Number;
       }
       void set(int value)
       {
           m_Number=value;
       }
    }
};
```

```
Hashtable_Example.cpp

#include "stdafx.h"
#include "Element.h"

using namespace System;
using namespace System::Collections;

int main(array<System::String ^> ^args)
{
    Hashtable ^m_Hash=gcnew Hashtable;
    for (int x=0; x<20;x++)
    {
        m_Hash->Add(x, gcnew Element(x));
    }
    Element ^m_Element=dynamic_cast< Element ^ >(m_Hash[7]);
    Console::WriteLine(m_Element->Number);

    return 0;
}
```

20.2. Sorted List Class

A SortedList is a collection of key and value pairs that are sorted by key. Because of this sorting, this collection class combines the functionality of both list type and dictionary type collections. As a result, elements in the collection are accessible by either their unique key or their zero-based index. Be aware that the sorting process of a SortedList will have implications on performance relative to a Hashtable, which has no sorting. In general though, the flexibility of the SortedList usually makes it an attractive collection to work with.

20.3. Sample Code: SortedList_Example

In this example, Element objects are added to a SortedList. In the first section, the elements are accessed by index as with a list. In the second, they are accessed by enumeration using for..each.

```
SortedList_Example.cpp

#include "stdafx.h"
#include "Element.h"
using namespace System;
using namespace System::Collections;

int main(array<System::String ^> ^args)
{
    // Create a SortedList and add four elements.
    SortedList ^m_SortedList=gcnew SortedList;
    m_SortedList->Add("A", gcnew Element(1));
    m_SortedList->Add("B", gcnew Element(2));
    m_SortedList->Add("C", gcnew Element(3));
    m_SortedList->Add("D", gcnew Element(4));

    int a;
    // Loop through the SortedList by index.
    for (int x=0; x <= 3; x++)
    {
        a=dynamic_cast< Element ^ >(m_SortedList->GetByIndex(x))->Number;
        Console::WriteLine(a.ToString());
    }

    // Enumerate through the SortedList.
    IDictionaryEnumerator ^m_Enum=m_SortedList->GetEnumerator();
    while (m_Enum->MoveNext())
    {
        a=dynamic_cast< Element ^ >(m_Enum->Value)->Number;
        Console::WriteLine(a.ToString());
    }
```

```
    // Use for..each to iterate throught SortedList.
    for each(DictionaryEntry ^x in m_SortedList)
    {
        a=dynamic_cast< Element ^ >(x->Value)->Number;
        Console::WriteLine(a.ToString());
    }
    return 0;
}
```

20.4. Thread Safety

It may be the case in a multithreaded application that more than one enumerator is reading a collection at the same time. SortedLists support this functionality as long as one thread does not modify the collection in the process. To guarantee thread safety in this case, all operations on the elements of a SortedList should be done through a thread-safe wrapper provided for by the collection's Synchronized method.

However, enumeration is not a thread-safe procedure even when the collection is synchronized. Other threads could still modify the collection, causing an error. The only way to guarantee thread safety is to lock the collection during the enumeration or to catch the exceptions thrown by changes being made by other threads.

In a later chapter we will look more closely at synchronizing and locking.

20.5. Generics

We can also create generic collections using the classes in the System::Collections::Generic namespace, including Dictionary, List, and LinkedList. Generic collections allow us to create strongly typed collections that provide better type safety and performance than non-generic collections. Here is an example showing the use of the LinkedList generic class.

20.6. Sample Code: LinkedList_Example

```
MyClass.h

#pragma once

ref class MyClass
{
private:
    int m_Value;
public:
    MyClass(int x) : m_Value(x) {}
    int get_Value() { return m_Value; }
};
```

```
LinkedList_Example.cpp

#include "stdafx.h"
#include "MyClass.h"

using namespace System;
using namespace System::Collections::Generic;

int main(array<System::String ^> ^args)
{
    LinkedList < MyClass ^ > ^m_List=gcnew LinkedList< MyClass ^ >;
    for (int x=0; x < 10; x++)
    {
        m_List->AddFirst(gcnew MyClass(x));
    }
    m_List->AddLast(gcnew MyClass(25));
    m_List->RemoveFirst();

    for each(MyClass ^x in m_List)
    {
        Console::WriteLine(x->get_Value().ToString());
    }

    return 0;
}
```

Here is an example showing the syntax to create your own generic type. Any managed type can potentially be generic.

20.7. Sample Code: Generics_Example

```
MyClass.h

#pragma once

generic<typename T>
public ref class MyClass
{
private:
    T m_Value;

public:
    MyClass(T);
    T get_Value();
};
```

```
MyClass.cpp

#include "StdAfx.h"
#include "MyClass.h"

generic<typename T>
MyClass<T>::MyClass(T v)
{
      m_Value=v;
}


generic< typename T >
T MyClass< T >::get_Value()
{
      return m_Value;
}
```

```
Generics_Example.cpp

#include "stdafx.h"
#include "MyClass.h"

using namespace System;

int main(array<System::String ^> ^args)
{
     MyClass<int> ^m_Obj=gcnew MyClass<int>(3);

     Console::WriteLine(m_Obj->get_Value());
     return 0;
}
```

Classes in the System::Collections namespace use the base Object type to store elements. Usually, we have to explicitly cast a pointer to an Object as a pointer to some other type when accessing it as a collection member. Strongly typed generic collections solve this problem.

There are subtle differences between generics and traditional C++ templates. For example, templates are instantiated at compile time, whereas generics are compiled at run time. However, both are type safe.

20.8.   Summary

This chapter examined the System::Collections and System::Collections::Generic namespaces. Because we use multiple instances of the same class so often, it is important to learn to manage groups of objects using collections. The following chapter will continue this discussion and look at the new STL.NET technology, which should make things much easier for those familiar with the C++ standard template library.

CHAPTER · 21

STL/STL.NET

Standard Template Library classes are available as unmanaged types to our VC++ 2005 projects. In addition, Microsoft is developing STL.NET, which is not yet available to a wider audience as of writing of this text.

STL.NET will allow the traditional STL collection classes, with their traditional interfaces, to be used as managed types. For VC++ 2005, the header files for STL.NET will be contained in a directory named "cli" or "cliext" in the VC\include directory and including anyone of them will be accomplished by adding the cliext path, e.g., <cli/vector>.

21.1. Sample Code: STL.NET_Example

```
#include "stdafx.h"
#include <cli/vector>

using namespace System;
using namespace cli;

int main(array<System::String ^> ^args)
{
    vector<String ^> ^m_Vector=gcnew vector<String ^>;
    m_Vector->push_back("Hello");
    return 0;
}
```

Again, STL.NET is not yet available. Microsoft has said that it should be available as a web download sometime soon. In the meantime, you can still use the traditional STL with unmanaged types.

21.2. Sample Code: STL_Example

```
#include "stdafx.h"
#include <vector>

using namespace System;

using namespace std;

int main(array<System::String ^> ^args)
{
    vector< int > m_Vector;
    m_Vector.push_back(3);
    m_Vector.push_back(4);

    Console::WriteLine(m_Vector.at(1));

    return 0;
}
```

21.3. Summary

The parameterization model implemented by the System::Collections classes is cumbersome to work with and furthermore is unsafe. In general, one would not use these classes in real-world applications in all but the simplest applications and instead would use the System::Collections::Generic classes. (Although for simplicity's sake I will continue to use the former in later examples.) However, when your applications address real-world problems, you need to provide more sophisticated solutions. The System::Collections::Generic library consists of collections based on a more conventional C++ model. STL.NET, which we have looked at briefly in this chapter, will be an even better solution still, especially for experienced C++ programmers who are used to STL. Besides, STL.NET will provide better performance.

CHAPTER • 22

DataSets

A DataSet can be thought of as in-memory representation of a relational database, complete with tables, columns, rows, and relationships, but is separate and distinct from any data source; does not interact directly with the database; and is only a cache of data, with database-like structures within it. DataSets can be used for storing, remoting, and programming against flat, XML, and relational data.

There are the many important public properties and methods of the DataSet class, including the Tables property that returns a pointer to a table in the collection of DataTables.

DataSets are made up of a collection of DataTables and DataRelations. DataTables are in turn made up of collections of DataColumns, DataRows, and Constraints. As with a database, the actual data is contained in the Rows collection of DataRow objects, and constraints maintain the data, entity, and relational integrity of the data through the ForeignKeyConstraints, the UniqueContraints, and the PrimaryKey. The DataRelation collection acts as an interface between related rows in different tables (Table 22-1).

In the following code sample, we will see code snippets to build a DataSet with a DataTable. In many situations, however, an OleDbDataAdapter will build these structures automatically. Nonetheless, because an understanding of how a DataSet is constructed is absolutely necessary, we will build a DataSet from the ground up.

TABLE 22-1

DataSet Object

DataTable Collection	DataRelation Collection
Columns (DataColumnCollection)	
DataColumns	
Rows (DataRowCollection)	
DataRows	
Constrains	
Constraint	

22.1.   Sample Code: DataSet_Example

Step 1.   Create a new CLR Console Application program named DataSet_Example.
Step 2.   In the main function, create a new DataSet.

```
DataSet ^m_DataSet=gcnew DataSet;
```

Because DataTables actually hold the data in a DataSet, DataTables are the main topic of discussion. A DataTable holds a Columns collection, which defines the table's schema; a Rows collection, which contains the records in DataRow objects; and Constraints, which ensure the integrity of the data along with the PrimaryKey of the DataTable. We can add a DataTable to a DataSet's collection of Tables using the overloaded Add method.

Step 3.   Now create a DataTable.

```
DataTable ^m_DataTable=gcnew DataTable("MyStockData");
```

The DataTable's Columns property returns a pointer to a DataColumnCollection, an object that holds a collection of DataColumn objects and defines the schema of the table. Usually the DataColumnCollection is defined automatically by a DataAdapter's Fill method, and we can then access the DataColumnCollection through the DataTable's Columns property. Because the DataColumnCollection inherits from the CollectionBase class, it uses the Add, Remove, Item, and Count methods to insert, delete, get a specified DataColumn from, and count the number of DataColumn objects within it. As we will see, in some cases, we may want to define the schema ourselves using the DataTable's Columns properties and methods.

We can add DataColums to the DataColumnCollection using the Columns.Add method.

Step 4.   Create a DataColumn and add it to the DataTable.

```
DataColumn ^m_DataColumn=gcnew DataColumn("ClosingPrices");
m_DataTable->Columns->Add(m_DataColumn);
```

22.2.   Rows, DataRowCollections, and DataRows

The Rows property of a DataTable returns a reference to a DataRowCollection, a collection that contains the data in DataRow objects. Because the DataRowCollection inherits from the Collection class, it uses the Add, Remove, Item, and Count methods to insert, delete, get a specified DataRow from, and count the number of DataColumn objects within it. As a result, we can add DataRows to the DataTable through its Rows property using the Rows.Add method.

Step 5. Create a new DataRow, adding it to the DataTable, and define a value for the first row's item 0.

```
m_DataTable->Rows->Add(m_DataTable->NewRow());
m_DataTable->Rows[0][0]=65.24;
```

Step 6. Finally, add the DataTable to the DataSet.

```
m_DataSet->Tables->Add(m_DataTable);
```

We can reference a specific cell to retrieve the data:

```
Console::WriteLine(m_DataSet->Tables[0]->Rows[0][0]->ToString());
```

Let's take a look at the entire program.

```
#include "stdafx.h"

using namespace System;
using namespace System::Data;

int main(array<System::String ^> ^args)
{
    // Create a DataSet, a DataTable and a DataColumn.
    DataSet ^m_DataSet=gcnew DataSet;
    DataTable ^m_DataTable=gcnew DataTable("MyStockData");
    DataColumn ^m_DataColumn=gcnew DataColumn("ClosingPrices");

    m_DataTable->Columns->Add(m_DataColumn);
    m_DataTable->Rows->Add(m_DataTable->NewRow());
    m_DataTable->Rows[0][0]=65.24;
    m_DataSet->Tables->Add(m_DataTable);

    Console::WriteLine(m_DataSet->Tables[0]->Rows[0][0]->ToString());
    return 0;
}
```

22.3. Summary

This chapter looked specifically at the DataSet object. A DataSet is a collection of DataTables, which are themselves collections of DataColumns and DataRows. DataSets are an important part of Microsoft's ADO.NET model, which we will review in a later chapter.

CHAPTER • 23

Connecting to Databases

ADO.NET is an application programming interface for interaction with data sources using .NET programming code. ADO.NET consists of a proprietary set of Microsoft objects that allow developers to access and efficiently manage data from relational and nonrelational databases, including MS Access, Sybase, MS SQL Server, Oracle, and even Excel just to name a few. As a result, if we need to write a program that provides connection to a database, we can use ADO.NET objects in our application to perform database transactions. The System::Data namespace consists of the subnamespaces and classes that constitute Microsoft's ADO.NET architecture.

ADO.NET is part of an overall Microsoft data access strategy for universal data access, which attempts to permit connectivity to the vast array of existing and future data sources. (Using the optimized objects in the System::Data::SqlClient namespace, we can connect to MS SQL Server databases.) In order for universal data access to work, Microsoft provides for interfaces between .NET programs and third-party data sources. This is where OleDb comes in.

Using the objects in the System::Data::OleDb namespace we can connect to OleDb data sources. OleDb objects enable connection to just about any data source.

The primary focus of this chapter is on the ADO.NET classes that enable us to open a connection to a data source, get data from it, and put the data into a DataSet, which we examined in a previous chapter. We can then close the connection to the data source. In a nutshell, ADO.NET allows us to connect to and disconnect from a data source, get data from a data source, and view and manipulate data. We will then look at an alternative to the DataSet construct and use a DataReader.

23.1. Database Connection

To interact with a database, we first need to establish a persistent connection to it through the use of an OleDbConnection object, which represents a unique connection to a data source. An instance of this class specifies the connection provider and the name and path of the database to which our application will connect.

119

23.2.   DataAdapter

An OleDbDataAdapter is a conduit object that allows us to retrieve data from a database using Structured Query Language, which we will look at in depth in a later chapter. Then, if need be the DataAdapter can also send updated data back to the database to make changes in the data based on operations performed while the DataSet held the data. In an effort to make multitiered applications more efficient, data processing is turning to a message-based approach that revolves around chunks of information.

After we have created an OleDbDataAdapter, we will create a DataSet object in which to place the data the DataAdapter returns to us. Unlike the DataSet example shown in a previous chapter, we will not have to construct the DataSet's DataTable ourselves. Rather, the DataAdapter will create the DataSet's schema for us.

23.3.   Sample Code: ADO.NET_Example

Let's create a simple VC++.NET program that will illustrate the use of ADO.NET objects for database connectivity.

Step 1.   Create a new VC++ Windows Application named ADONET_Example.

Step 2.   On your Form1, place a button, two textboxes, and a large datagridview. You can leave the controls with their default names.

Step 3.   To your Form1 code window, add the code to use the namespaces System:: Data::OleDb and System::Text.

Step 4.   To Form1, add managed pointers for an OleDbConnection object named m_Conn, an OleDbDataAdapter named m_Adapter, and a DataSet named m_DataSet as shown.

Step 5.   Add the code for the button1_Click event as shown, as well as the code for the ColumnAverage function.

```
Form1.h

#pragma once

namespace ADONET_Example
{
    using namespace System;
    using namespace System::ComponentModel;
    using namespace System::Collections;
    using namespace System::Windows::Forms;
    using namespace System::Data;
    using namespace System::Drawing;
    using namespace System::Data::OleDb;
    using namespace System::Text;

public ref class Form1 : public System::Windows::Forms::Form
{
// Windows generated code here.

    OleDbConnection ^m_Conn;
    OleDbDataAdapter ^m_Adapter;
```

```
   DataSet ^m_DataSet;

private: System::Void button1_Click(System::Object^ sender, System::EventArgs^ e)
{
   m_Conn=gcnew OleDbConnection("Provider=Microsoft.Jet.OLEDB.4.0;
                                 Data Source=C:\Finance.mdb");
   m_Adapter=gcnew OleDbDataAdapter("Select * From AXP", m_Conn);
   m_DataSet=gcnew DataSet;

   // Get the data from the database.
   m_Adapter->Fill(m_DataSet, "AXPData");

   // Close the connection.
   m_Conn->Close();

   // Bind the DataSource to the DataGrid.
   dataGridView1->DataSource=m_DataSet->Tables[0];

   // Refer to a specific element in the DataSet.
   textBox1->Text=m_DataSet->Tables[0]->Rows[0][5]->ToString();

   // Pass the collection of DataRows to a function.
   double m_Avg=ColumnAverage(m_DataSet->Tables[0]->Rows, 5);

   textBox2->Text=m_Avg.ToString();
}

double ColumnAverage(DataRowCollection ^m_DataPoints, int m_Column)
{
   double m_Total=0;
   for(int x=0; x < m_DataPoints->Count; x++)
   {
      m_Total+=Convert::ToDouble(m_DataPoints[x]->ItemArray[m_Column]);
   }
   return m_Total / m_DataPoints->Count;
}
};
}
```

In the button1_Click event given earlier, the first line creates an OleDbConnection object called m_Conn and supplies the connection string. In this case, the Microsoft JET driver is specified as well as the path to the MS Access database known as Finance.mdb. A few lines later, we call the m_Conn->Open() method. At that point, the database connection is made.

The second line of code creates an OleDbDataAdapter object. Two arguments are passed to its constructor: a string containing an SQL statement and the database connection against which the SQL statement will be executed, namely m_Conn. The third line of code creates a DataSet object called m_DataSet.

Once our three objects are created and the connection is open, we can execute the SQL statement by calling the m_Adapter->Fill() method. This method can take two arguments.

The first argument is the DataSet that will hold all of the data returned by the SQL query and the second is a String that represents our name for the resulting DataTable. Once the data is in the DataSet, we close the connection to the database.

At this point in the program, all of the data from the table named AXP in the database now exist in memory in m_DataSet. We display the data by binding dataGridView1 to the specified DataSet and DataTable. (Incidentally, the DataGridView is an excellent grid object.)

As in the DataSet example we looked at earlier in the chapter, we can retrieve any specific element in the DataTable by referencing its DataSet, its DataTable, its row, and column. As you will see, the DataAdapter has constructed the DataSet with a schema identical to the AXP table in the Finance database.

Now that the data are in memory we can perform mathematical operations on it. In its current form, the DataSet consists of a data column and open, high low, close, and volume columns. In the example, we have created a function that will simply average the elements in a column. As a result, we can pass a managed pointer to the DataRowCollection.

Notice that the ColumnAverage() function accepts a reference to a DataRowCollection and an integer specifying the column to be averaged. In this case, we are averaging column number 5, the volume column, so our program will print the average volume into the label. The calling statement uses the Rows property, which returns a reference to a DataRowCollection as mentioned earlier.

23.4. Enumerating Through All the Data in a DataSet

DataSets are collections of DataTables, which themselves are collections of DataRows, which are themselves collections of DataColumns. As a result, we can enumerate through every field of every row of every DataTable in the entire DataSet. It's a bit academic, but worth noting.

```
Ienumerator ^m_Enum=m_DataSet->Tables->GetEnumerator();

while (m_Enum->MoveNext())
{
    DataTable ^m_Table=safe_cast< DataTable ^ >(m_Enum->Current);
    Ienumerator ^m_RowEnum=m_Table->Rows->GetEnumerator();

    while (m_RowEnum->MoveNext())
    {
        DataRow ^m_Row=safe_cast< DataRow ^ >(m_RowEnum->Current);
        IEnumerator^ m_ColEnum=m_Table->Columns->GetEnumerator();
        while (m_ColEnum->MoveNext())
        {
            DataColumn ^m_Column=safe_cast< DataColumn ^ (m_ColEnum->Current);
            Console::WriteLine(m_Row[m_Column].ToString());
        }
    }
}
```

23.5. Using Excel as a Data Source

Had we wanted to use Excel as a data source, we could easily accomplish this. First off, we would create an Excel spreadsheet named Book1.xls. Then, in Excel we name a range in the spreadsheet to be used as the table name, e.g., "Prices." Then we simply modify the following lines of code:

```
m_Conn=gcnew OleDbConnection("Provider=Microsoft.Jet.OLEDB.4.0;
        Data Source=C:\Book1.xls;Extended Properties=Excel 8.0");
m_Adapter=gcnew OleDbDataAdapter("Select * From Prices" , m_Conn);
```

23.6. Writing XML from a DataSet

In the button2_Click event function, we can call the m_DataSet->WriteXML() method. In one line of code, the method will convert the entire DataSet into an XML document and, in this case, save it in the path defined.

Step 6.   Add another button, button2, to your Form1.

Step 7.   Add the following code to the button2_Click event handler as shown.

```
<bb.private: System::Void button2_Click(System::Object^ sender, System::EventArgs^ e)
{
    m_DataSet->WriteXml("C:\myXML.xml");
}
```

23.7. Updating a Database with Changes in a Dataset

If we make a change to the DataSet and want to have the database itself reflect the change, we can use the OleDbDataAdapter's Update method to automatically create and execute the proper SQL INSERT, UPDATE, or DELETE statements for each inserted, updated, or deleted row in the DataSet.

Step 8.   Add another button, button3, to your Form1.

Step 9.   Add the following code to the button3_Click event handler as shown.

Step 10. Run the program and click button1. Once the data appears in the DataGridView, change the data in one of the cells and then click button3.

```
private: System::Void button3_Click(System::Object^ sender, System::EventArgs^ e)
{
    m_Conn->Open();
    OleDbCommandBuilder ^m_Builder=gcnew OleDbCommandBuilder(m_Adapter);
    int m_Int=m_Adapter->Update(m_DataSet->Tables[0]);
    m_Conn->Close();
}
```

Step 11.   Close your application and reopen it. Again, click button1 and you should see that the change you made to the DataSet in STEP 10, which was saved to the database, is now in fact changed in the database.

23.8.   Retrieving Data with a DataReader

As we have chosen to use it in this chapter, a DataSet is essentially an in-memory representation of a database. Not all times, however, are we interested in pulling all the data into memory and storing it. As you can imagine, this has performance implications. If we are interested only in reading data, and not storing it, there is a faster way using a OleDbDataReader. A DataReader allows us to read very quickly a stream of data rows as they arrive from a data source. Once we have read it, we can choose to save the data or drop it. If we don't need to store the data, we are better off using a DataReader performance-wise.

Step 12.   Add another button, button4, to your Form1 and a large textbox, textBox3, with the Multiline property set to true.

Step 13.   Add the following code to the button4_Click event handler as shown.

```
private: System::Void button4_Click(System::Object^ sender, System::EventArgs^ e)
{
    m_Conn->Open();
    OleDbCommand ^m_Command=gcnew OleDbCommand("SELECT * FROM IBM", m_Conn);

    OleDbDataReader ^m_Reader=m_Command->ExecuteReader();

    while (m_Reader->Read())
    {
        textBox3->AppendText(m_Reader->GetDateTime(0)+"t"+
                             m_Reader->GetDouble(4)+Environment::NewLine);
    }
    m_Reader->Close();
    m_Conn->Close();
}
```

23.9.   Summary

In this chapter, we learned how to use the basic functionalities of Microsoft's ADO.NET technology. Specifically, we reviewed OleDbConnections, OleDbDataAdapters, DataSets, DataGridViews, and DataRowCollections to view and manipulate data from a database. Also, we looked at using Excel as a data source, updating data sources, and using a DataReader as an alternative to the DataSet model.

CHAPTER • 24

Structured Query Language

Structured Query Language (SQL) is a computer language for communication and interaction with databases and was created to be a cross-platform syntax to extract and manipulate data from disparate database systems. So in theory the same SQL queries written for an Oracle database will work on a Sybase database or an Access database and so on. However, database vendors have also developed their own versions of SQL, such as Transact-SQL and Oracle's PL/SQL, which extend ANSI/ISO SQL. This chapter focuses on writing standard SQL and does not use any vendor-specific SQL syntax.

In our database connection program in the previous chapter, the communicating parties were a "front end," our VC++.NET application that sent an SQL statement via an OleDbDataAdapter, and a "back end" data source that held the data. The statement, the SQL code, can contain instructions that can read or change the data within the database or manipulate the database itself in some way. We can embed SQL statements into our VC++.NET programs to perform everything from simple data retrieval to high-level operations on databases.

The SQL statements that we may most often be concerned with when developing quantitative trading or risk management systems are those that retrieve data, called queries. However, we will at times also need to write, change, or delete data in a database. By the end of this chapter you should have a good understanding of the basic syntax of SQL, which consists of only several dozen or so words. SQL statements are simply groups of those words logically arranged to pull specific data from the data source or manipulate data in the data source. These types of SQL statements are referred to as data manipulation language (DML). Also, however, SQL can be used to actually manipulate the database itself. These SQL statements are called data definition language (DDL).

24.1. Data Manipulation Language

We use DML to retrieve, alter, and otherwise work with actual data held within a database.

125

24.1.1. The SELECT Statement

Reading data is the most common task we want to perform against a database. A SELECT statement queries the database and retrieves selected data that match the criteria that we specify. The SELECT statement has five main clauses, although a FROM clause is the only required one. Each of the clauses has a wide array of options and parameters. Here, we will show the general structure of a SELECT statement with clauses. However, each of them will be covered in more detail later in the chapter.

```
SELECT [ALL | DISTINCT] column1,column2
FROM table1,table2
[WHERE "conditions"]
[GROUP BY "column-list"]
[HAVING "conditions"]
[ORDER BY "column-list" [ASC (Default) | DESC]];
```

A SELECT statement means that we want to choose columns from a table. When selecting multiple columns, a comma must delimit each of them except for the last column. Also, be aware that as with VC++.NET, SQL is not case sensitive. Upper- or lowercase letters will do just fine. Be aware too that most, but not all, databases require the SQL statement to be terminated by a semicolon.

Before we get too in depth, let's create a VC++.NET program to test out the SQL statements we look at as we go along.

Step 1.   Create a new VC++ Windows Application named SQL_Example.

Step 2.   To your Form1, add a textbox, three buttons, and a large DataGridView.

Step 3.   In the Form1 code window add the following code. Notice that we will be using the Options.mdb database.

```
#pragma once
namespace SQL_Example
{
    using namespace System;
    using namespace System::ComponentModel;
    using namespace System::Collections;
    using namespace System::Windows::Forms;
    using namespace System::Data;
    using namespace System::Drawing;
    using namespace System::Data::OleDb;

public ref class Form1 : public System::Windows::Forms::Form
{
public:
    Form1(void)
    {
        InitializeComponent();
        m_Connection=gcnew OleDbConnection("Provider=Microsoft.Jet.OLEDB.4.0;
                                     Data Source=C:\\Options.mdb");
    }
```

```
// Windows generated code in here.

private: OleDbConnection ^m_Connection;
private: OleDbDataAdapter ^m_Adapter;
private: DataSet ^m_DataSet;
private: System::Void button1_Click(System::Object^ sender, System::EventArgs^ e)
{
    try
    {
        m_Connection->Open();
        m_Adapter=gcnew OleDbDataAdapter(textBox1->Text, m_Connection);
        m_DataSet=gcnew DataSet;
        m_Adapter->Fill(m_DataSet);
        dataGridView1->DataSource=m_DataSet->Tables[0];
    }
    catch (Exception ^e)
    {
        MessageBox::Show("Enter a valid SQL statement.");
    }
    finally
    {
        m_Connection->Close();
    }
}
};
}
```

This program will allow you to provide an SQL statement during runtime. Furthermore, we will be able to test out several SQL statements without having to rerun the program, as we have also included a Try...Catch block so that the program won't crash if you make a mistake in the SQL statement.

Step 4.   Run the program and enter the simple SQL statement shown in the textbox.

```
SELECT OptionSymbol,StockSymbol,Year,Month,Strike,Bid,Ask,OpenInt FROM OptionContracts;
```

Step 5.   Click button1. For each of the following SQL statements, we will always be clicking button1.

Note that the columns are displayed in the order that they appear in the SELECT statement. If all columns from a table were needed to be part of the result set, we do not need to explicitly specify them. Rather, in the case where all columns are to be selected, we can use the * symbol. As shown in the previous chapter's example, the resulting SQL statement would look like this:

```
SELECT * FROM OptionContracts;
```

For now, leave your SQL_Example Windows application running. You can test out the SQL statements as you read through the rest of the chapter.

24.1.2. The WHERE Clause

The previous example retrieved a result set that included all the rows in the table from the specified columns. However, we may want to filter some rows out according to some condition or based upon some comparison. This is where the WHERE clause comes in. For comparison in SQL, we use the operators shown in Table 24-1.

So, if we were interested in only the option contracts with open interest greater than 1,000, our SQL would look like this:

```
SELECT * FROM OptionContracts WHERE OpenInt > 1000;
```

The WHERE clause can also have multiple conditions using AND or OR. If we wanted to see all contracts where open interest is over 1000 and the bid is greater than 0, it would look like this:

```
SELECT * FROM OptionContracts WHERE OpenInt > 1000 AND Bid > 0;
```

If we needed to build a **WHERE** clause for such a field, MS Access requires that we use single quotes for string comparison like this:

```
SELECT * FROM OptionContracts WHERE StockSymbol = 'IBM';
```

Date comparison requires the use of the pound sign, #. For example, if we wanted to see all of the options trades done in February of 2003:

TABLE 24-1

Comparison Operator	Description
<	Contents of the field are less than the value.
<=	Contents of the field are less than or equal to the value.
>	Contents of the field are greater than the value.
>=	Contents of the field are greater than or equal to the value.
=	Contents of the field are equal to the value.
<>	Contents of the field are not equal to the value.
BETWEEN	Contents of the field fall between a range of values.
LIKE	Contents of the field match a certain pattern.
IN	Contents of the field match one of a number of criteria.

```
SELECT * FROM OptionTrades
WHERE TradeDateTime>=#2/01/2003# AND TradeDateTime<=#2/28/2003#;
```

24.1.3. The ORDER BY Clause

We can sort our result set with the ORDER BY clause. ORDER BY is an optional clause that allows us to display the results of our query in a sorted order, either ascending or descending, based on the columns that we specify to order by. Here is an example:

```
SELECT * FROM OptionContracts
WHERE StockSymbol='MSFT' ORDER BY OpenInt;
```

This statement selects all the MSFT option contracts and orders data from the lowest open interest to the highest. To view data in descending order, we simply add DESC to the end.

```
SELECT * FROM OptionContracts
WHERE StockSymbol='MSFT' ORDER BY OpenInt DESC;
```

If we need to order based on multiple columns, we must separate the columns with commas.

```
SELECT * FROM OptionContracts
WHERE StockSymbol='MSFT' ORDER BY OpenInt DESC, Strike;
```

Notice now that the contracts that have the same open interest are now listed in order of strike price. Also, the DESC applies only to the OpenInt. Strike is sorted with the default ASC order.

24.1.4. The LIKE Clause

So far we have learned how to find exact matches with SQL. However, there may be times that we need to search for partial strings. SQL provides a LIKE operator for just this type of query.

The LIKE operator can only be used on fields that have one of the string types set as their data type. LIKE cannot be used on dates or numbers.

String comparison employs a wildcard sign, %, which can be used to match any possible character that might appear before or after the characters specified. If you want to view all of the IBM option contracts with an 80 strike:

```
SELECT * FROM OptionContracts
WHERE StockSymbol='IBM' AND OptionSymbol LIKE '%P';
```

The LIKE operator proves to be very useful as we write more complex SQL statements, as it enables us to find partial matches without performing any complicated string manipulation. Keep in mind, however, that the LIKE operator is not the most efficient SQL command and will degrade overall performance. If we know the exact string that we are looking for in a field, then we should use the = operator instead of LIKE.

In addition to the % wildcard, there are two other important wildcards used with the LIKE operator—the underscore (_) and the square brackets ([]). Whereas the % wildcard is used to find a string with any number of characters before and/or after the specified characters, the underscore is used to limit the search to a single leading or trailing character. A search of '%D%' would return MCDRE and IBMDP. Say, for example, we wanted to find all the April calls for all the stocks. Omitting the IBM WHERE class and changing the LIKE expression to '%D_' would limit the return values to just those calls with April expiration, as we are now looking for any option contract with a D as the second to last letter in its symbol.

```
SELECT * FROM OptionContracts WHERE OptionSymbol LIKE '%D_';
```

Additionally, we can use the brackets ([]) to further limit ranges of characters. With the brackets, we can specify particular characters that must appear in a particular position. For instance, if we were looking for April and May calls, then we need to modify our criteria. We limit our search to option contracts that have either D or E in the second to last position, so we specify this by putting these characters within brackets, in the appropriate place:

```
SELECT * FROM OptionContracts WHERE OptionSymbol LIKE '%[DE]_';
```

Keep in mind that because the brackets may only contain single characters, we cannot use them for lists of strings. This is the biggest limitation to the bracket wildcard, but there are still a large number of possibilities for expression searching in strings.

24.1.5.   Aggregate SQL Functions

So far the SQL that we have been using retrieves rows of data from the database. However, SQL can do a lot more. Among other things, SQL has a few built-in functions that can tell us things about data as a whole. For example, what if we wanted to know what contract has the largest open interest? How about the total number of trades for a given month? As you can see, these numbers are not contained within the columns of a table. Rather, they must be computed.

ANSI/ISO SQL contains aggregate functions that can compute simple information from data in a database. Specific RDBMSs may support additional aggregate functions that are proprietary and also very useful. Supported ANSI/ISO SQL aggregates functions (Table 24-2).

24.1.5.1.   The SUM Function

Let's begin by taking a look at the SUM function. It is used within a SELECT statement and, predictably, returns the summation of a series of values. In this example, we will compute the total number of shares traded in the month of January 2003.

TABLE 24-2

Aggregate Function	Description
AVG	Returns the average of the values in a column.
COUNT	Returns the total number of values in a column.
COUNT(*)	Returns the number of rows in a table.
MAX	Returns the largest value in a column.
MIN	Returns the smallest value in a column.
SUM	Returns the sum of the numeric values in a column.

```
SELECT SUM(Quantity) FROM StockTrades
WHERE TradeDateTime >= #1/1/2003# AND TradeDateTime <= #1/31/2003#;
```

```
SELECT * FROM StockTrades
WHERE TradeDateTime BETWEEN #01/01/2003# AND #1/31/2003#;
```

Notice that the result set only contains one row of data. This is to be expected when using any of the SQL aggregate functions. Also notice the name of the column. Since we asked SQL to return an aggregate value, SQL named the column for us. When this occurs, we say that an SQL-computed column is being used.

Of course, the column name 'Expr1000' is not descriptive of the data it contains. Fortunately, SQL column naming is simple. To rename computed columns, use the AS modifier. The AS modifier allows us to give meaningful names to any computed columns. If we wanted to give a meaningful name, say TotalShares, to the computed column in the SQL statement written earlier, we could write it as

```
SELECT SUM(Quantity) AS TotalShares FROM StockTrades
WHERE TradeDateTime >= #1/1/2003# AND TradeDateTime <= #1/31/2003#;
```

24.1.5.2. The AVG/COUNT/MIN/MAX Functions

Predictably, these aggregate functions will return the average of data in a column, the lowest and highest values in a column, and the count or number of elements in a column. If we wanted to obtain the respective values for the month of January 2003, our SQL statements would look as follows:

```
SELECT MIN (Quantity) FROM StockTrades
WHERE TradeDateTime >= #01/01/2003# AND TradeDateTime <= #1/31/2003#;
```

```
SELECT MAX (Quantity) FROM StockTrades
WHERE TradeDateTime >= #01/01/2003# AND TradeDateTime <= #1/31/2003#;
```

```
SELECT AVG (Quantity) FROM StockTrades
WHERE TradeDateTime >= #01/01/2003# AND TradeDateTime <= #1/31/2003#;
```

```
SELECT COUNT (*) FROM StockTrades
WHERE TradeDateTime>=#01/01/2003# AND TradeDateTime<=#1/31/2003#;
```

24.1.6. The DISTINCT Function

The SQL DISTINCT function is useful when only the first occurrence of a desired series of data is needed. For example, if we were interested in seeing a list of all the stocks that have been traded, we would not care to see duplicates. That is, we may have traded MSFT several times and we don't care to see it listed more than once. We can filter out duplicates with the DISTINCT function.

```
SELECT DISTINCT (StockSymbol)
FROM StockTrades
ORDER BY StockSymbol;
```

24.1.7. The GROUP BY Clause

As we have just seen, using aggregate functions such as SUM and MIN will get us a computed value for a group of records. What if, however, we wanted to write a SQL statement that would show the SUMs of the quantities traded each individual option symbol? The GROUP BY will return the results of aggregate functions for a group of values.

```
SELECT OptionSymbol,SUM (Quantity)
FROM OptionTrades
GROUP BY OptionSymbol;
```

Notice that option symbols are only displayed when they have a greater than zero value. If, for example, the summation of the quantity for AXPDZ were zero, it would not be included in the result set. The GROUP BY clause can only be used when selecting multiple columns from a table(s) and at least one aggregate function appears in the SELECT statement.

When there are multiple columns beyond the one being aggregated, we can GROUP BY all the other selected columns. For example, if we wanted the total quantity for all option symbols by BuySell, the SQL would look like the following:

```
SELECT OptionSymbol,BuySell,SUM (Quantity)
FROM OptionTrades
GROUP BY OptionSymbol,BuySell;
```

Note that the previous SQL has two columns in the GROUP BY clause. Remember, if the column appears in the SELECT and the SELECT has aggregate functions, the column must appear in a GROUP BY clause.

24.1.8. The HAVING Clause

The HAVING clause is like a WHERE clause for groups. By definition, an SQL statement that uses a GROUP BY clause cannot use a WHERE clause. We must use a HAVING clause instead. For example, if we wanted to see only those option contracts that have total quantities traded of greater than or equal to 50, the SQL statement would look like this

```
SELECT OptionSymbol,SUM (Quantity)
FROM OptionTrades
GROUP BY OptionSymbol HAVING SUM (Quantity)>=50;
```

The HAVING clause is reserved for aggregate functions and is usually placed at the end of an SQL statement. Also, an SQL statement with a HAVING clause may or may not necessarily include the GROUP BY clause. The following SQL statement is valid:

```
SELECT COUNT (OptionSymbol)
FROM OptionTrades
HAVING SUM (Quantity)>=50;
```

24.1.9. Mathematical Operations

We can also make mathematical calculations in our SQL statements—add, subtract, multiply, divide, and modulus. The following SQL uses a column alias to describe the (quantity * price) of a trade:

```
SELECT OptionSymbol,Price,Quantity,(Price * Quantity * 100)
AS TradeCost
FROM OptionTrades;
```

24.1.10. Aliasing

Tables in a database can be aliased in a FROM clause. The following example creates an alias named "OT" for the OptionTrades table.

```
SELECT * FROM OptionTrades OT;
```

This is convenient when you want to retrieve information from two or more separate tables (an operation known as joining). The advantage of using a table alias when joining will become apparent as our SQL statements become more complex.

24.1.11.   Joining Tables

So far in our examples, we have retrieved data from only one table. In many instances, however, we may need to retrieve data from two or more tables.

The Stock table and the OptionContracts table shown previously contain information about individual stocks and options contracts on those stocks and we may be interested in returning data from both tables in a single SQL statement. To join these two tables we must first identify a column in each table that contains the same data. In this example, the OptionContracts table contains a StockSymbol column, which matches the StockSymbol column in the Stock table.

The two tables can be joined on these StockSymbol columns, although it is just a coincidence that both these tables are named the same. In order to join tables, data must match, not necessarily the column names. Here is an example using table aliasing for readability.

```
SELECT * FROM Stock S,OptionContracts OC
WHERE S.StockSymbol=OC.StockSymbol;
```

In this example the join is performed within the WHERE clause. The previous SQL will return all columns for each table joined by the stock symbol. With the two tables joined, the SELECT and the WHERE clause can now be modified. For example:

```
SELECT
OC.OptionSymbol,OC.StockSymbol,OC.Bid,OC.Ask,S.DividendAmount
FROM Stock S,OptionContracts OC
WHERE S.StockSymbol=OC.StockSymbol AND S.StockSymbol='IBM';
```

24.1.11.1.   The UNION Keyword

A UNION is useful if you want to get data from two tables within the same result set. For example, if we wanted to see the bid and ask for INTC as well as the bids and ask for all the INTC options in one result set, the SQL statement would read as follows:

```
SELECT StockSymbol,Bid,Ask FROM Stock
WHERE StockSymbol='IBM'
UNION
SELECT OptionSymbol,Bid,Ask FROM OptionContracts
WHERE StockSymbol='IBM';
```

The data type for the columns in each SELECT statement must match for a UNION to work. This is not an issue in the example given earlier because each of the tables has identical column sets.

24.1.11.2. The Inner Join Clause

If we need to include data from two or more tables in the result set, we can use the INNER JOIN or OUTER JOIN statements SQL to do so. An INNER JOIN allows us to join two tables that have values from one or more columns in common. An OUTER JOIN allows us to join two tables that have one or more columns in common. That is, the difference between an INNER JOIN and an OUTER JOIN is that in an INNER JOIN, records from the first, or source, table that do not have a match in the second, or joining, table are excluded from the result set. In an OUTER JOIN, records from the source table that do not have a match in the joining table are still included in the result set.

We use an INNER JOIN to join two tables that have values in common from at least one column.

```
SELECT ST.StockSymbol,ST.Price,OC.OptionSymbol,OC.Bid,OC.Ask
FROM StockTrades ST
INNER JOIN OptionContracts OC
ON ST.StockSymbol = OC.StockSymbol
```

In the statement just shown, the StockTrades and OptionContracts tables are joined based on values in their common StockSymbol column. For rows in the StockTrades table that have a match in the OptionContract table, data for the matching rows are included. Rows in the StockTrades table that do not have a match in the OptionContract table are excluded by the Inner Join.

24.1.11.3. The Outer Join Clause

We use an OUTER JOIN to join two tables that have in common at least one column. When the fields from the two tables are compared in the ON clause, those fields in the joining table for records in the source table that do not match will have null values.

Here is an example of an OUTER JOIN:

```
SELECT S.StockSymbol,S.Bid,S.Ask,ST.Price
FROM Stock S
LEFT OUTER JOIN StockTrades ST
ON S.StockSymbol = ST.StockSymbol
```

For rows from the Stock table that do not have a matching value between the StockSymbol column and the StockSymbol column from StockTrades, notice that the StockTrades.Price column contains a null value. The Price field for KO is null since no trades were placed in that stock.

The use of the LEFT modifier in the OUTER JOIN means that all rows from the table on the left of the OUTER JOIN operator, i.e., the Stock table, will be included in the result set, whether or not there are matches in the table to the right, the StockTrades table. If, however, we used the RIGHT modifier, all rows from the table on the right of the OUTER JOIN will be included with or without matches. Finally, we could also use the FULL modifier so that all rows from both tables will be included in the result set.

24.1.12.   The INSERT Statement

Up to this point, we have only queried the Option.mdb database and looked at the results. We may, however, also be interested in changing the data. In order to add, delete, or modify data in the Options.mdb database, we will first need to add some elements to our SQL_ Example program.

Step 6.   Add another button to your form.
Step 7.   Add the following code to the button2_Click event.

```
private: System::Void button2_Click(System::Object^ sender, System::EventArgs^ e)
{
   try
   {
      m_Connection->Open();
      OleDbCommand ^m_Command = gcnew OleDbCommand(textBox1->Text, m_Connection);
      m_Command->ExecuteNonQuery();
   }
   catch (Exception ^e)
   {
      MessageBox::Show("Enter a valid SQL statement.");
   }
   finally
   {
      m_Connection->Close();
   }
}
```

An OleDbCommand object is an SQL statement, which we can use to perform transactions against a database. We use the ExecuteNonQuery() member method to execute UPDATE, INSERT, and DELETE statements.

For the remainder of the chapter, SELECT statements should be executed using the first button and all other transactions should be executed using this new, second button.

The SQL INSERT statement enables us to add data to a table in a database. Here is an example showing the syntax for adding a record to the OptionTrades table:

```
INSERT INTO OptionTrades
(TradeDateTime,OptionSymbol,BuySell,Price,Quantity,TradeStatus)
VALUES (#02/27/2003#,'IBMDP','B',2.60,10,'F');
```

Step 8.   Click button2. For the remainder of the chapter, we will be clicking button2.

You can verify that this data has been added to the table by writing a simple SELECT statement on the OptionTrades table and clicking button1.

Notice that all values for all columns have been supplied, save for the TradeID column, which is generated automatically. If a value for a column is to be left blank, the keyword NULL could be used to represent a blank columns value.

Regarding data types, notice that strings are delimited by single quotes, numerical data do not need single quotes, and dates are defined with pound signs. As mentioned previously, because each RDBMS is different, you should look into the documentation of your system for how to define the data types. Whatever your RDBMS, the comma-delimited list of values must match the table structure exactly in the number of attributes and the data type of each attribute.

24.1.13. The UPDATE Statement

The SQL UPDATE clause is used to modify data in a database table existing in one or several rows. The following SQL updates one row in the stock table, the dividend amount for IBM:

```
UPDATE Stock SET DividendAmount = .55
WHERE StockSymbol = 'IBM';
```

SQL does not limit us to updating only one column. The following SQL statement updates both the dividend amount and the dividend date columns in the stock table.

```
UPDATE Stock SET DividendAmount = .50, DividendDate = #03/18/2003#
WHERE StockSymbol = 'IBM';
```

The update expression can be a constant, any computed value, or even the result of a SELECT statement that returns a single row and a single column. If the WHERE clause is omitted, then the specified attribute is set to the same value in every row of the table. Also, we can also set multiple attribute values at the same time with a comma-delimited list of attribute-equals-expression pairs.

24.1.14. The DELETE Statement

As its name implies, we use an SQL DELETE statement to remove data from a table in a database. Like the UPDATE statement, either single rows or multiple rows can be deleted. The following SQL statement deletes one row of data from the StockTrades table:

```
DELETE FROM StockTrades
WHERE TradeID = 40 ;
```

The following SQL statement will delete all records from the StockTrades table that represent trades before January 4, 2003.

```
DELETE FROM StockTrades
WHERE TradeDateTime < #01/04/2003# ;
```

If the WHERE clause is omitted, then every row of the table is deleted, which of course should be done with great caution.

We can avoid writing INSERT, UPDATE, and DELETE statements by using the functionalities of a DataAdapter object as we have seen.

24.2.   Updating a Database with Changes in a DataSet

As discussed in the previous chapter on ADO.NET, we can also make changes to data in the database. This method uses the OleDbDataAdapter's Update function to automatically create and execute the proper SQL INSERT, UPDATE, or DELETE statements for each inserted, updated, or deleted row in the DataSet.

```
m_Connection->Open () ;
OleDbCommandBuilder ^m_Builder=gcnew OleDbCommandBuilder(m_Adapter) ;

// Change some data in the DataSet
m_DataSet->Tables[0]->Rows[0] [5]=200 ;

// Call the Update method.
int m_Int=m_Adapter->Update(m_DataSet->Tables[0]) ;
m_Connection->Close() ;
```

24.3.   Data Definition Language

We use DDL to create or modify the structure of tables in a database. When we execute a DDL statement, it takes effect immediately. Again, for all transactions, you should click Button2 to execute these nonqueries. You will be able to verify the results of the SQL statements by creating simple SELECT statements and executing a query with Button1 in your program.

24.3.1.   Creating Views

A view is a saved, read-only SQL statement. Views are very useful when you find yourself writing the same SQL statement over and over again. Here is a sample SELECT statement to find all the IBM option contracts with an 80 strike:

```
SELECT * FROM OptionContracts
WHERE StockSymbol='IBM' AND OptionSymbol LIKE '%P' ;
```

Although not overly complicated, the SQL statement just shown is not overly simplistic either. Instead of typing it over and over again, we can create a VIEW. The syntax for creating a view is as follows:

```
CREATE VIEW IBM80s AS SELECT * FROM OptionContracts
WHERE StockSymbol='IBM' AND OptionSymbol LIKE '%P' ;
```

This code creates a VIEW named IBM80s. Now to run it, simply type in the following SQL statement.

```
SELECT * FROM IBM80s;
```

Views can be deleted as well using the DROP keyword.

```
Mbb>DROP VIEW IBM80s;
```

24.3.2. Creating Tables

As you know by now database tables are the basic structure in which data are stored. In the examples we have used so far, the tables have been preexisting. Often times, however, we need to build a table ourselves. While we are certainly able to build tables ourselves with an RDBMS such as MS Access, we will cover the SQL code to create tables in VC++.NET.

As a review, tables contain rows and columns. Each row represents one piece of data, called a record, and each column, called a field, represents a component of that data. When we create a table, we need to specify the columns' names as well as their data types. Data types are usually database specific but usually can be broken into integers, numerical values, strings, and Date/Time. The following SQL statement builds a simple table named Trades:

```
CREATE TABLE MyTrades
(MyInstr Char(4) NOT NULL,
MyPrice Numeric(8, 2) NOT NULL,
MyTime Date NOT NULL) ;
```

The general syntax for the CREATE TABLE statement is as follows:

```
CREATE TABLE TableName (Column1 DataType1 Null/Not Null, …);
```

The data types that you will use most frequently are the VARCHAR2(n), a variable-length character field where n is its maximum width; CHAR(n), a fixed-length character field of width n; NUMERIC(w.d), where w is the total width of the field and d is the number of places after the decimal point (omitting it produces an integer); and DATE, which stores both date and time in a unique internal format. NULL and NOT NULL indicate whether a specific field may be left blank.

Tables can be dropped as well. When a table is dropped, all of the data it contains is lost.

```
DROP TABLE MyTrades;
```

24.3.3. Altering Tables

We have already seen that the INSERT statement can be used to add rows. Columns as well can be added or removed from a table. For example, if we wanted to add a column named Exchange to the StockTrades table, we can use the ALTER TABLE statement. The syntax is supplied next:

```
ALTER TABLE StockTrades ADD Exchange char(4) ;
```

As discussed in the previous chapter, all tables must have a primary key. We can use the ALTER TABLE statement to specify TradeID in the Trades table created previously.

```
ALTER TABLE Trades ADD PRIMARY KEY(TradeID) ;
```

Columns can be removed as well using the ALTER TABLE statement.

```
ALTER TABLE StockTrades DROP Exchange;
```

24.4. Summary

Over the course of this chapter, we have taken a pretty good look at SQL, from simple select statements to joining tables to updating databases and finally altering the structure of a database. Because financial markets produce so much data every day, it is important to understand SQL as a tool to interacting with large relational databases for research and testing.

CHAPTER · 25

XML

XML is a meta-language for communicating data between disparate technologies. That is, we can create new markup languages using XML to communicate, in this case, financial data, from one application to another. Many segments of the financial industry have already done this specifically for their own domains.

XML allows us to represent the contextual meaning of the data we wish to describe and transmit. This is done through the definition of customized tags. As long as the application that sends an XML message and the application that receives it agree on what these tags mean, they can communicate and exchange data.

25.1. Well-Formed XML Documents

Every XML document must be well formed, i.e., it must follow all of the structural rules for XML. Programs that read XML, called parsers, will reject any message that does not follow the structural rules for being well formed. Among the most important rules are that XML is case sensitive and that unclosed tags and overlapping tags are not permitted.

Every start tag must have an end tag. The start tag begins an enclosed area of text, known as an item, according to the tag name. <Ticker> is a start tag. </Ticker> is an end tag. The element, defined by a tag, ends with the end tag. XML tags may also include one of a list of attributes consisting of an attribute name and an attribute value. A tag that opens inside another tag must close before the containing tag closes. Put differently, the structure of an XML document must be strictly hierarchical. However, just because an XML document is well formed, does not mean it is valid.

25.2. Valid XML Documents

When tags in a well-formed XML document are queried for their meanings, we say the document is being validated. A valid XML message means that both the sending and the receiving parties are able to correctly identify the document's content according to an agreed-upon set of tag definitions.

We will use an XML Schema to validate an XML stream that is shared between the two parts of our application. Financial organizations publish schemas that outline the format of XML documents according to their protocol. Trading firms that wish to exchange data can then build their XML documents according to these agreed-upon schemas so that their counterparts will understand the messages.

Here is a simple XML document that contains data about a trade.

```
Trade.xml

<Trade>
    <TradeID>10FI58B6034</TradeID>
    <Exchange Acronym="CME" />
    <Contract Symbol="ES" Expiry="Sep06"/>
    <Price>110525</Price>
    <Quantity>10</Quantity>
    <Time>26 Jul 2006 11:05:01.1452</Time>
    <Account>00123</Account>
</Trade>
```

25.3. XML Schema Documents

XML Schemas are documents that use XML Schema Definition (XSD) language to define and validate XML documents. For example, an OTC derivatives trade represented in XML can be validated with an XML Schema before it is sent. This validation verifies that all of the required data is present and is in the proper order and data type. This ensures that the recipient of the trade will be able to interpret the data correctly when it is received.

25.4. Parsers

As discussed previously, an XML message's structure should be validated against an XSD. This is done through the use of a parser, a program that actually reads the data and conducts the validation. A parser that has access to an XSD guarantees that all the proper elements and attributes are present in an XML document. As with XML itself, the rules for validation are very strict.

XML validation is order sensitive and elements must appear in the same order as they are specified in the XSD. Additional fields may not be added without first defining them in the XSD or in the XML message itself.

25.5. Sample Code: Traders.xsd

Given the XML document shown earlier, we can generate an XML Schema using Microsoft's XML Schema definition tool (xsd.exe). This tool, though not without its short-comings, will generate an XSD file against which subsequent XML data can be validated. In the command window, just type xsd, the path, and the file name.

```
C:\>xsd ./Trade.xml
```

The XSD file generated by this tool on my machine was not correct. It would not validate the XML file used to create the XML Schema itself. However, by simply copying and pasting the italicized code shown into the proper location in sequence, it worked just fine.

```
<?xml version="1.0" encoding="utf-8"?>
<xs:schema id="NewDataSet" xmlns=" " xmlns:xs="http://www.w3.org/2001/XMLSchema"
xmlns:msdata="urn:schemas-microsoft-com:xml-msdata">
   <xs:element name="Trade">
     <xs:complexType>
        <xs:sequence>
           <xs:element name="TradeID" type="xs:string" minOccurs="0" />
           <xs:element name="Exchange" minOccurs="0" maxOccurs="unbounded">
             <xs:complexType>
               <xs:attribute name="Acronym" type="xs:string" />
             </xs:complexType>
           </xs:element>
           <xs:element name="Contract" minOccurs="0" maxOccurs="unbounded">
             <xs:complexType>
                 <xs:attribute name="Symbol" type="xs:string"/>
                 <xs:attribute name="Expiry" type="xs:string"/>
             </xs:complexType>
           </xs:element>
           <xs:element name="Price" type="xs:string" minOccurs="0" />
           <xs:element name="Quantity" type="xs:string" minOccurs="0" />
           <xs:element name="Time" type="xs:string" minOccurs="0" />
           <xs:element name="Account" type="xs:string" minOccurs="0" />
        </xs:sequence>
     </xs:complexType>
   </xs:element>
   <xs:element name="NewDataSet" msdata:IsDataSet="true">
      <xs:complexType>
        <xs:choice maxOccurs="unbounded">
           <xs:element ref="Trade" />
        </xs:choice>
      </xs:complexType>
   </xs:element>
</xs:schema>
```

In the simple examples shown here, we will see how to write and read an XML document and validate it against the XML Schema.

25.6.   Sample Code: XmlWriter_Example

```cpp
#include "stdafx.h"
using namespace System;
using namespace System::Xml;
using namespace System::Text;
int main(array<System::String ^> ^args)
{
    XmlTextWriter ^m_Writer=gcnew XmlTextWriter("C:\\Trade.xml", Encoding::ASCII);

    m_Writer->WriteStartDocument();
    m_Writer->WriteDocType("Trade", nullptr, nullptr, nullptr);

    m_Writer->WriteStartElement("Trade");
    m_Writer->WriteElementString("TradeID", "10FI58B6034");

    m_Writer->WriteStartElement("Exchange");
    m_Writer->WriteAttributeString("Acronym", "CME");
    m_Writer->WriteEndElement();

    m_Writer->WriteStartElement("Contract");
    m_Writer->WriteAttributeString("Symbol", "ES");
    m_Writer->WriteAttributeString("Expiry", "Sep06");
    m_Writer->WriteEndElement();

    m_Writer->WriteElementString("Price", "110525");
    m_Writer->WriteElementString("Quantity", "10");
    m_Writer->WriteElementString("Time", "26 Jul 2006 11:05:01.1452");
    m_Writer->WriteElementString("Account", "00123");

    m_Writer->WriteEndElement();
    m_Writer->Formatting=Formatting::Indented;

    m_Writer->Flush();
    m_Writer->Close();
    return 0;
}
```

25.7.   Sample Code: XmlReader_Example

```cpp
MyClass.h

#pragma once
using namespace System;
using namespace System::Xml;
```

```
using namespace System::Xml::Schema;

ref class MyClass
{
private:
     bool m_Valid;
public:
    MyClass(void);
    bool Validate();
    void Validate_EventHandler(Object ^, ValidationEventArgs ^);
};
```

MyClass.cpp

```
#include "StdAfx.h"
#include ".\myclass.h"

MyClass::MyClass(void)
{
    m_Valid=true;
}

bool MyClass::Validate()
{
    XmlReaderSettings ^m_Settings=gcnew XmlReaderSettings();

    m_Settings->ProhibitDtd=false;
    m_Settings->Schemas->Add(nullptr, "C:\\Trade.xsd");
    m_Settings->ValidationType=ValidationType::Schema;
    m_Settings->ValidationEventHandler+=gcnew ValidationEventHandler(
                                  this, &MyClass::Validate_EventHandler);

    XmlReader ^m_Reader=XmlReader::Create("C:\\Trade.xml", m_Settings);

    while (m_Reader->Read())
    {
        switch (m_Reader->NodeType)
        {
            case XmlNodeType::Element:
                if (m_Reader->HasAttributes)
                {
                    while(m_Reader->MoveToNextAttribute())
                    {
                        Console::WriteLine(m_Reader->Value);
                    }
                }
                break;
```

```
                case XmlNodeType::Text:
                    Console::WriteLine(m_Reader->Value);
                    break;
                case XmlNodeType::EndElement:
                    break;
            }
        }
    m_Reader->Close();
    return m_Valid;
}


void MyClass::Validate_EventHandler(Object ^m_Source, ValidationEventArgs ^e)
{
    // In the event a problem is encountered during the read/validation,
    // this event will be raised.
    m_Valid=false;
    Console::WriteLine(String::Concat("Validation: ", e->Message));
}
```

XmlReader.cpp

```
#include "stdafx.h"
#include "MyClass.h"
using namespace System;

int main(array<System::String ^> ^args)
{
    MyClass m_Obj;
    bool m_Bool=m_Obj.Validate();
    Console::WriteLine(m_Bool);
}
```

25.8. Summary

Performance wise, XML documents are large, relative to ones with binary formats, and use more bandwidth, more storage space, and require more processor time for compression. Furthermore, parsing XML documents is generally a slower process and requires more memory. Good application design can help avoid some of these problems.

As an alternative to using the XmlReader and XmlWriter classes, we can, given an XML Schema, run the XML Schema Definition (xsd.exe) tool to generate classes that, when serialized, will conform to the XML Schema. As shown in a later chapter, we can use an XmlSerializer object when the XML document adheres to an XML Schema.

CHAPTER • 26

Financial Information Exchange Protocol

26.1. XML Protocols in Financial Markets

Within the financial markets industry, consortiums and organizations of firms have developed several XML and non-XML-based protocols. These XML standards provide a framework for encoding information relating to different parts of the industry. The most interesting of these XML protocols are:

- Financial Information Exchange (FIX)/FAST/FIXML: FIXML is the XML version of FIX.
- FpML: Financial Products Markup Language.
- Swift/SwiftML: SwiftML is the XML version of Swift.
- RIXML: Research Information Exchange Markup Language.
- MDDL: Market Data Definition Language.
- FinXML.
- SFXL: Securities Financing Extensible Markup Language.
- OFX: Open Financial Exchange.
- XBRL: Extensible Business Reporting Language.
- IFX: Interactive Financial Exchange.
- IRML: Investment Research Markup Language.
- XFRML: Extensible Financial Research Markup Language.
- MDML: Market Data Markup Language.
- WeatherML: Weather Markup Language.
- STPML: Straight Through Processing Markup Language.

As you can imagine, an institution of any size may need to support a multiplicity of standards within its trading, risk management, and back office systems. Of the most widely used of the protocols mentioned earlier, however, is the non-XML protocol FIX, promoted by FIX Protocol, Ltd. (FPL).

26.2.   Overview of FIX

Financial institutions use the industry standard FIX protocol to quickly communicate trades and trade information electronically between exchanges and counterparties. Because FIX has been adopted by nearly every major stock and futures exchange, investment and money management and trading firm, and the Bond Market Association, it has become an integral part of global, real-time trading. If your firm has or intends to build an automated order management system, FIX is or will be an integral part of it. One of the nice things about FIX is that there is so much vendor support for it that you can employ FIX without knowing or even seeing it by purchasing or licensing something known as a FIX engine.

(There is, unfortunately, little public documentation of FIX so I will provide a brief overview of FIX, adapted from the FIX Protocol, Ltd., website, www.fixprotocol.org, and conversations with FIX professionals.)

Building an order management system (OMS) is a big endeavor, requiring forethought, planning, and investment in hardware and software. Employing FIX as part of an OMS on a small scale can be inexpensive, in the neighborhood of a few thousand dollars. Large-scale implementation can run into the millions of dollars.

When planning an electronic trading infrastructure, choosing the right network model is important. Routing networks, leased lines (24-hour T1-line, direct connections between two counterparties over a telecommunications circuit), the Internet (which, as you can imagine, can be inexpensive, but slow and unsecure), and Virtual Private Networks (VPNs) are all options with various strengths and weaknesses to each.

26.2.1.   Point-to-Point VPN

In a point-to-point VPN, each firm has one physical connection into the network, but separate logical connections to each of its counterparties. Typically, point-to-point VPNs take sent data and pass it untouched to the recipient. The main advantage here is a reduction in complexity and cost of managing multiple connections to multiple counterparties. Regardless of the number of trading partners, each firm has only to manage one physical line into the network. Point-to-point VPNs are generally very fast.

26.2.2.   Hub-and-Spoke Network

In the hub-and-spoke network model, each firm makes one physical and one logical connection into the network. All communications between counterparties pass via the hub's FIX engine. Each firm's own FIX engine sends messages containing the recipient's information into the hub, which parses the message and routes it on to the appropriate place.

As a result, in a hub-and-spoke network, every firm can communicate with every other firm through the single logical connection without having to establish new ones for each counterparty, with all the complications that would create. For a hub, the underlying physical network could be the Internet, a network proprietary to the hub, or a point-to-point network run by a third-party vendor. In this way, a hub consists of two separate layers—one providing hub functionalities and one providing the network.

Hub-and-spoke networks are a simple and cost-effective way to reach multiple trading partners. Some hub-and-spoke networks have a FIX certification, where all parties test their functionality against the hub to ensure compliance before going online. Firms then only have one test to perform, as opposed to testing against every counterparty. If the hub fails, however, all ability to communicate with trading partners is lost. Redundancy, while expensive, is important.

In general, the costs associated with operating a FIX network increase with the level of redundancy, hardware encryption, and the number of connections and messages sent.

26.2.3. Costs for FIX Networks

Costs for operating a FIX network can be broken down into infrastructure development costs and usage costs. Network vendors charge installation fees, although routers usually retain the ownership of routers. Also, each firm will usually need to purchase a local tail, a very small leased line, to provide connectivity from the network's point of presence to the firm's office.

Usage costs come in many flavors—per message fees that may include volume discounts, bandwidth fees where a monthly fee buys a level of bandwidth, and percentage of trade value where the network provider charges basis points on the total value traded with fixed caps per month.

In summary, your firm should thoughtfully forecast trading volumes and the number of required connections and then analyze potential expenses under the competing pricing structures. As with any business decision, service has a price. Installation times, high availability, service level agreements, redundancy, and support have value and total cost should be considered.

26.2.4. FIX Engines

A FIX engine is a piece of software that creates outgoing FIX messages and parses incoming ones. A FIX engine manages the session and application layers and is the single piece of software your firm needs in order to FIX enable your trading or order management systems.

In the context of an order management system, a FIX engine is your interface, which, together with a network, connects you to the outside world. Thus, to FIX enable an application refers to the integration of a FIX engine and connection to a routing network. Purchasing or licensing a FIX engine means that no one in your firm needs to know FIX for your firm to enjoy its benefits.

If your firm uses or purchases an off-the-shelf order management system, your vendor may or may not allow you to select a FIX engine for integration. In the case where your firm has or intends to build its own order management system, you will of course have your pick of the over 100 FIX engine vendors. Whatever the case, be aware that while FIX engines are essentially commodity software packages, not all are created equal.

There are several vendor support options for different capabilities (Table 26-1). Also, many different technologies may be offered (Table 26-2). Different support services are also available (Table 26-3).

When considering the purchase or licensing of a FIX engine, your firm should think about many things—performance requirements, hardware requirements, prebuilt interfaces to electronic communication networks (ECNs) and counterparties, monitoring and testing requirements, and costs.

Be aware that advertised "messages per second" often sound impressive, but you may not experience those same speeds on your infrastructure. In addition, the nature of your trading should dictate the value of high speeds. High-frequency systems, where speed

TABLE 26-1

FIX Engine Capabilities

Support for different versions of FIX

Support for multiple asset classes

High availability, load balancing, and scalability

Speed and robustness

Backup logging of data

Encryption

Support for per connection business logic

TABLE 26-2

FIX Engine Technologies

Support for different platforms

Architectual flexibility

Class library APIs or "FIX in a box" solutions

TABLE 26-3

FIX Engine Vendor Support Services

Access to source code

24/7 call center

Upgrades

Documentation

Pricing

Monitoring tools

is a competitive advantage, require fast FIX engines. If your firm employs strategies that don't depend on nanoseconds for performance, speed is of lesser value. Also, performance of a given FIX engine on your firm's existing hardware should be understood ahead of time.

Common nowadays are FIX engines that offer connectivity to ECNs and certifications against major trading counterparties. These prebuilt interfaces to liquidity sources will save your firm time and money. Less common, but growing in popularity for obvious reasons, are FIX engines where business logic, such as validation, translation, and version mapping, is built in to the system.

More and more too, FIX engines are providing connection monitoring tools, alerting functionalities, automated testing tools for certification that can speed up implementation.

Most FIX engine vendors charge a per month or per quarter licensing fee and possibly pay-as-you-go support fees. Whatever the case, cost should not be a major issue.

In summary, when selecting a FIX engine, FIX Protocol, LTD., suggests that performance is important, but that the value of performance should be weighed against the competitive advantage gained. Also, your firm should look for vendors who have proven themselves in the marketplace and should look for those engines that include business logic and alerting, testing, and monitoring tools. Finally, price should be a consideration, but total cost should not be ignored.

26.2.5. FIX Adapted for Streaming (FAST)

The FAST protocol is a new, open source data compaction methodology developed by the FIX organization, FIX Protocol, Ltd., that is gaining rapid acceptance in the financial industry. According to FIX Protocol, Ltd., FAST employs implicit tagging, field encoding, and serialization to reduce by up to 90% message size and bandwidth utilization. As a result, FAST significantly improves the communication efficiencies for exchange data feeds without incurring trade-offs in processing and latency. The FASTAPI allows for easy access to the FAST functions used to compress data streams. You will likely hear more about FAST in the near future.

26.3. Summary

This brief chapter reviewed FIX, a widely used, non-XML protocol for real-time messaging of trade and trade information in the financial markets. While it may be unlikely that you ever use FIX yourself, need to understand the construction of FIX messages, or even see a FIX message, it is important to understand, at least conceptually, FIX and FIX engines, as they may impact the success of your firm's automated trading systems.

CHAPTER • 27

Serialization

XML serialization is the process of converting an object's public data members into an XML stream that can be transported readily. On the other end, deserialization reconstructs the object and its data from an XML stream. XML serialization will not convert methods, nor will it convert private data. To serialize public and private data you should use a BinaryFormatter instead.

27.1. Serialization_Example

The Serialize and Deserialize methods of an XmlSerializer object serialize public data of an object.

```
Tick.h

#pragma once
using namespace System;

public ref struct Tick
{
    DateTime Time;
    double Price;
    double Qty;
};
```

```
Serialization_Example.cpp

#include "stdafx.h"
#include "Tick.h"
using namespace System;
using namespace System::IO;
using namespace System::Xml::Serialization;
```

```
int main(array<System::String ^> ^args)
{
    // Serialize a Tick object.
    Tick ^m_Tick=gcnew Tick;
    m_Tick->Time=DateTime::Now;
    m_Tick->Price=51.25;
    m_Tick->Qty=1000;

    XmlSerializer ^m_Serializer=gcnew XmlSerializer(Tick::typeid);
    StreamWriter ^m_Writer=gcnew StreamWriter("MyFile.xml");
    m_Serializer->Serialize(m_Writer, m_Tick);
    m_Writer->Close();

    // Deserialize a Tick object.
    FileStream ^m_FileStream=gcnew FileStream("myFile.xml", FileMode::Open);
    Tick ^m_Tick1=(Tick ^) m_Serializer->Deserialize(m_FileStream);

    Console::WriteLine(m_Tick1->Time.ToString() +
                       "\t"+m_Tick1->Price +
                       "\t"+m_Tick1->Qty);
    return 0;
}
```

27.2.   Summary

As mentioned, if we have an XSD, we can run the XML Schema Definition tool to generate classes that are strongly typed to the schema. In the example given earlier, we are assuming that the tick class conforms to a known XML Schema. It is advantageous to use the XmlSerializer instead of the XmlReader and XmlWriter described in a previous chapter.

CHAPTER ◆ 28

Windows Services

A Windows Service is a type of application that can be used to create long-running server-based programs that run locally or across a network. Services generally do not have user interfaces and run in the background on the client computer or server and can start automatically when your computer boots.

28.1.   Sample Code: WindowsService_Example

In order to gain an understanding of Windows Services in .NET, let's create a simple service application.

Step 1.   In Visual C++, open a new Windows Service solution named WindowsService_Example.

Note that the template wizard generates the following code:

```
WindowsService_ExampleWinService.h

#pragma once

using namespace System;
using namespace System::Collections;
using namespace System::ServiceProcess;
using namespace System::ComponentModel;

namespace WindowsService_Example {

public ref class WindowsService_ExampleWinService : public
System::ServiceProcess::ServiceBase
{
    public:
```

```
            WindowsService_ExampleWinService()
            {
                    InitializeComponent();
            }
        protected:
            ~WindowsService_ExampleWinService()
            {
                    if (components)
                    {
                        delete components;
                    }
            }
            virtual void OnStart(array<String^>^ args) override
            {
                    // TODO: Add code here to start your service.
            }
            virtual void OnStop() override
            {
                    // TODO: Add code here to perform any tear-down necessary ...
            }
        private:
            System::ComponentModel::Container ^components;

#pragma region Windows Form Designer generated code
            void InitializeComponent(void)
            {
                    this->components = gcnew System::ComponentModel::Container();
                    this->CanStop = true;
                    this->CanPauseAndContinue = true;
                    this->AutoLog = true;
                    this->ServiceName = L"WindowsService_ExampleWinService";
            }
#pragma endregion
        };
}
```

```
WindowsService_ExampleWinService.cpp

#include "stdafx.h"
#include <string.h>
#include "WindowsService_ExampleWinService.h"

using namespace WindowsService_Example;
using namespace System::Text;
using namespace System::Security::Policy;
using namespace System::Reflection;

//To install/uninstall type: "WindowsService_Example.exe -Install [-u]"
int _tmain(int argc, _TCHAR* argv[])
```

```
{
    if (argc>=2)
    {
        if (argv[1][0]==_T('/'))
        {
            argv[1][0]=_T('-');
        }
        if (_tcsicmp(argv[1], _T("-Install"))==0)
        {
            array<String^>^ myargs=System::Environment::GetCommandLineArgs();
            array<String^>^ args=gcnew array<String^>(myargs->Length - 1);

            // Set args[0] with the full path to the assembly,
            Assembly^ assem=Assembly::GetExecutingAssembly();
            args[0]=assem->Location;

            Array::Copy(myargs, 2, args, 1, args->Length - 1);
            AppDomain^ dom=AppDomain::CreateDomain(L"execDom");
            Type^ type=System::Object::typeid;
            String^ path=type->Assembly->Location;
            StringBuilder^ sb=gcnew StringBuilder(path->Substring
                                                (0, path->LastIndexOf(L "\\")));
            sb->Append(L "\\InstallUtil.exe");
            Evidence^ evidence=gcnew Evidence();
            dom->ExecuteAssembly(sb->ToString(), evidence, args);
        }
    }
    else
    {
        ServiceBase::Run(gcnew WindowsService_ExampleWinService());
    }
}
```

Next, we need to create the installers for your service.

Step 2.   In the Design View window for WindowsService_ExampleWinService.h,
right click the background in the design window and select Add Installer.
A component named ProjectInstaller, which contains a ServiceInstaller object
and a ServiceProcessInstaller object, will be added to your service project.

Step 3.   In the Properties window for your ServiceInstaller object, set the StartType
property to Automatic.

Step 4.   In the Properties window for your ServiceProcessInstaller object, set the
Account property to LocalSystem.

The Windows Service program that we have created so far doesn't do anything. Let's add
some code to be sure that it runs.

Step 5.   Add the following class to your project.

```
MyClass.h

#pragma once
using namespace System;
using namespace System::IO;

ref class MyClass
{
private:
    FileStream ^m_File;
    StreamWriter ^m_Writer;
public:
    MyClass(void);
    void WriteMessage(String ^);
};
```

```
MyClass.cpp

#include "StdAfx.h"
#include "MyClass.h"

MyClass::MyClass(void)
{
    m_File=gcnew FileStream("C:/MyFile.txt", FileMode::OpenOrCreate);
    m_Writer=gcnew StreamWriter(m_File);
}

void MyClass::WriteMessage(String ^m_Message)
{
    m_Writer->Write(m_Message);
    m_Writer->Flush();
    m_Writer->Close();
    m_File->Close();
}
```

Step 6.   In your WindowsService_ExampleWinService.h class, #include "MyClass.
h", add a pointer to an instance of MyClass as a member, and, to the OnStart
method, add the following code.

```
virtual void OnStart(array<String^>^ args) override
{
    myObj=gcnew MyClass;
    myObj->WriteMessage("Hello, World!");
}
```

Step 7. Build your project.

In order to install a Windows Service, we do not use the Setup Project. Rather, we must go to the command line and install from there.

Step 1. In your command window, navigate to the directory that contains Windows Service_Example.exe.

```
C:\>cd WindowsService_Example/Debug
```

Step 2. Install the .exe thusly:

```
C:WindowsService_Example\Debug>WindowsService_Example.exe -Install
```

If you need to uninstall the service, which you should do before debugging and reinstalling:

```
C:WindowsService_Example\Debug>WindowsService_Example.exe -Install\u
```

Next, you need to start your service, as it will only start automatically when you boot your computer.

Step 3. On your Windows desktop, right click on My Computer and select Manage.
Step 4. In the Computer Management window, expand Services and Applications and double click Services. A list of all the Windows Services on your computer will appear.
Step 5. Navigate down to WindowsService_Example and click start.

When your service starts, it should create the file named MyFile.txt. Open this text file and get your message.

28.2. Summary

A Windows Service is a type of application that can be used to create long-running server-based programs. Because automated trading systems make use of Windows Service applications a great deal, being comfortable with them is important.

CHAPTER • 29

Setup and Installation Packages

Visual Studio 2005 provides a setup project template that allows us to create installers, which will enable us to distribute an application. The output of a setup project is an MS Installer file with the .msi extension. This file will contain the application we intend to install as well as any .dlls the application depends on and other information and instructions for installation. You can take this .msi file to other computers and be assured that everything necessary for installation will be there.

29.1. Code Sample: Installation_Example

First, we will need to create an application to install.

Step 1.   Create a new Windows Forms Application solution named Installation_ Example.
Step 2.   In the Properties window for your Form1, change the Text property to Installation_Example.
Step 3.   Build your application.

Next, we will need to add a setup project that will install the project files and run the necessary installers for your Windows application.

Step 1.   Click on File menu item and select Add and then New Project.
Step 2.   In the Project Types window, select Other Project Types, Setup, and Deployment and, in the Templates window, select Setup Project. Name your project Installation_Setup.

Now we need to add the output from the Installation_Example project to the setup project.

Step 3.   In Solution Explorer, right click Installation_Setup, select Add, and then select Project Output. The Add Project Output Group window will appear.
Step 4.   Installation_Example should already be selected in the Project box. In the list box, select Primary Output and then click OK.

Step 5.   In the Solution Explorer, right click Installation_Setup and select Build.

Now, in Windows Explorer navigate to the Installation_Setup directory. In the Debug or Release subfolder, you will find a file named setup.exe or one called Installation_Setup.msi. Double click this file and it will walk you through the process for installing Installation_Example.exe.

29.2.   Summary

Adding an installer to your project can make your project look much more professional. Also, when working with clients or other departments, installers are usually a good idea to prevent user mistakes during installation.

SECTION • II

Concurrency

CHAPTER ◆ 30

Threading

At any given time, your computer may be executing several different applications or services concurrently. These programs run as processes within the Windows operating system, which allocates time on the processor (or processors) to different threads that execute code. As a result, by dividing the processor's time among the multiple threads, the operating system can create the appearance of simultaneous execution of multiple programs. One after the other, the operating system allocates a very small slice of time to each thread according to their respective priorities. When the processor switches from one thread to another thread, the operating system saves all the needed information about the thread, called the thread context. When the thread restarts, its thread context will be reloaded, enabling execution to resume. (Futher, the .NET Framework breaks down processes into subprocesses called application domains; the managed class System::AppDomain represents these subprocesses. An AppDomain is essentially a safe, isolated place where your program code can execute.) Of course, the number of threads that can run at the same time is a function of the number of processors on your computer or server.

The term *multithreading* essentially means the ability to have different parts of our computer program running at the same time. Multiple threads allow our programs to perform multiple blocks of code concurrently, or in parallel, and we can use them to, for example, communicate over a network or with a database, perform time-consuming calculations, or distinguish between operations with different priorities. High-priority threads can be used to manage real-time data feeds and calculations while low-priority ones can be used to perform less critical tasks.

In general, however, while multithreading is advantageous, fewer threads are still better than more. Managing multiple threads can eat up a large amount of processor time (not to mention a programmer's time!) and create new problems. Namely, multithreading can create conflicts between threads that are trying to use the same resource. In order to make our multithreaded programs safe, we may have to control access to different resources or blocks of code or objects, a process called synchronization. Incorrect synchronization of resources can create deadlocks or race conditions. (A deadlock happens when two threads stop responding because each is waiting for the other to finish. A race condition happens when abnormal events or results are generated due to an unknown dependence between events in different threads.) Fortunately, the .NET Framework system provides several objects that we can use to control access to resources, as shown in a later chapter.

Parallel execution can bring performance gains and in .NET and it's not that hard to do. The hard part of multithreading is making sure that the different threads do not interfere with one another in an unwanted or unexpected way. Again, we will look at that topic in a later chapter; for now let's look at threads. Using the classes in the System::Threading namespace, we can create and control multiple threads in our programs.

30.1.   Threading Namespace

The System::Threading namespace contains types that allow us to create and manage multithreaded programs. In .NET, a thread is either a foreground thread or a background thread. One difference between a foreground thread and a background thread is that a background thread will not keep an application running after all of the foreground threads have been stopped. Once all foreground threads are stopped, the operating system will automatically stop any and all background threads. Also, background threads will only run when the foreground thread is idle.

The Thread class allows us to create and manage foreground threads in our applications. The Thread's constructor accepts a new ThreadStart delegate as a parameter. The ThreadStart delegate accepts the address of a static or instance method.

30.2.   Sample Code: Thread_Example

```
MyClass.h

#pragma once
using namespace System;
using namespace System::Threading;

ref class MyClass
{
private:
        int m_Value;

public:
        MyClass(void);
        void Go();
        void set_Data(int);
};
```

```
MyClass.cpp

#include "StdAfx.h"
#include ".\myclass.h"

MyClass::MyClass(void)
{
}
```

```
void MyClass::Go()
{
    Thread::Sleep(5000);
    Console::WriteLine("Hello from the other thread: "+m_Value);
}

void MyClass::set_Data(int x)
{
    m_Value=x;
}
```

```
Thread_Example.cpp

#include "stdafx.h"
#include "MyClass.h"

using namespace System;
using namespace System::Threading;

int main(array<System::String ^> ^args)
{
    MyClass ^m_Obj=gcnew MyClass;
    m_Obj->set_Data(4);

    Thread ^m_Thread=gcnew Thread(gcnew ThreadStart(m_Obj, &MyClass::Go));
    m_Thread->Start();

    Console::WriteLine("Hello from the main thread.");

    return 0;
}
```

Be aware that on a single processor machine, calling the Thread::Start method will not necessarily start thread execution. Execution will wait for the current thread to yield the processor over to it.

Relative to the Thread class, the ThreadPool class discussed later will, in general, be an easier way to handle multiple threads, especially for short-lived operations that don't require blocking or prioritization of threads or necessitate a stable identity for the thread.

30.3. Sample Code: ThreadAbort_Example

Calling the Thread class' Abort method throws a ThreadAbortException within the worker thread. In this example the while loop will continue forever until the thread is aborted and not reset. Because the Abort method does not cause the foreground Thread to stop immediately, we need to call Join. The Join method blocks the calling thread until the worker thread terminates.

```
MyClass.h

#pragma once
using namespace System;
using namespace System::Threading;

ref class MyClass
{
public:
    MyClass(void);
    static void Go();
};
```

```
MyClass.cpp

#include "StdAfx.h"
#include ".\myclass.h"

MyClass::MyClass(void)
{
}

void MyClass::Go()
{

    while (true)
    {

        try
        {
            Console::WriteLine(".");
            Thread::Sleep(300);
        }
        catch(ThreadAbortException ^e)
        {
            if (String::Equals(e->ExceptionState, "RESET"))
            {
                Thread::ResetAbort();
                Console::WriteLine("Thread: Reset.");
            }
            else
            {
                Console::WriteLine("Thread: Aborted.");
            }
        }
    }
}
```

```
ThreadAbort_Example.cpp

#include "stdafx.h"
#include "MyClass.h"
using namespace System;
using namespace System::Threading;

int main(array<System::String ^> ^args)
{
    Thread ^m_Thread=gcnew Thread(gcnew ThreadStart(&MyClass::Go));
    m_Thread->Start();

    Thread::Sleep(1000);

    m_Thread->Abort("RESET");

    Thread::Sleep(1000);

    m_Thread->Abort("TERMINATE");
    m_Thread->Join();

    Console::WriteLine("Main thread ending.");
    return 0;
}
```

In general, it may not be a good idea to use Thread::Abort to terminate threads. Because it throws an exception in that thread, you will never know where that thread is in terms of processing.

30.4. Thread Priority

The ThreadPriority enumeration lets us specify the scheduling priority of a particular thread relative to other threads. Table 30-1 shows the available priorities.

At any given time, the thread with the highest priority will always execute first. Threads with the same priority will be cycled through with fixed time slices allocated to each. Threads with lower priorities will run last and will be relegated if a new thread with a higher priority becomes available.

TABLE 30-1

Thread Priority Members
AboveNormal
BelowNormal
Highest
Lowest
Normal (default)

30.5.   Sample Code: ThreadPriority_Example

```
MyClass.h

#pragma once
using namespace System;
using namespace System::Threading;
ref class MyClass
{
public:
    static void ThreadInfo()
    {
        Thread ^m_Thread_2 = Thread::CurrentThread;
        m_Thread_2->Sleep(5000);

        Console::WriteLine(m_Thread_2->Name);
        Console::WriteLine(m_Thread_2->ThreadState);
        Console::WriteLine(m_Thread_2->Priority);
    }
};
```

```
ThreadPriority_Example.cpp

#include "stdafx.h"
#include "MyClass.h"
using namespace System;
using namespace System::Threading;

int main(array<System::String ^> ^args)
{
    Thread ^m_Thread = gcnew Thread(gcnew ThreadStart(&MyClass::ThreadInfo));
    m_Thread->Name = "My Thread";
    m_Thread->Priority = ThreadPriority::Highest;
    m_Thread->Start();

    Console::WriteLine("Main thread ending.");
    return 0;
}
```

30.6.   ThreadState Enumeration

The ThreadState enumeration specifies one of eight states of a thread (Table 30-2).

TABLE 30-2

State	Description
Initialized	Thread is initialized but not started.
Ready	Thread is waiting to use a processor and is ready to run on the next available processor.
Running	Thread is currently using a processor.
Standby	Thread is about to use a processor.
Terminated	Thread has exited and no longer using a processor.
Transition	Thread cannot execute because it is waiting for a resource other than the processor.
Unknown	Thread state is unknown.
Wait	Thread is not ready because it is waiting for some other operation or for a resource to become available.

30.7. ThreadPool Class

The ThreadPool class makes threading simpler and easier through the use of a group, or pool, of worker threads that are managed by the operating system. This pool consists of 25 background threads. As a result, in our programs, a foreground thread can monitor the pool of background threads. We can run work items on separate background thread by calling the QueueUserWorkItem method, as shown in the example given later. This method accepts a new WaitCallback delegate. The delegate accepts the address of a static or instance method. A later chapter will show how to use ThreadPools to manage a pool of wait operations using callback functions.

30.8. Sample Code: ThreadPool_Example

```
MyClass.h

#pragma once
using namespace System;
using namespace System::Threading;

ref class MyClass
{
public:
    MyClass(void);
    static void MyFunction(Object ^);
};
```

```
MyClass.cpp

#include "StdAfx.h"
#include ".\myclass.h"

MyClass::MyClass(void)
{
}


void MyClass::MyFunction(Object ^m_Obj)
{
    Console::WriteLine("Hello from MyFunction thread.");
}
```

```
ThreadPool_Example.cpp

#include "stdafx.h"
#include "MyClass.h"
using namespace System;
using namespace System::Threading;

int main(array<System::String ^> ^args)
{
    ThreadPool::QueueUserWorkItem(gcnew WaitCallback(&MyClass::MyFunction));

    Console::WriteLine("Main thread ending.");
    return 0;
}
```

30.9.   Updating Forms from Other Threads

Here is an example. Suppose an instance of Form1 is created on the main thread. Suppose too that we start another thread, the calculations thread. When new calculations are made, we wish to have those new values sent to Form1. Using the synchronous event architecture discussed in a previous chapter, when the event is raised in the calculation thread and the event handler in Form1 is invoked, the method will nonetheless execute on calculations thread. In this case, a runtime exception will be thrown.

Updating a GUI form from a thread other than the one on which the form itself was created is illegal. However, we can execute a delegate asynchronously on the main thread using the Form1->BeginInvoke() method inherited from System::Windows::Forms::Control.

30.10.   Sample Code: FormUpdate_Example

In this example, notice that Form1 contains a pointer to an instance of MyClass and that MyClass contains a pointer to an instance of Form1. (In some cases, because the C++ compiler would not allow this type of circular dependency, a forward declaration to the other class would have to be made prior to each class declaration.)

Also in this Windows Forms Application example, notice that Form1 inherits from the Control class that contains a method called BeginInvoke, which will execute a delegate asynchronously on the thread on which the Control's handle was created. The GUI for this example will simply be a form with a button, button1, and a textbox, textBox1.

```
MyClass.h

#pragma once
#include "Delegates.h"

using namespace System::Threading;
using namespace System::Diagnostics;
using namespace System::Windows::Forms;

ref class MyClass
{
private:
     Form ^m_Form;
     Thread ^m_Thread;

public:
     MyClass(Form ^m_Form);

     MyUpdateHandler ^UpdateForm;

     void RunThread();
};
```

```
MyClass.cpp

#include "stdafx.h"
#include "MyClass.h"

MyClass::MyClass(Form ^m_F)
{
     m_Form=m_F;

     m_Thread=gcnew Thread(gcnew ThreadStart(this, &MyClass::RunThread));
     m_Thread->Name="Calculations";
     m_Thread->Start();
}

void MyClass::RunThread()
{
   for (int x=0; x < 4; x++)
```

```
    {
        Thread::Sleep(3000);
        Debug::WriteLine("MyClass Thread: "+Thread::CurrentThread->Name);

        m_Form->BeginInvoke(UpdateForm, x);

        Debug::WriteLine("MyClass Thread again: "+Thread::CurrentThread->Name);
    }
}
```

```
Delegates.h
#pragma once

public delegate void MyUpdateHandler(int);
```

```
Form1.h

MyClass ^m_Obj;

private: System::Void button1_Click(…)
{
    Thread::CurrentThread->Name="Main";
    m_Obj=gcnew MyClass(this);
    m_Obj->UpdateForm+=gcnew MyUpdateHandler(this, &Form1::UpdateFormEventHandler);
}
private: void UpdateFormEventHandler(int x)
{
    Debug::WriteLine("Form Thread: "+Thread::CurrentThread->Name);
    TextBox1->Text=x.ToString();
}
```

In this example, the Calculations thread starts at the MyClass::RunThread() method. We call BeginInvoke on the Form, which invokes the UpdateForm delegate handler, UpdateFormEventHandler, on the Main thread.

30.11.   Thread Safety

In .NET, all public static class members support concurrent access in a multithreaded project. As a result, it is possible that any such member could be accessed simultaneously from two different threads as discussed. Be sure to check the Thread Safety section in the .NET help files for information on specific classes. If you need to use a class that is not thread safe, you will need to wrap it with code that will add the synchronization constructs that will be required.

30.12. Summary

Understanding concurrency, i.e., multithreading, is a key to building fast, robust trading systems. This chapter looked at some of the basics of multithreading in .NET, including the Thread and ThreadPool classes, and how to start and stop threads in code. We will continue our discussion of threading in the coming chapters.

CHAPTER • 31

Synchronization Classes

Generally speaking, collection classes are not thread safe. This means that while multiple threads can read collection at the same time, any changes to the elements in the collection by a thread will cause problems for any other threads that are accessing it. However, a collection can be made thread safe by creating a thread-safe wrapper around it.

We can create a wrapped collection by simply calling the collection object's Synchronized method. In the end, only hashtables are guaranteed to be thread safe, while arrays can never be so.

31.1. Sample Code: Synchronize_Example

```
#include "stdafx.h"

using namespace System;
using namespace System::Collections;

int main(array<System::String ^> ^args)
{

    Hashtable ^m_HT = gcnew Hashtable;

    m_HT->Add("A", "Zero");
    m_HT->Add("B", "One");
    m_HT->Add("C", "Two");

    // Create a synchronized wrapper around the Hashtable.
    Hashtable ^m_HTSync = Hashtable::Synchronized(m_HT);

    Console::WriteLine(String::Concat("m_HT is ",
        m_HT->IsSynchronized ? "synchronized" : "not synchronized"));
```

```
    Console::WriteLine(String::Concat("m_HTSync is ",
        m_HTSync->IsSynchronized ? "synchronized" : "not synchronized"));

    return 0;
}
```

We can even create our own synchronized objects. When the Synchronization attribute is added to a class, only one thread is allowed to be executing on a specific instance.

ContextBoundObjects are objects that can be bound to a set of properties or policies regarding synchronization.

```
#pragma once
using namespace System;
using namespace System::Runtime::Remoting::Contexts;

[Synchronization]
ref class MyClass : public ContextBoundObject
{
public:
    MyClass(void);
    ~MyClass(void);
};
```

The System::Threading namespace contains objects for managing access to resources shared between threads. These classes are derived from the WaitHandle class, which exposes WaitAll, WaitAny, and WaitOne methods that block the current thread's access until a signal is received.

31.2.   Mutex Class

When two or more threads in our program need to access the same resource at the same time, we may need a mechanism to make sure that only one thread at a time is allowed to enter a block of code. This is where a Mutex, derived from WaitHandle, comes in. When one thread acquires a Mutex, all subsequent threads that attempt to acquire it will be suspended, or blocked, until the original thread releases the Mutex. As a result, a Mutex object will grant exclusive access to a critical section of code. Also, a Mutex will automatically release when the thread that owns it terminates.

31.3.   Example Code: Mutex_Example

In this example, we will start three threads at the MyClass::RunCalculations static method. As you can see, this method will take 3 seconds to run since the executing thread is put to sleep. Note that once the first thread acquires the Mutex via the WaitOne method, the second thread is blocked from entering the method body until after the first thread releases the Mutex. The third thread can then follow once the second thread has released the Mutex.

MyClass.h

```
#pragma once
using namespace System;
using namespace System::Threading;

ref class MyClass
{
private:
    static Mutex ^m_Mutex=gcnew Mutex;

public:
    MyClass(void);
    static void RunCalcs();
};
```

MyClass.cpp

```
#include "StdAfx.h"
#include ".\myclass.h"

MyClass::MyClass(void)
{
}

void MyClass::RunCalcs()
{
    // Thread will wait until all other threads have exited protected area.
    m_Mutex->WaitOne();

    Console::WriteLine(Thread::CurrentThread->Name+
                                        "has entered protected the area.");
    // Simulate some time-intensive process here.
    Thread::Sleep(3000);

    Console::WriteLine(Thread::CurrentThread->Name+"is leaving protected the area.");

    // Release the Mutex.
    m_Mutex->ReleaseMutex();
}
```

Mutex_Example.cpp

```
#include "stdafx.h"
#include "MyClass.h"
```

```
using namespace System;
using namespace System::Threading;
int main(array<System::String ^> ^args)
{

   for (int i=1; i < 4; i++)
   {
      // Start 3 new threads.
      Thread ^m_Thread=gcnew Thread(gcnew ThreadStart(&MyClass::RunCalcs));
      m_Thread->Name="Thread"+i.ToString();
      m_Thread->Start();
   }
   return 0;
}
```

31.4. Semaphore Class

A Semaphore, which is again derived from the WaitHandle class, will limit the number of threads that can access a block of code at the same time. Similar to a Mutex, threads enter the semaphore by calling the WaitOne method and then Release it on the way out. Be aware though that there is no guarantee of the order in which blocked and queued threads will enter a semaphore.

31.5. Sample Code: Semaphore_Example

This example creates a semaphore with a total capacity of three threads. Further, the starting capacity is zero. We start five threads and send them into the restricted method. Each thread will then be blocked while it waits for the semaphore. When the main thread Releases, three threads will enter the semaphore and two will remain blocked. When two of the three Release the semaphore, the remaining two will be allowed to enter.

```
MyClass.h

#pragma once

using namespace System;
using namespace System::Threading;

ref class MyClass
{
private:
      static Semaphore ^m_Semaphore;

public:
      MyClass();
      static void Worker(Object ^);
};
```

MyClass.cpp

```cpp
#include "stdafx.h"
#include "MyClass.h"

MyClass::MyClass()
{
    m_Semaphore = gcnew Semaphore(0, 3);

    for (int x = 1; x <= 10; x++)
    {
        Thread ^m_Thread = gcnew Thread(gcnew ParameterizedThreadStart(&MyClass::Worker));
        m_Thread->Start(x);
    }
    Thread::Sleep(500);

    // Calling release(3) will allow 3 thread to enter.
    m_Semaphore->Release(3);

    Thread::Sleep(5000);
    Console::WriteLine("Main thread exits.");
}

void MyClass::Worker(Object ^m_Thread)
{
    // All threads are blocked here until semaphore release is called.
    m_Semaphore->WaitOne();

    Console::WriteLine("Thread: {0} entering semaphore.", m_Thread);

    Thread::Sleep(1000);

    Console::WriteLine("Thread: {0} releasing semaphore.", m_Thread);

    // As each thread releases, others are allowed to enter.
    m_Semaphore->Release();
}
```

Semaphore_Example.cpp

```cpp
#include "stdafx.h"
#include "MyClass.h"

using namespace System;
using namespace System::Threading;

int main(array<System::String ^> ^args)
{
```

```
    MyClass ^m_Obj=gcnew MyClass;
    return 0;
}
```

31.6.   Monitor Class

Monitors give us the ability to synchronize access to an object by obtaining and releasing a lock on it. Monitors lock reference types and limit access to them to a single thread. While a thread owns the lock for an object, no other thread can acquire a lock on it.

31.7.   Sample Code: Monitor

In this example, if one thread has obtained a lock using the Monitor::Enter method on m_Hashtable, but has not yet released it using Monitor::Exit, then the current thread will be blocked until the other thread releases the lock on the object. Also, once the current thread obtains the lock, no other thread will be able to obtain a lock until the current thread releases it.

```
Monitor::Enter(m_Hashtable);

Ienumerator ^m_Enum=m_Hashtable->GetEnumerator();

while(m_Enum->MoveNext())
{
    Console::WriteLine(m_Enum->Current->ToString());
}

Monitor::Exit(m_Hashtable);
```

31.8.   Summary

This chapter looked at using Synchronization and Monitor, Mutex, and Semaphore objects to control access to resources by multiple threads. As most trading systems are multi-threaded, it is important to understand the topics in this chapter.

CHAPTER • 32

Sockets

This chapter provides a very brief overview of sockets in .NET.

When we send messages from one computer to another, they are sent to a queue, which holds the messages, provides routing services, and guarantees delivery. A queue manager relays the message from its sender to its intended receiver. If the receiver is not available, the queue will hold the message until it becomes available. Queue communication can be either synchronous or asynchronous.

By asynchronous we mean that messages are sent and received to and from the queue in separate processes. An application using asynchronous communication can send a message to a queue and immediately go on to other tasks without waiting for a reply. In synchronous communication, however, the sender of a message must wait an indeterminate amount of time for a response from the receiver before continuing on. In .NET we use sockets to manage both synchronous and asynchronous communications of messages.

As you can imagine, a synchronous socket would generally not be preferable in trading applications, which use networks heavily for price updates and order routing, but they work just fine for simpler applications. Rather, asynchronous sockets that do not suspend processing while waiting for network operations would be a better choice. Asynchronous sockets use what is known as the .NET Framework Asynchronous Programming Model to control network connections on one thread while the application continues to run on other threads.

In .NET, asynchronous operations provide an optional callback method to return a result. Asynchronous sockets use ThreadPool threads to initiate sending or receiving data and complete the network connection. The .NET Socket class provides the services of the Winsock32 API by marshaling managed data to native types and as said provide for both synchronous and asynchronous communications using TCP/IP, UDP, or any of many other protocols contained in the ProtocolType enumeration.

The NetworkStream class provides methods for sending and receiving data over sockets, and we can again use the NetworkStream class for both synchronous and asynchronous communications. When we create a NetworkStream object, we must provide a connected Socket as you will see. An IPEndPoint represents a network end point as an IP address and a port number.

32.1.   Sample Code: SynchronousServer_Example

The following example uses synchronous socket communications, albeit on a separate thread, to illustrate some asynchronous attributes; only the ServerThread in this example and the ClientThread in the next wait for network operations, while the main thread in each continues to run.

```
Form1.h

#pragma once
#include "Delegates.h"

namespace SynchronousServer_Example {

using namespace System;
using namespace System::ComponentModel;
using namespace System::Collections;
using namespace System::Windows::Forms;
using namespace System::Data;
using namespace System::Drawing;
using namespace System::Threading;
using namespace System::Net;
using namespace System::Net::Sockets;
using namespace System::IO;

public ref class Form1 : public System::Windows::Forms::Form
{
// Windows generated code here.

Socket ^m_Socket;
NetworkStream ^m_Stream;
BinaryWriter ^m_Writer;
BinaryReader ^m_Reader;
Thread ^m_ServerThread;
FormUpdateHandler ^UpdateForm;

private: System::Void Form1_Load(System::Object^ sender, System::EventArgs^ e)
{
    // Subscribe to the delegate.
    UpdateForm += gcnew FormUpdateHandler(this, &Form1::OnUpdateForm);
    // Start a new thread for the socket to listen on.
    m_ServerThread=gcnew Thread(gcnew ThreadStart(this, &Form1::RunServer));
    m_ServerThread->Start();
}
private: void RunServer()
{
    try
```

```
{
    // Create an endpoint for the socket on your local machine.
    IPEndPoint ^m_EP=gcnew IPEndPoint(IPAddress::Parse("127.0.0.1"), 11000);

    // Create a TCP/IP socket.
    m_Socket=gcnew Socket(AddressFamily::InterNetwork, SocketType::Stream,
                          ProtocolType::Tcp);
    try
    {
        // Bind the socket to the endpoint and wait for incoming connections.
        m_Socket->Bind(m_EP);
        m_Socket->Listen(10);

        while (true)
        {
            // Update the form on the main thread.
            this->BeginInvoke(UpdateForm, "Waiting for connection.");

            // Thread will be blocked here until a new connection is made.
            Socket ^m_Handler=m_Socket->Accept();

            // Create a new network stream, and binary reader and writer.
            m_Stream=gcnew NetworkStream(m_Handler);
            m_Writer=gcnew BinaryWriter(m_Stream);
            m_Reader=gcnew BinaryReader(m_Stream);

            // Update the form on the main thread.
            this->BeginInvoke(UpdateForm, "Connection received.");

            // Write a reply to the client.
            m_Writer->Write("SERVER: Connection successful!");
            String ^m_Reply;
            while (m_Reply != "CLIENT: Exit" && m_Handler->Connected)
            {
                // Keep the connection open until the client types "Exit."
                try
                {
                    // Read the incoming message.
                    m_Reply=m_Reader->ReadString();
                    // Update the form on the main thread.
                    this->BeginInvoke(UpdateForm, m_Reply);
                }
                catch (Exception ^e)
                {
                    // Debug::WriteLine(e->Message);
                }
            }
            // Update the form on the main thread.
            this->BeginInvoke(UpdateForm, "User terminated connection.");
```

```
                    // Close everything.
                    m_Writer->Close();
                    m_Reader->Close();
                    m_Stream->Close();
                    m_Socket->Shutdown(SocketShutdown::Both);
                    m_Socket->Close();
                }
            }
            catch (Exception ^e)
            {
                // Debug::WriteLine(e->Message);
            }
        }
        catch (Exception ^e)
        {
            // Debug::WriteLine(e->Message);
        }
    }

    private: System::Void textBox1_KeyDown(System::Object^ sender, KeyEventArgs^ e)
    {
        try
        {
            if(e->KeyCode == Keys::Enter && m_Socket != nullptr)
            {
                // When the user hits enter, write to the binary writer.
                m_Writer->Write("SERVER:"+textBox1->Text);
                textBox2->Text += "SERVER:"+textBox1->Text+Environment::NewLine;

                if (textBox1->Text == "Exit")
                {
                    // If the user types "Exit," close the socket.
                    m_Socket->Close();
                    textBox1->Clear();
                }
            }
        }
        catch (Exception ^e)
        {
            // Debug::WriteLine(e->Message);
        }
    }

    private: void OnUpdateForm(String ^m_Data)
    {
        // Update the form.
        textBox2->Text += m_Data+Environment::NewLine;
    }
};
}
```

32.2. Sample Code: SynchronousClient_Example

```
Form1.h

#pragma once
#include "Delegates.h"

namespace SynchronousClient_Example {

using namespace System;
using namespace System::ComponentModel;
using namespace System::Collections;
using namespace System::Windows::Forms;
using namespace System::Data;
using namespace System::Drawing;
using namespace System::Threading;
using namespace System::Net;
using namespace System::Net::Sockets;
using namespace System::IO;


public ref class Form1 : public System::Windows::Forms::Form
{
// Windows generated code here.
Socket ^m_Socket;
NetworkStream ^m_Output;
BinaryWriter ^m_Writer;
BinaryReader ^m_Reader;
Thread ^m_ClientThread;
String ^m_Message;


FormUpdateHandler ^UpdateForm;

private: System::Void Form1_Load(System::Object^ sender, System::EventArgs^ e)
{
    // Subscribe to the delegate.
    UpdateForm+=gcnew FormUpdateHandler(this, &Form1::OnUpdateForm);
    // Start a new thread for the socket.
    m_ClientThread=gcnew Thread(gcnew ThreadStart(this, &Form1::RunClient));
    m_ClientThread->Start();
}
private: void RunClient()
{
    // Create an endpoint for the socket on your local machine.
    IPEndPoint ^m_EP=gcnew IPEndPoint(IPAddress::Parse("127.0.0.1"), 11000);

    // Create a TCP/IP socket.
    m_Socket=gcnew Socket(AddressFamily::InterNetwork, SocketType::Stream,
                ProtocolType::Tcp);
```

```
        try
        {
            // Connect the socket to the endpoint.
            m_Socket->Connect(m_EP);
            // Create a new network stream, and binary reader and writer.
            m_Output=gcnew NetworkStream(m_Socket);
            m_Writer=gcnew BinaryWriter(m_Output);
            m_Reader=gcnew BinaryReader(m_Output);

            while (m_Message != "CLIENT: Exit" && m_Socket->Connected)
            {
                // Keep the connection open until we type "Exit"
                try
                {
                    // Read the incoming message.
                    m_Message=m_Reader->ReadString();
                    // Update the form on the main thread.
                    this->BeginInvoke(UpdateForm, m_Message);
                }
                catch (Exception ^e)
                {
                    // Debug::WriteLine(e->Message);
                }
            }
            // Close everything.
            m_Writer->Close();
            m_Reader->Close();
            m_Output->Close();
            m_Socket->Shutdown(SocketShutdown::Both);
            m_Socket->Close();
        }
        catch (Exception ^e)
        {
            // Debug::WriteLine(e->Message);
        }
    }
private: System::Void textBox1_KeyDown(System::Object^ sender, KeyEventArgs^ e)
    {
        try
        {
            if (e->KeyCode == Keys::Enter)
            {
                // When the user hits enter, write to the binary writer.
                m_Writer->Write("CLIENT:"+textBox1->Text);
                textBox2->Text += "CLIENT:"+textBox1->Text+Environment::NewLine;
                textBox1->Clear();
            }
        }
        catch (Exception ^e)
```

```
    {
        // Debug::WriteLine(e->Message);
    }
}
private: void OnUpdateForm(String ^m_Data)
{
    // Update the form.
    textBox2->Text += m_Data+Environment::NewLine;
}
};
}
```

32.3. Summary

In this chapter we have taken a very brief look at a very large topic, messaging in .NET, including the Socket class. Network communications can be synchronous or asynchronous. For trading system development, asynchronous communications would be preferred, although a thorough discussion of asynchronous communications is beyond the scope of this text. Further investigation would certainly be beneficial. The Visual Studio Documentation help files contain an extensive treatment of the .NET Asynchronous Programming Model.

In many cases, the messaging technology would be encompassed within a FIX engine or a third-party API that you can connect to for data feeds and order routing. Whether or not you ever become an expert at sockets and asynchronous communications, at a minimum, a general knowledge of the topic is important, as messaging technologies form the backbone of modern financial markets.

SECTION • III

Interoperability and Connectivity

CHAPTER • 33

Marshaling

Marshaling activities, performed by the common language runtime (CLR) marshaling service, are concerned with how data are passed back and forth between managed and unmanaged memory during runtime, making it appear as if both managed and unmanaged codes are operating on the same data when in fact they each have a copy. As shown in later chapters, the CLR provides mechanisms for interoperating with unmanaged code through Platform Invoke, for calls to functions and objects exported from native C++ libraries, and COM Interop, for interaction with objects in COM libraries. Underneath the hood, both of these mechanisms use the same interop marshaling service, although certain data types are at times supported only by one or the other.

Most data types have common representations in both managed and unmanaged codes, called blittable types, as mentioned previously. Other types may have ambiguous representations, called nonblittable types. For example, multiple unmanaged representations may map to the same managed type. Also, there may be type information lost in the marshaling process. Managed types are nonblittable, including delegates. As an example, Strings are nonblittable types—they have several unmanaged representations, some of which require conversion, as we will see. While there may be default or alternative representations presented by the interop marshaler, we can also supply explicit marshaling instructions for ambiguous types.

Instead of using the interop marshaler, we can design a custom marshaler for an interface that introduces different marshaling behavior or exposes the interface to unmanaged types in a different way. By using a custom marshaler, we can minimize the distinction between new .NET components and existing native or COM components.

33.1. Marshal Class

The Marshal class provides static methods for customizing the marshaling process—controlling and interacting with unmanaged memory and converting managed and unmanaged types. In the following example, the Marshal::StringToHGlobalAnsi method copies the ANSI characters from a managed String into a char * on the unmanaged heap and back.

33.2.   Sample Code: StringToCharArray_Example

```
#include "stdafx.h"

using namespace System;
using namespace System::Runtime::InteropServices;

int main(array<System::String ^> ^args)
{
    String ^m_Sym="IBM";

    // Marshall: :StringToHGlobalAnsi method copies the contents of a
    // managed String into unmanaged memory.
    char* m_C=(char *)(void *)Marshal::StringToHGlobalAnsi(m_Sym);

    // Convert char array to String.
    String ^m_String=gcnew String(m_C);

    Console::WriteLine(m_String);

    // Marshal::FreeHGlobal frees memory previously allocated on
    // the unmanaged memory
    Marshal::FreeHGlobal((IntPtr) m_C);

    return 0;
}
```

33.3.   Summary

If you need interoperability, use Platform Invoke or COM Interop. In such cases, as shown in later chapters, it is important to understand marshaling of integers, arrays, objects, and so on.

CHAPTER • 34

Interior and Pinning Pointers

A native C++ pointer cannot point to a location on the managed heap since the common language runtime (CLR) moves things around from time to time. As a result, for a native pointer to work, the CLR must update the pointer to the new location. This is where an interior pointer comes in.

An interior pointer can be assigned to anything that can be assigned to a native pointer and most often is used to point to member types—reference or value—inside reference types. Then the interior pointer can perform all of the regular pointer operations and pointer arithmetic. Here is a quick look at using an interior pointer.

34.1. Sample Code: InteriorPointer_Example

```
ManagedStruct.h

#pragma once

ref struct ManagedStruct
{
    ManagedStruct(int x) : m_Value(x) {}
    int m_Value;
};
```

```
ManagedStruct.cpp

#include "stdafx.h"
#include "ManagedStruct.h"
using namespace System;

int main(array<System::String ^> ^args)
{
```

```
    ManagedStruct ^m_Struct=gcnew ManagedStruct(3);
    interior_ptr< int > m_Pin=&(m_Struct->m_Value);
    Console::WriteLine(*m_Pin);

    return 0;
}
```

34.2. Pinning Pointers

If we need to pass a managed object into an unmanaged function or a method of an unmanaged object, we need to make sure that the managed object will not be moved around by the CLR during execution of the unmanaged function. To accomplish this, we can pin the managed object.

A pinning pointer is an interior pointer that will prevent the CLR from moving a reference type around until the pointer goes out of scope or is set to nullptr. We can pin an entire object or a member of an object, although in both cases the effect will be to pin the entire object. Be aware that pinning pointers cannot be used as function input or return values or as a member of a class.

34.3. Sample Code: Pinning_Example

```
ManagedClass.h

#pragma once

ref class ManagedClass
{
private:
    int m_Value;

public:
    ManagedClass(int);
    int get_Value();
};
```

```
ManagedClass.cpp

#include "StdAfx.h"
#include ".\managedclass.h"

ManagedClass::ManagedClass(int x) : m_Value(x)
{
}

int ManagedClass::get_Value()
```

```
{
    return m_Value;
}
```

UnmanagedClass.h

```
#pragma once
#include "ManagedClass.h"

class UnmanagedClass
{
public:
    static int GetFromManaged(ManagedClass ^);
};
```

UnmanagedClass.cpp

```
#include "StdAfx.h"
#include ".\unmanagedclass.h"

int UnmanagedClass::GetFromManaged(ManagedClass ^m_PinnedObj)
{
    return m_PinnedObj->get_Value();
}
```

Pinning_Example.cpp

```
#include "stdafx.h"
#include "ManagedClass.h"
#include "UnmanagedClass.h"
using namespace System;

int main(array<System::String ^> ^args)
{
    // Pass the managed object into the unmanaged
    // function after it's been pinned.

    ManagedClass ^m_Obj=gcnew ManagedClass(4);
    pin_ptr < ManagedClass ^ > m_PinnedObj=&m_Obj;

    int x=UnmanagedClass::GetFromManaged(m_Obj);

    m_PinnedObj=nullptr;

    Console::WriteLine(x);
    return 0;
}
```

Notice that the instance of the managed class continues to exist after the pinning pointer, m_PinnedObj, is set to nullptr and is not subject to garbage collection. It is still referenced by the managed pointer m_Obj.

34.4.   Summary

When the CLR marshals an object, the object is pinned for the duration of the Platform Invoke call so that the garbage collector does not move the object around in memory or destroy it.

CHAPTER • 35

Connecting to Managed DLLs

35.1. Example Code: DLL_Example

Let's create our own .dll file. In our .dll, we will include class definitions. In later programs we can add a reference to our .dll and create instances of the classes it contains.

Step 1. In Visual C++, open a new Class Library solution application. Give your application the name MyLibrary.

Step 2. In the MyLibrary.h file, include the following class definition.

```
MyLibrary.h

#pragma once

using namespace System;

namespace MyLibrary
{
    public ref class InstrObj
    {
    public: double get_Bid()
            {
                return 25.5;
            }
    };
}
```

Step 3. Now, add a new ref class called OrderObj.

Step 4. Add the following class definition to the OrderObj.h file.

```
OrderObj.h

#pragma once

using namespace System;

namespace MyLibrary
{
    public ref class OrderObj
    {
    private:
        int m_Price;
    public:
        OrderObj();
        int get_Price();
    };
    }
```

Step 5.   Finally, add Order.cpp with the following code and build the application.

```
OrderObj.cpp

#include "stdafx.h"
#include "./orderobj.h"

namespace MyLibrary
{
    OrderObj::OrderObj()
    {
        m_Price=100025;
    }
    int OrderObj::get_Price()
    {
        return m_Price;
    }
}
```

Now let's create a program that uses the MyLibrary.dll.

Step 1.   Create a new CLR Console Application named DLL_Example.
Step 2.   In the Solution Explorer, right click on the project name, DLL_Example, and select References… The Property Pages window will appear.
Step 3.   Click on the Add New Reference button and the Add Reference window will appear.

Step 4.   Click on the Browse tab and navigate to the MyLibrary.dll file created in the previous project and click OK. You should see MyLibrary show up in the References list in the Property Pages window.

Step 5.   In the DLL_Example code window, include the following code:

```
DLL_Example.cpp

#include "stdafx.h"

using namespace System;
using namespace MyLibrary;

int main(array<System::String ^> ^args)
{
    InstrObj ^m_Instr=gcnew InstrObj();
    Console::WriteLine(m_Instr->get_Bid());

    OrderObj m_Order;
    Console::WriteLine(m_Order.get_Price());

    return 0;
}
```

35.2.   Summary

In this short chapter, we looked at creating .dll files in VC++. Other programs can reference dlls and use the code as its own. In financial markets, we make use of "APIs," which most often take the form of .dll files.

CHAPTER • 36

Connecting to Component Object Model (COM) DLLs with COM Interop

In .NET, we can create instances of Component Object Model (COM) coclasses through the use of a runtime callable wrapper (RCW), which the .NET Framework creates for us automatically when we add a reference to a COM library. The RCW creates a managed wrapper around the unmanaged COM object, marshals method calls, and, if necessary, converts data between the managed wrapper and the unmanaged object. From the perspective of our managed code, the wrapped COM object will look and feel just like any other managed object. Through the RCW, managed classes can even inherit from COM coclasses.

In this case the derived, managed classes can then expose all the methods and properties of the COM object as well as any new methods defined in the managed class itself. The resulting object, then, exists partly in managed code and partly in unmanaged code. As for object destruction, the Common Language Runtime (CLR) will perform garbage collection on the RCW.

In any case, it is always advisable when using COM objects to make "chunky" method calls as opposed to "chatty" ones. A chunky call is a single method call that performs as many tasks as possible, whereas a chatty call is one that does only a very simple task and may then require many successive calls to accomplish the work of one chunky call. You can reduce overhead by designing your projects to make chunky calls when overhead is high as it is with COM.

36.1. Sample Code: MyCOMLibrary

In order to gain an understanding of COMInterop in .NET, let's start by creating a COM .dll that will contain an unmanaged class.

Step 1.   In Visual C++, open a new Active Template Library (ATL) Project named MyCOMLibrary. When the ATL Project Wizard appears, click Finish.

The ATL, which wraps the Win32 API, consists of template classes in C++ that let us create COM objects.

Step 2.   From the View menu, select Class View to open the Class View window.
Step 3.   In the Class View window, right click on MyCOMLibrary and select Add and then Add Class.
Step 4.   In the Add Class window, select the ATL category and ATL Simple Object. The ATL Simple Object Wizard window should appear.
Step 5.   In the ATL Simple Object Wizard, give the class a short name of Instrument and click Finish.
Step 6.   In the Class View window, you should now see IInstrument added to the list under MyCOMLibrary. Right click IInstrument and select Add and Add Method. The Add Method Wizard should appear.

In the Add Method Wizard, we will define the name of the method, the types and names of the input parameters, and the return type and name.

Step 7.   Enter a method name of Square. In Parameter attributes, click In. Enter a Parameter type of DOUBLE and a Parameter name of x. Click add (see Figure 36-1).

Now we need to set the return value.

Step 8.   Click on Parameter type of DOUBLE * and give a Parameter name of answer. You should see the out and retval check boxes become active. Click them both on and then click Add.
Step 9.   Click Finish (see Figure 36-2).

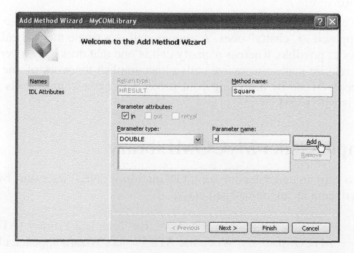

FIGURE 36-1

FIGURE 36-2

Step 10.   Add another method named Get by repeating the same steps given earlier. The Get method should accept a CHAR * named value and return a DOUBLE * named answer.

The Instrument.h file should look like this.

```
#pragma once
#include "resource.h"                        // main symbols

#include "MyCOMLibrary.h"

#if defined(_WIN32_WCE) && !defined(_CE_DCOM) &&
!defined(_CE_ALLOW_SINGLE_THREADED_OBJECTS_IN_MTA)
#error "Single-threaded COM…"
#endif


// CInstrument

class ATL_NO_VTABLE CInstrument :
      public CComObjectRootEx<CComSingleThreadModel>,
      public CComCoClass<CInstrument, &CLSID_Instrument>,
      public IDispatchImpl<IInstrument, &IID_IInstrument,
&LIBID_MyCOMLibraryLib, /*wMajor=*/ 1, /*wMinor=*/ 0>
{
public:
      CInstrument()
      {
      }

DECLARE_REGISTRY_RESOURCEID(IDR_INSTRUMENT)

BEGIN_COM_MAP(CInstrument)
      COM_INTERFACE_ENTRY(IInstrument)
      COM_INTERFACE_ENTRY(IDispatch)
END_COM_MAP()
      DECLARE_PROTECT_FINAL_CONSTRUCT()

      HRESULT FinalConstruct()
      {
            return S_OK;
      }
      void FinalRelease()
```

```
        {
        }
public:

public:
        STDMETHOD(Square)(DOUBLE x, DOUBLE* answer);
public:
        STDMETHOD(Get)(CHAR* value, DOUBLE* answer);
};

OBJECT_ENTRY_AUTO(__uuidof(Instrument), CInstrument)
```

Step 11.   In the Instrument.cpp file, provide the following code for the function definitions.

```
// Instrument.cpp : Implementation of CInstrument

#include "stdafx.h"
#include "Instrument.h"

// CInstrument

STDMETHODIMP CInstrument::Square(DOUBLE x, DOUBLE* answer)
{
        *answer=x * x;
        return S_OK;
}
STDMETHODIMP CInstrument::Get(CHAR* value, DOUBLE* answer)
{
        if (strcmp(value, "LAST") <=0)
        {
                *answer=120125;
        }
        else
        {
                *answer=0;
        }
        return S_OK;
}
```

Step 12.   Build MyCOMLibrary.
Step 13.   When you compile, your dll should be registered automatically. If not, use regsvr32 C://pathname.dll in the command window.

36.2. Sample Code: UsingCOMDLL_Example

Let's create a new program to test our COM dll.

Step 1.   Open a new CLR Console Application named UsingCOMDLL_Example.

Step 2.   Add a reference to MyCOMLibrary.dll. MyCOMLibrary 1.0 Type Library should be listed under the COM tab in the Add Reference window. Note that the namespace is now Interop::MyCOMLibrary. Through .NET's COMInterop, we will now have a managed wrapper around any unmanaged object.

Step 3.   Add the following code to the main code window. Notice the name MyCOMLibraryLib.

```cpp
#include "stdafx.h"

using namespace System;
using namespace MyCOMLibraryLib;

int main(array<System::String ^> ^args)
{
    InstrumentClass ^m_Instr=gcnew InstrumentClass;

    double c=m_Instr->Square(2);

    Console::WriteLine(c);

    delete m_Instr;

    return 0;
}
```

36.3. Summary

COM dlls are prevalent. Lots of financial industry software is developed in COM. While we delved only briefly into developing a COM program in this chapter, it is important to understand what COM is and how to connect to COM libraries in .NET programs.

CHAPTER • 37

Connecting to C++ DLLs with Platform Invocation Services

Via the Platform Invocation Services (PInvoke) of the common language runtime (CLR), we can use unmanaged application programming interfaces (APIs) directly. The DLLImport attribute provides us with the information needed to call unmanaged C-style functions and C++ style methods that are exported from a native, Win32 custom .dll.

In order to invoke one of these functions, we must supply the name of the .dll file and the entry point, either as the function name or as the ordinal entry point. If the name of the function in our application is the same as the name in the .dll, we do not have to explicitly provide that name as the entry point.

Be aware that the interop marshaler will always attempt to free memory allocated by unmanaged code. If you expect traditional C++ behavior, you may be surprised when using PInvoke, which will automatically free memory for pointers.

37.1. Calling C-Style Functions

According to Microsoft, Platform Invoke "has an overhead of between 10 and 30×86 instructions per call." Additionally, marshaling between data types will create additional overhead, although not between types that have the representation in both managed and unmanaged memory, called blittable types. So, for example, there is no overhead to translate between int and Int32.

As with COM Interop calls, though, in order to achieve higher performance, it is preferable to have chunky classes as opposed to chatty ones.

37.2. Sample Code: MyWin32Library

In order to gain an understanding of Platform Invoke in .NET, let's start by creating a Win32 custom .dll that will contain unmanaged functions.

Step 1.   In Visual C++, open a new Win32 Project named MyWin32Lib. The Win32 Project Wizard appears.

Step 2.   In the Project Wizard, click on Application Settings. In the Application Type list, check DLL. In the Additional Options list, check Export Symbols. Click Finish.

Step 3.   The MyWin32Lib.h and .cpp code window will be generated as shown. Also, modify the .cpp code and the .h file, adding a function prototype and definition named Add, as shown. Be sure to #include <cmath> header file.

```
MyWin32Lib.h

#ifdef MYWIN32LIB_EXPORTS
#define MYWIN32LIB_API __declspec(dllexport)
#else
#define MYWIN32LIB_API __declspec(dllimport)
#endif


// This class is exported from the MyWin32Lib.dll
class MYWIN32LIB_API CMyWin32Lib {
public:
    CMyWin32Lib(void);
    // TO DO: Add your code here.
};

extern MYWIN32LIB_API int nMyWin32Lib;

MYWIN32LIB_API int fnMyWin32Lib(void);

extern "C" MYWIN32LIB_API int Add(int, int);
```

```
MyWin32Lib.cpp

#include "stdafx.h"
#include "MyWin32Lib.h"

#ifdef _MANAGED
#pragma managed(push, off)
#endif

BOOL APIENTRY DllMain(HMODULE hModule,
                      DWORD ul_reason_for_call,
                      LPVOID lpReserved
                      )
{
    switch (ul_reason_for_call)
    {
    case DLL_PROCESS_ATTACH:
    case DLL_THREAD_ATTACH:
    case DLL_THREAD_DETACH:
```

```
          case DLL_PROCESS_DETACH:
               break;
          }
     return TRUE;
}


#ifdef _MANAGED
#pragma managed(pop)
#endif

// This is an example of an exported variable
MYWIN32LIB_API int nMyWin32Lib=0;

// This is an example of an exported function.
MYWIN32LIB_API int fnMyWin32Lib(void)
{
     return 42;
}
// This is the constructor of a class that has been exported.
// see MyWin32Lib.h for the class definition
CMyWin32Lib::CMyWin32Lib()
{
     return;
}
extern "C" MYWIN32LIB_API int Add(int x, int y)
{
     return x + y;
}
```

Step 4.   Build your solution.

The extern "C" syntax in the example declares the function and specifies that its name is visible from external files.

37.3.   Sample Code: UsingWin32DLL_Example

Let's create a new program to test our Win32 custom .dll.

Step 1.   Create a new Visual C++ CLR Console Application named UsingWin32DLL_
           Example.
Step 2.   In Windows Explorer, from the MyWin32Lib project folder, copy the file
           named MyWin32Lib.dll into the project folder for this new solution.
Step 3.   In the code window, add the following code.

```
UsingWin32Library_Example.cpp

#include "stdafx.h"

using namespace System;
using namespace System::Runtime::InteropServices;

[DllImport("MyWin32Lib", EntryPoint="Add")]
int Add(int a, int b);

int main(array<System::String ^> ^args)
{
    Console::WriteLine(Add(2, 3).ToString());
    return 0;
}
```

Step 4.   Build and run your solution.

37.4.   Creating Objects

Now let's look at a more complex problem. What if we need to create an instance of a class?

37.5.   Sample Code: MyWin32ClassLibrary

Step 1.   Create a new Win32 Project DLL as before. Be sure to check DLL and Export symbols under the Application Setting window in the Project Wizard.

Step 2.   Add a class named MyClass to your project. Add the code as shown.

```
MyClass.h

#ifdef MYWIN32CLASSLIB_EXPORTS
#define MYWIN32CLASSLIB_API __declspec(dllexport)
#else
#define MYWIN32CLASSLIB_API __declspec(dllimport)
#endif

class MYWIN32CLASSLIB_API MyClass
{
private:
     int myValue;
public:
    MyClass(int x);
    ~MyClass(void);
    int get_Value();
};
```

```
MyClass.cpp

#include "StdAfx.h"
#include "MyClass.h"

MyClass::MyClass(int x)
{
     myValue=x;
}

MyClass::~MyClass(void)
{
}

int MyClass::get_Value()
{
     return myValue;
}
```

Step 3.   You can remove MyWin32ClassLib.h from your project.
Step 4.   In the file named MyWin32ClassLib.cpp, modify the code as shown here.

```
MyWin32ClassLibrary.cpp

#include "stdafx.h"
#include "MyClass.h"

#ifdef _MANAGED
#pragma managed(push, off)
#endif

BOOL APIENTRY DllMain(HMODULE hModule, DWORD ul_reason_for_call, LPVOID lpReserved)
{
     switch (ul_reason_for_call)
     {
     case DLL_PROCESS_ATTACH:
     case DLL_THREAD_ATTACH:
     case DLL_THREAD_DETACH:
     case DLL_PROCESS_DETACH:
          break;
     }
     return TRUE;
}

#ifdef _MANAGED
#pragma managed(pop)
```

```
#endif
extern "C" MYWIN32CLASSLIB_API MyClass *CreateMyObject(int x)
{
        return new MyClass(x);
}
extern "C" MYWIN32CLASSLIB_API void DeleteMyObject(MyClass *myObj)
{
        delete myObj;
}
```

Step 5.   Build your solution.

37.6.   Sample Code: UsingWin32Class_Example

Let's create a new program to test our Win32 class.

Step 1.   Create a new Visual C++ CLR Console Application named UsingWin32-ClassLib_Example.

Step 2.   In Windows Explorer, from the MyWin32ClassLib project folder for the .dll that we just created, copy the file named MyWin32ClassLib.dll into the project folder for this solution.

Step 3.   On the menu bar, click Project and Add New Item and add a new .h code window named MyWrapperClass.h to your project. Add the following code:

```
#pragma once
using namespace System;
using namespace System::Runtime::InteropServices;

ref class MyWrapperClass
{
public:
        [DllImport("MyWin32ClassLib", EntryPoint="?get_Value@MyClass@@QAEHXZ",
                CallingConvention=CallingConvention::ThisCall) ]
        static int get_Value(int *myInstance);
};
```

Here you see that we used the ordinal entry point. We can find the ordinal entry point by using the Windows Command window and navigating to the directory containing the compiled Win32 .dll file. Once there, type the following:

```
C:\MyWin32ClassLib\release>link -dump -exports MyWin32ClassLib.dll
```

You will see a list of data showing the ordinals for the different functions in the .dll. The class member functions will include the class name.

	ordinal	hint	RVA	name
	1	0	00001010	??0MyClass@@QAE@H@Z
	2	1	00001020	??1MyClass@@QAE@XZ
	3	2	00001000	??4MyClass@@QAEAAV0@ ABV0@@Z
	4	3	00001030	?get_Value@MyClass@@QAEHXZ
	5	4	00001050	CreateMyObject
	6	5	00001070	DeleteMyObject

Step 4. Add the following code to the main file:

```
#include "stdafx.h"
#include "MyWrapperClass.h"

using namespace System;
using namespace System::Runtime::InteropServices;

[DllImport("MyWin32ClassLib", EntryPoint="CreateMyObject") ]
int *CreateMyObject(int);

[DllImport("MyWin32ClassLib", EntryPoint="DeleteMyObject") ]
void DeleteMyObject(int *);

int main(array<System::String ^> ^args)
{
    int *m_Obj=CreateMyObject (4);
    int a=MyWrapperClass::get_Value(m_Obj);

    Console::WriteLine(a);

    DeleteMyObject(m_Obj);
    return 0;
}
```

Step 5. Build your solution.

37.7. CallingConventionEnumeration

You may have noticed use of the CallingConvention in the example. This enumeration specifies the convention or protocol that will be required to call the unmanaged functions. We use ThisCall to call class member functions using the "this" pointer. In the example, we pass the pointer myObj into the static member get_Value.

37.8.   Summary

In financial engineering, we often have native C++ .dlls that contain many functions and classes. You may be familiar with native C++ libraries for financial markets, such as Bernt Ødegaard's excellent "Financial Numerical Recipes in C++" or potentially QuantLib, which contain dozens of C-style functions and C++ classes for financial calculations. (Of course, algorithms in these resources make extensive use of STL and other libraries such as Loki and Boost, in the case of QuantLib, which certainly add to the complexity of the problem.) Dlls written in native C++ can be integrated into managed, .NET applications using PInvoke, as we have seen over the course of this chapter.

CHAPTER • 38

Connecting to Excel

At times it may be necessary to connect a Visual C++.NET application to Excel. Through the Component Object Model (COM) libraries and COM Interop, Microsoft allows us to fully control an Excel spreadsheet in code. Of course, the implementations of this technology are endless.

38.1. Sample Code: ControllingExcel_Example

In order to gain understanding as to how to control Excel using COM libraries, let's create a simple C++.NET application.

Step 1. In Visual Studio, open a new Visual C++.NET console application named ControllingExcel_Example.

Step 2. In the Add Reference window, select the COM tab and navigate to and select Microsoft Excel Object Library.

Step 3. Add the following code to the main function. For readability, I have broken the code down into subsections.

In addition to System and Excel, we will need to use two namespaces in our program—the System::Reflection namespace, which includes Missing::Value and BindingFlags enumeration, and the InteropServices namespace, which contains the COMException class.

```
ControllingExcel_Example.cpp

#include "stdafx.h"

using namespace System;
using namespace System::Reflection; // For Missing.Value and BindingFlags
using namespace System::Runtime::InteropServices; // For COMException
using namespace Excel;
```

This section creates instances of the COM classes that represent an Excel application, a new workbook, and a worksheet.

```
int main(array<System::String ^> ^args)
{
    ApplicationClass ^m_XL = gcnew ApplicationClass();
    Workbook ^m_WB = m_XL->Workbooks->Add(Missing::Value);
    Worksheet ^m_WS = dynamic_cast< Worksheet ^ >(m_WB->Worksheets->Item[1]);

    m_XL->Visible = true;
    m_XL->UserControl = true;
```

Had we wanted to open an existing workbook, we could create an instance of the workbook class thusly.

```
Workbook ^m_WB = m_XL->Workbooks->Open("C:\\MyTestXL.xls", Missing::Value,
    Missing::Value, Missing::Value, Missing::Value, Missing::Value, Missing::Value,
    Missing::Value, Missing::Value, Missing::Value, Missing::Value, Missing::Value,
    Missing::Value);
```

To start, let's simply put a value into a cell.

```
// Enter a value into a cell
Range ^m_Range = m_WS->Range::get("A1", Missing::Value);
m_Range->Value2 = 5;
```

Now let's put a one-dimensional array into a range of cells.

```
// Enter one dimensional array to Excel
array<int> ^m_1DArray = gcnew array<int>(5);

for (int x = 0; x < 5; x++)
{
    m_1DArray[x] = 10 + x;
}
m_WS->Range::get("B1", "F1")->Value2 = m_1DArray;
```

We can format the range as well.

```
// Format the range
m_WS->Range::get("B1", "F1")->Font->Bold = true;
m_WS->Range::get("B1", "F1")->HorizontalAlignment = XlVAlign::xlVAlignCenter;
m_WS->Range::get("B1", "F1")->NumberFormat = "$0.00";
```

In order to enter an array vertically, i.e., as a column vector, we need to actually create a two-dimensional array.

```
// Show the array vertically
array< int, 2 > ^m_1DVertArray=gcnew array< int, 2 >(5, 1);

for (int x=0; x < 5; x++)
{
    m_1DVertArray[x, 0]=10+x;
}
m_WS->Range::get("G1", "G5")->Value2=m_1DVertArray;
```

Here is the code for a real, two-dimensional array, which differs essentially only by the array size from the previous example.

```
// This code sends two dimension array to Excel
array< double, 2 > ^m_2DArray=gcnew array< double, 2 >(3, 3);

for (int x=0; x < 3; x++)
{
    for (int y=0; y < 3; y++)
    {
        m_2DArray[x, y]=Math::Exp(x * y);
    }
}
m_WS->Range::get("H1", "J3")->Value2=m_2DArray;
```

Now let's read the range from Excel back into a managed, two-dimensional array in C++.

```
// This paragraph reads two dimensional array from Excel
array< Object ^, 2 > ^m_2DReadArray=dynamic_cast< array< Object ^, 2 > ^ >
                                    (m_WS->Range::get("H1", "J3")->Value2);

Console::WriteLine(m_2DReadArray[1, 1]);
Console::WriteLine(m_2DReadArray[3, 3]);
```

We can also enter formulae into cells.

```
// This shows how to put formulae into cells
m_WS->Range::get("B5", "D5")->Formula="=B1+C1";
m_WS->Range::get("K1", "K1")->Formula="=MDETERM(H1:J3)";
```

Now let's save the workbook and close Excel. If an exception is thrown during this process, it will be a COM one. Nonetheless, it will be wrapped and subsequently handled as a managed object.

```
try
{
    // If user interacted with Excel it will not close
    // when the app object is destroyed, so we close it explicitly
    m_WB->SaveAs("C:\\MyTestXL.xls", XlFileFormat::xlWorkbookNormal,
                Missing::Value, Missing::Value, Missing::Value,
                Missing::Value, XlSaveAsAccessMode::xlNoChange,
                Missing::Value, Missing::Value, Missing::Value,
                Missing::Value);
    m_WB->Close(Missing::Value, Missing::Value, Missing::Value);
    m_XL->UserControl = false;
    m_XL->Quit();
}
catch (COMException ^e)
{
    Console::WriteLine("Error in closing Excel.");
}

// GC is required to be sure that the XL application object is released.
GC::Collect();
return 0;
}
```

The next section simply extends the previous program to illustrate the creation of chart in Excel.

38.2.   Sample Code: ExcelChart_Example

First, let's create a two-dimensional array to hold data we intend to graph.

```
// This code sends a two dimension array to Excel
array< int, 2 > ^m_DataArray = gcnew array< int, 2 >(2, 10);
for (int x = 0; x < 10; x++)
{
    m_DataArray[0, x] = x;
    m_DataArray[1, x] = x / 2;
}
Range ^m_Range = m_WS->Range::get("A1", "J2");
m_Range->Value2 = m_DataArray;
```

Next, draw the chart and set its size and position.

```
// The following code draws the chart
m_Range->Select();
ChartObjects ^m_ChartObjects = dynamic_cast< ChartObjects ^ >
                        (m_WS->ChartObjects(Missing::Value));
```

```
// Set the chart position to 0, 50 and size to 400, 200
ChartObject ^m_ChartObj=dynamic_cast< ChartObject ^ >
                        (m_ChartObjects->Add(0, 50, 400, 200));
Chart ^m_Chart=dynamic_cast< Chart ^ >(m_ChartObj->Chart);
```

Using the ChartWizard, we can format the chart.

```
// Format the chart using ChartWizard
array< Object ^ > ^m_ChartFormat=gcnew array< Object ^ >(11);

m_ChartFormat [0]=m_Range;                              // Chart Data Source
m_ChartFormat[1]=XlChartType::xl3DColumn;              // Chart Gallery Type
m_ChartFormat[2]=Missing::Value;                       // Format
m_ChartFormat[3]=XlRowCol::xlRows;                     // Plot By Rows or Columns
m_ChartFormat[4]=Missing::Value;;                      // Category Labels
m_ChartFormat[5]=Missing::Value;;                      // Series Labels
m_ChartFormat[6]=true;                                 // Legend
m_ChartFormat[7]="Portfolio Value";                    // Chart Title
m_ChartFormat[8]="Years";                              // X-Axis Title
m_ChartFormat[9]="Value";                              // Y-Axis Title
m_ChartFormat[10]=Missing::Value;                      // Extra Title

m_Chart->GetType()->InvokeMember("ChartWizard", BindingFlags::InvokeMethod,
                        nullptr, m_Chart, m_ChartFormat);
```

38.3. Summary

This chapter looked at how to control Excel, a COM object, through managed VC++.NET. As Excel is the most popular software development platform in the front office, learning how to interoperate with it can be very useful.

CHAPTER • 39

Connecting to TraderAPI

TraderAPI is a .NET .dll that emulates the XTAPI offered by Trading Technologies, Inc., a Chicago-based software company that licenses its X_Trader platform to futures traders worldwide. (You can download a free demo version of X_Trader along with XTAPI at the company website, www.tradingtechnolgies.com.) Through X_Trader, we can trade futures contracts on many, many exchanges through one user-friendly graphical user interface. XTAPI, installed as part of X_Trader Pro, contains Component Object Model (COM) classes we can instantiate in our .NET programs to, among other functionalities, get real-time market price feeds, route orders, and receive fill notifications. (XTAPI is discussed in greater detail in another chapter.) TraderAPI mimics the look, feel, and behavior of this popular tool for electronic market connectivity.

The classes in TraderAPI, described in this chapter, are a one-for-one match to real-life classes in XTAPI, although without all of the methods, and the method calls I have included are very similar. However, TraderAPI is not COM as is XTAPI; because TraderAPI was written in .NET, there are differences (again discussed in another chapter). Nevertheless, using TraderAPI we can build trading applications with all (or nearly all) the functionality of the real thing.

39.1. TraderAPI Overview

TraderAPI has a random, internal price generation mechanism for E-Mini S&P 500, symbol ES, and E-Mini Nasdaq 100, symbol NQ, futures contracts traded on the Chicago Mercantile Exchange. Further, we can route market and limit orders and receive fill notifications to and from the simulated "exchange."

When a valid connection is made to TraderAPI for a futures contract, a window will appear that shows the exchange view of the instrument, including the bid and ask prices, the quantity on the bid and ask, the last trade price, and the quantity of the last trade, as well as the order book showing working limit orders we have in the market by order ID number (Key) and price (Figure 39-1).

Now let's take a look at the TraderAPI classes in alphabetical order.

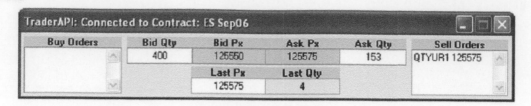

FIGURE 39-1

39.2.   FillObj

When a fill is received from the exchange, the OrderSetClass' OnOrderFillData event will fire and pass in information regarding a fill in the form of a FillObj. The get_Get() method will allow us to retrieve this information (Table 39-1).

TABLE 39-1

Methods	Description
get_Get(String ^)	Returns BUYSELL, CONTRACT, FFT, KEY, PRICE, PRODUCT, ORDERQTY, and/or TIME for a fill.

39.3.   InstrObjClass

An instance of the InstrObjClass represents a tradable instrument on the exchange, in this case a futures contract (Table 39-2).

TABLE 39-2

Methods	Description
get_Get(String ^)	Returns ASK, ASKQTY, BID, BIDQTY, LAST, LASTQTY, and/or NETPOS for the instrument
Open(bool)	Opens the InstrObjClass object for updates
Properties	**Description**
CreateNotifyObject	Returns a pointer to a new InstrNotifyClass (observer)
Contract	Gets/sets the contract name (e.g. "Dec06")
Exchange	Gets/sets the exchange name (e.g. "CME-A")
OrderSet	Gets/sets OrderSetClass object associated with the instrument
ProdType	Gets/sets the product type ("FUTURE")
Product	Gets/sets the product ("ES" or "NQ")
TickSize	Gets the tick size of the contract

39.4. InstrNotifyClass

An InstrNotifyClass object is an observer that will raise an event when an update is received from the exchange for its associated InstrObjClass (Table 39.3). We can set the filter to receive updates only for specific occurrences.

TABLE 39-3

Methods	Description
InstrNotifyClass (InstrObjClass)	Constructor
Properties	**Description**
EnablePriceUpdates	Sets ability to receive price updates to true or false
UpdateFilter	Sets filter for update events (e.g. "BID,BIDQTY,ASK,ASKQTY,LAST, LASTQTY")
Events	**Description**
OnNotifyFound	Fires the first time an instrument update is received
OnNotifyUpdate	Fires everytime after the first that an update is received according to the update filter

39.5. OrderObj

An OrderObj represents a working order in the order book (OrderSetClass)(Table 39-4). Every order is given a unique "Key."

TABLE 39-4

Methods	Description
get_Get(String ^)	Returns ACCT, BUYSELL, ORDERTYPE, PRICE, ORDERQTY, FFT, PRODUCT, CONTRACT, KEY for a working order
Properties	**Description**
Delete	Cancels and deletes the order

39.6. OrderProfileClass

An OrderProfileClass object contains all of the information about a trade. To enter an order, we create an OrderProfileClass object and pass it to the SendOrder() method of the OrderSetClass (Table 39-5).

TABLE 39-5

Methods	Description
get_Get(String ^)	Returns ACCT, BUYSELL, ORDERTYPE, LIMIT, ORDERQTY, FFT, PRODUCT, CONTRACT for the order profile
set_Set(String ^, String ^)	Sets the ACCT, BUYSELL, ORDERTYPE, LIMIT, ORDERQTY, FFT for the order profile

Properties	Description
Instrument	Associates an InstrObjClass with the order profile

39.7.   OrderSetClass

An OrderSetClass object is our order book and will contain a collection of OrderObj objects. Further, we use an OrderSetClass object to send orders to the exchange, cancel a specific working order, delete all working orders, and receive fill updates from the exchange (Table 39-6).

Instead of delving into each method of each object, here is a well-commented program that illustrates most of the functionality of TraderAPI.

TABLE 39-6

Methods	Description
Cancel(String ^)	Cancels an order with a particular key
DeleteOrders(bool)	Deletes all bids (true) and all offers (false)
get_SiteKeyLookup(String ^)	Returns an order with a particular key
Open(bool)	Opens the order set for order entry
SendOrder(OrderProfile ^)	Sends an order
set_Set(String ^, Object ^)	Sets MAXORDERS, MAXORDERQTY, MAXWORKING, MAXPOSITION limits for order entry

Properties	Description
EnableOrderAutoDelete	Enables deleting of orders
EnableOrderFillData	Enables fill data evens
EnableOrderSend	Enables order entry
Instrument	Associates an InstrObjClass with the order set

Events	Description
OnOrderFillData	Fires when a fill is received
OnOrderSetUpdate	Fires when an update to an order in the order set is received

39.8.   Sample Code: TraderAPIConnection_Example

This example shows how to use TraderAPI to get real-time market data, enter orders, and receive fill confirmations. In your Windows Forms Application, be sure to add a reference to TraderAPI, create the GUI, and add the appropriate code.

When you want to enter a limit order, be sure to enter the price in the text box on the lower right (Figure 39-2).

In this code example, I have left out much of the error-handling code to focus on the topic of TraderAPI.

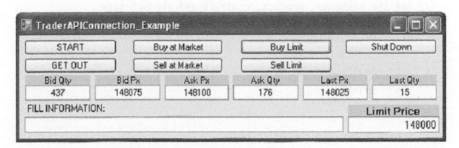

FIGURE 39-2

```cpp
#pragma once

namespace TraderAPIConnection
{
using namespace System;
using namespace System::ComponentModel;
using namespace System::Collections;
using namespace System::Windows::Forms;
using namespace System::Data;
using namespace System::Drawing;
using namespace TraderAPI;

public ref class Form1 : public System::Windows::Forms::Form
{
// Windows generated code in here.

private: InstrNotifyClass ^m_Notify;
private: InstrObjClass ^m_Instr;
private: OrderSetClass ^m_OrderSet;

private: System::Void button1_Click(System::Object^ sender, System::EventArgs^ e)
{
      // Create a new InstrObjClass object
      m_Instr=gcnew InstrObjClass;
```

```
    // Create a new InstrNotifyClass object from the InstrObjClass object.
    m_Notify=dynamic_cast< InstrNotifyClass ^ >(m_Instr->CreateNotifyObj);
    // Enable price updates.
    m_Notify->EnablePriceUpdates=true;
    // Set UpdateFilter so event will fire anytime any one of these changes in the
    // associated InstrObjClass object.
    m_Notify->UpdateFilter="BIDQTY,BID,ASK,ASKQTY,LAST,LASTQTY";
    // Subscribe to the OnNotifyUpdate event.
    m_Notify->OnNotifyUpdate+=gcnew InstrNotifyClass::OnNotifyUpdateEventHandler
                           (this, &TraderAPIConnection::Form1::OnUpdate);
    // Set the exchange, product, contract and product type.
    m_Instr->Exchange="CME";
    m_Instr->Product="NQ";
    m_Instr->Contract="Sep05";
    m_Instr->ProdType="FUTURE";
    // Open m_Instr.
    m_Instr->Open(true);


    // Create a new OrderSetClass object.
    m_OrderSet=gcnew OrderSetClass;
    // Set the limits accordingly. If any of these limits is reached,
    // trading through the API will be shut down automatically.
    m_OrderSet->set_Set("MAXORDERS", 1000);
    m_OrderSet->set_Set("MAXORDERQTY", 1000);
    m_OrderSet->set_Set("MAXWORKING", 1000);
    m_OrderSet->set_Set("MAXPOSITION", 1000);
    // Enable deleting of orders. Enable the OnOrderFillData event.
    // Enable order sending.
    m_OrderSet->EnableOrderAutoDelete=true;
    m_OrderSet->EnableOrderFillData=true;
    m_OrderSet->EnableOrderSend=true;
    // Subscribe to the OnOrderFillData event.
    m_OrderSet->OnOrderFillData+=gcnew
                            OrderSetClass:: OnOrderFillDataEventHandler(
                            this, &TraderAPIConnection::Form1::OnFill);


    // Open the m_OrderSet.
    m_OrderSet->Open(true);
    // Associate m_OrderSet with m_Instr.
    m_Instr->OrderSet=m_OrderSet;
}


private: void OnFill(FillObj ^pFill)
{
    // Get fill data here with chatty calls.
    // Chunky calls will be demonstrated in a later chapter.
    textBox7->Text=String::Concat("FILL RECEIVED: ",
                    pFill->get_Get("FFT3")->ToString(), " ID#: ",
                    pFill->get_Get("KEY")->ToString(), " Price: ",
```

```
                           pFill->get_Get("PRICE")->ToString(), " B/S: ",
                           pFill->get_Get("BUYSELL")->ToString(), " QTY: ",
                           pFill->get_Get("QTY")->ToString());
}


private: void OnUpdate(InstrNotifyClass ^pNotify, InstrObjClass ^pInstr)
{
     // Get new data from the InstrObjClass using chatty calls here.
     textBox1->Text=pInstr->get_Get("BIDQTY")->ToString();
     textBox2->Text=pInstr->get_Get("BID")->ToString();
     textBox3->Text=pInstr->get_Get("ASK")->ToString();
     textBox4->Text=pInstr->get_Get("ASKQTY")->ToString();
     textBox5->Text=pInstr->get_Get("LAST")->ToString();
     textBox6->Text=pInstr->get_Get("LASTQTY")->ToString();
}


private: System::Void button2_Click(System::Object^ sender, System::EventArgs^ e)
{
     SendMarketOrder("B");
}
private: System::Void button5_Click(System::Object^ sender, System::EventArgs^ e)
{
     SendMarketOrder("S");
}
private: System::Void button3_Click(System::Object^ sender, System::EventArgs^ e)
{
     SendLimitOrder("B", textBox8->Text);
}
private: System::Void button6_Click(System::Object^ sender, System::EventArgs^ e)
{
     SendLimitOrder("S", textBox8->Text);
}


private: void SendMarketOrder(String ^m_BS)
{
// Create an OrderProfileClass object to contain information about a market order.
     OrderProfileClass ^m_Profile=gcnew OrderProfileClass;
     m_Profile->Instrument=m_Instr;
     m_Profile->set_Set("ACCT", "12345");
     m_Profile->set_Set("BUYSELL", m_BS);
     m_Profile->set_Set("ORDERTYPE", "M");
     m_Profile->set_Set("ORDERQTY", Convert::ToString(6));
     m_Profile->set_Set("FFT3", "MKT ORDER");
     // Send the order through m_OrderSet.
     __int64 m_Result=m_OrderSet->SendOrder(m_Profile);
}


private: void SendLimitOrder(String ^m_BS, String ^m_Px)
{
```

```
        // Send a limit order here.
        OrderProfileClass ^m_Profile=gcnew OrderProfileClass;
        m_Profile->Instrument=m_Instr;
        m_Profile->set_Set("ACCT", "12345");
        m_Profile->set_Set("BUYSELL", m_BS);
        m_Profile->set_Set("ORDERTYPE", "L");
        m_Profile->set_Set("LIMIT", m_Px);
        m_Profile->set_Set("ORDERQTY", Convert::ToString(6));
        m_Profile->set_Set("FFT3", "LMT ORDER");
        __int64 m_Result=m_OrderSet->SendOrder(m_Profile);
}

private: System::Void button4_Click(System::Object^ sender, System::EventArgs^ e)
{
        // Delete all working buys and sells.
        __int64 m_Long=m_OrderSet->DeleteOrders(true);
        m_Long=m_OrderSet->DeleteOrders(false);
}


private: System::Void button7_Click(System::Object^ sender, System::EventArgs^ e)
{
        // Shut down should include explicit object destruction.
        m_Notify->OnNotifyUpdate-=gcnew
                                InstrNotifyClass:: OnNotifyUpdateEventHandler(this,
                                &TraderAPIConnection::Form1::OnUpdate);
        m_OrderSet->OnOrderFillData-=gcnew
                                OrderSetClass:: OnOrderFillDataEventHandler(this,
                                &TraderAPIConnection::Form1::OnFill);
        m_Instr=nullptr;
        m_OrderSet=nullptr;
        m_Notify=nullptr;
        GC::Collect(); }
};
}
```

39.9.   Summary

This chapter looked at TraderAPI, an XTAPI emulator, for simulating market connectivity. There are six classes in TraderAPI.dll and we use instances of these classes and their methods to work with real-time data and order execution. Later chapters will use TraderAPI to develop automated trading systems.

CHAPTER • 40

Connecting to XTAPI

XTAPI installs along with Trading Technologies, Inc.'s industry-leading X_Trader Pro platform. You can download a free demo version of X_Trader and XTAPI from the company website at www.tradingtechnologies.com. (At devnet.tradingtechnolgies.com, you can apply for a login to access all relevant XTAPI documentation, as well as sample code.) As you can imagine, Trading Technologies upgrades their platform and their API on a regular basis. The version I used to develop the code in this chapter was 6.2.7.27. The API file name was XTAPITTM_6.2.DLL. While this code will work for this version and file, future updates to the API may cause it to become outdated, but probably not in a significant way for quite some time.

As mentioned also, XTAPI contains Component Object Model (COM) classes that will be exposed to our .NET programs through an interop wrapper. (Because of this, you will see some changes from the TraderAPI connection code in a previous chapter, but the structure here is the same.) The .NET Framework will generate this wrapper automatically when you add a reference to the .DLL file. From there, be sure to add "using namespace XTAPI;" and you will be ready to go.

The XTAPI connectivity code presented in this chapter can substitute one for one with the code for connectivity to TraderAPI shown in a previous chapter. Everything else remains the same.

40.1. Sample Code: XTAPIConnection_Example

```
Setting Up XTAPI Objects

private: TTInstrNotifyClass ^m_Notify;
private: TTInstrObjClass ^m_Instr;
private: TTOrderSetClass ^m_OrderSet;
```

```
private: System::Void button1_Click(System::Object^ sender, System::EventArgs^ e)
{
    m_Instr=gcnew TTInstrObjClass;
    m_Notify=dynamic_cast< TTInstrNotifyClass ^ >(m_Instr->CreateNotifyObject);
    m_Notify->EnablePriceUpdates=true;
    m_Notify->UpdateFilter="LAST,LASTQTY";
    m_Notify->OnNotifyUpdate+=gcnew_ITTInstrNotifyEvents_OnNotifyUpdateEventHandler(
                             this, &Form1::OnUpdate);

    m_Instr->Exchange="TTSIM-A";
    m_Instr->Product="NQ";
    m_Instr->Contract="Sep05";
    m_Instr->ProdType="FUTURE";
    m_Instr->Open(true);

    m_OrderSet=gcnew TTOrderSetClass;
    m_OrderSet->Set("MAXORDERS", 1000);
    m_OrderSet->Set("MAXORDERQTY", 1000);
    m_OrderSet->Set("MAXWORKING", 1000);
    m_OrderSet->Set("MAXPOSITION", 1000);
    m_OrderSet->EnableOrderAutoDelete=true;
    m_OrderSet->EnableOrderFillData=true;
    m_OrderSet->EnableOrderSend=true;
    m_OrderSet->OnOrderFillData+=gcnew_ITTOrderSetEvents_OnOrderFillDataEventHandler(
                             this, &Form1::OnFill);
    m_OrderSet->Open(true);

    m_Instr->OrderSet=m_OrderSet;
}
```

Handling Order Fill Updates

```
private: void OnFill(TTFillObj ^pFill)
{
    textBox7->Text=String::Concat(pFill->Get["FFT3"]->ToString(), " ID#: ",
                         pFill->Get["KEY"]->ToString(), " Price: ",
                         pFill->Get["PRICE"]->ToString(), " B/S: ",
                         pFill->Get["BUYSELL"]->ToString(), " QTY: ",
                         pFill->Get["QTY"]->ToString());
}
```

Handling Instrument Data Updates

```
private: void OnUpdate(TTInstrNotify ^pNotify, TTInstrObj ^pInstr)
{
    textBox1->Text=pInstr->Get["BIDQTY"]->ToString();
    textBox2->Text=pInstr->Get["BID"]->ToString();
```

```
    textBox3->Text=pInstr->Get["ASK"]->ToString();
    textBox4->Text=pInstr->Get["ASKQTY"]->ToString();
    textBox5->Text=pInstr->Get["LAST"]->ToString();
    textBox6->Text=pInstr->Get["LASTQTY"]->ToString();
}
```

```
Sending Market and Limit Orders

private: void SendMarketOrder(String ^m_BS)
{
    TTOrderProfileClass ^m_Profile=gcnew TTOrderProfileClass;
    m_Profile->Instrument=m_Instr;
    m_Profile->Set("ACCT", "12345");
    m_Profile->Set("BUYSELL", m_BS);
    m_Profile->Set("ORDERTYPE", "M");
    m_Profile->Set("ORDERQTY", Convert::ToString(6));
    m_Profile->Set("FFT3", "MKT ORDER");
    __int64 myResult=m_OrderSet->SendOrder[m_Profile];
}

private: void SendLimitOrder(String ^m_BS, String ^m_Px)
{
    TTOrderProfileClass ^m_Profile=gcnew TTOrderProfileClass;
    m_Profile->Instrument=m_Instr;
    m_Profile->Set("ACCT", "12345");
    m_Profile->Set("BUYSELL", m_BS);
    m_Profile->Set("ORDERTYPE", "L");
    m_Profile->Set("LIMIT", m_Px);
    m_Profile->Set("ORDERQTY", Convert::ToString(6));
    m_Profile->Set("FFT3", "LMT ORDER");
    __int64 m_Result=m_OrderSet->SendOrder[m_Profile];
}
```

40.2. Summary

This chapter looked at code for connecting to Trading Technologies, Inc.'s XTAPI .DLL. XTAPI contains COM classes very similar to the ones presented earlier as part of TraderAPI, which emulates XTAPI. With this code, you should be able to easily convert anything you develop on TraderAPI for use with XTAPI.

SECTION · IV

Automated Trading Systems

CHAPTER • 41

Building Trading Systems

There are four disciplines that go into automated trading system development—computer science, quantitative finance, trading strategy, and quality. Successful implementation of an automated trading system demands that all of these activities be performed at a high level.

41.1. Buy vs. Build

Application programming interfaces (APIs) can be thought of as "pipelines" to the market over which exchange member trading firms can access exchange data and place orders electronically. Installing and maintaining a communications network for data and order execution, however, involve complex networks, servers, routers, and FIX engines, not to mention constant software redevelopment as exchanges upgrade their APIs.

Rather than incurring the time and expense it takes to build electronic exchange connections from scratch, it is also possible and much less capital intensive to license third-party trading software and to take advantage of their exchange connections and built-in functionality for data feeds, order entry, and risk management. Then, proprietary analytics and trading algorithms can be added on top of this software via their own APIs. The added layer of a front-end API usually will add minimal latency to the overall system. Many of these third-party vendors have years of experience building systems for trading and are, in terms of the development cycle, well ahead of even some major proprietary houses. We can extend the discussion of commercial-off-the-shelf (COTS) software to research and back office processes as well.

COTS is a term that describes commercially available software that offers specific functionalities required by a larger system—in our case, a trading system. Very often purchasing or licensing COTS for execution, database, and back office systems is a lower cost (and lower-hassle) solution than in-house development, even though loss of control over functionality and performance is an obvious trade-off. However it is done, integrating COTS, which uses disparate systems built often in disparate technologies, into a working trading system requires development of glue code. That is, glue code is that programming code that integrates the components of a COTS-based system.

Developing a profitable trading system with software and hardware is no small task. One well-known options trader estimates that it takes a $10 million investment just to get in the game. That $10 million pays for building network infrastructure, hiring high-level quantitative analysts and programmers, and at least a year of research and development before you even make your first trade. Much of this expense, though, is dedicated to licensing COTS and integrating it into a system with glue code, developing proprietary software, and buying hardware that connects to the exchanges. One limitation to this architecture is that no single COTS front-end trading system connects to all markets around the world. As a result, it may be necessary to create proprietary software that connects to a multiplicity of front-end APIs to provide access to all the different markets and products (Figure 41-1).

Again, a complete trading system consists of many subsystems and data sources—a proprietary trade selection and order management engine, an execution system, a risk management system, a back office accounting system, and historical, fundamental, quantitative, and economic databases—and no COTS package does it all here either. Integrating these disparate systems into a working order management system requires development of lots of glue code for connectivity and interoperability (Figure 41-2).

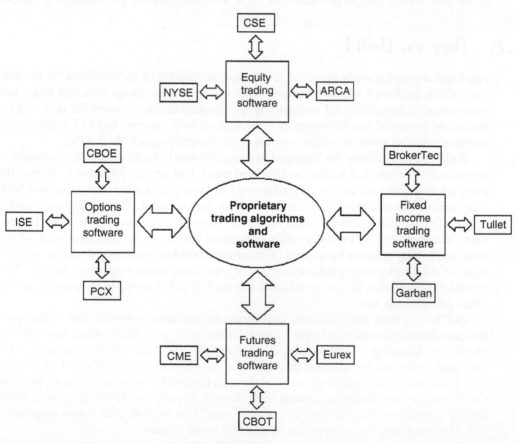

FIGURE 41-1

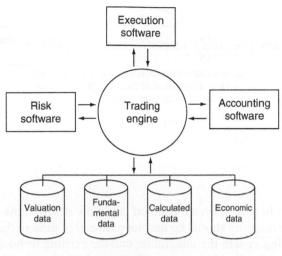

FIGURE 41-2

41.2. Data Mapping

The diagram shown in Figure 41-2 presents several challenges to the glue code developer (glue code is shown as lines connecting the components). Beyond the connectivity issues are issues of data mapping. Data mapping is the process of creating blueprints and plans for converting data from format to format for communication among components in COTS-based trading systems. Several questions must be answered and documented.

- What data do I want to save?
- What data flow into and out of the calculation engine?
- What data flow into and out of the trade engine?
- What data flow into and out of the risk engine?
- What data flow into and out of the accounting engine?
- What if I need to look at my positions in Bloomberg?
- What functions will be performed by the front-end, third-party execution system?
- What functions can be performed by COTS software and what data flow into and out of such software?

It is inconceivable that a professional organization would design a trading system without reference to the problem of transferring data from one component of the system to another or from one software engine to another. However, this often happens when management pushes for reduction in cost, with no regard for total cost. Data and the software components may each be of excellent quality, but they may not work well together in production.

Often analysts and traders build out trading systems only to end up complaining about how long it takes to get it operational due to difficulties in mapping data to the external software—accounting, risk management, and pricing systems.

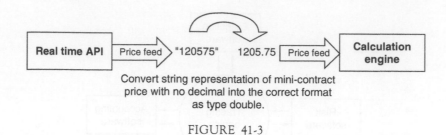

FIGURE 41-3

The solution here is to create detailed data flow descriptions and proposed structures for results. Data mapping should be developed ahead of time so that during development in code of the trading system the integration into the existing technological environment will be well understood and well documented. Figure 41-3 gives a quick example.

In the example given in Figure 41-3, the real-time price updates come as strings from the API. Furthermore, the price format leaves out the decimal. Clearly, conversion must take place so that the price in the proper format enters the calculation engine.

41.3. Speed of Development

When building automated trading systems, there are trade-offs to be made. One such trade-off may be between the speed of the system and the speed of development. Presumably, fast systems that minimize slippage are more profitable than slower ones that may miss opportunities that exist for only milliseconds. However, faster systems may take longer to develop, may require more expensive hardware, and may require higher salary network administrators and programmers. For trading strategies that may only remain profitable for a few months to a year, somewhat slower technologies and programming languages that offer rapid development may offer advantages.

If, for example, we intend to build a high-frequency trading system, the optimal solution would be to develop it in C++ on a Unix platform. However, if we assume that the system will remain profitable for only 12 months, development on a Windows operating system may make more sense. Just for round numbers, let's estimate that development in Windows and C++ takes 3 months, whereas development in Unix may take 6 months. Furthermore, Unix C++ programmers are far more expensive and Unix system administrators are far more expensive than Microsoft professionals, which will also cut into the profitability of the system. As a result, while the Unix implementation would be preferred, it may not feasible given the time constraints, scalability of the strategy, and return on investment constraints of the firm. For this reason, the world of automated trading systems will, I believe, become more and more dominated by Microsoft implementations. The Windows .NET Integrated Development Environment provides so many tools and streamlines the development process so much that Unix is often not considered, even though every technology professional knows that it is a faster and more stable platform.

In any case, while this text for simplicity focuses on development of a client-based system, automated trading systems are very often implemented in n-tier architectures where the calculation engine sits on a server to which the RTD/exchange gateway server, database server(s), and client GUI connect (Figure 41-4).

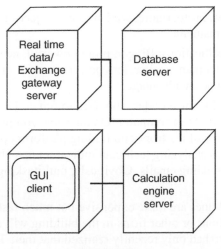

FIGURE 41-4

Bigger still are trading systems that use grid-computing architectures to take advantage of multiple processors on the same network to concurrently calculate complex algorithms. Discussion and presentation of code examples of these architectures are beyond the scope of this text, although many of the programming concepts are the same.

When it comes to building high-frequency, real-time automated trading systems, the entire conversation revolves around speed, especially for well-understood trades like calendar spreads. However, it's important to understand that the speed of an automated trading system is not constant. Rather speeds of individual messages to and from an electronic exchange fall into a generally lognormal distribution. One of the goals of a firm's technology budget should be to lower the mean and narrow the standard deviation of this distribution.

41.4. Ten Things that Affect the Speed of a Trading System

What factors affect the speed of an automated trading system? Here is a list of the 10 things that affect the speed of a real-time automated trading system, in no particular order.

1. Programming language and efficiency of the code: The programming language and compiler used to implement an automated trading system will affect the speed of the trading system. Some languages built on some compilers will run faster than others. Applications developed in MS Excel will suffer from serious problems, not the least of which will be slowness of Dynamic Data Exchange (DDE) technology. Serious automated trading systems should be developed in a more robust environment or created from scratch in code using, for example, C++, Visual Basic.NET, or C#. Traditionally, C++ has been viewed as the premier language for trading system development, although the advent of Microsoft's .NET Framework makes Visual Basic.NET and C#.NET viable implementation languages. The efficiency of the code and the use and management of multiple threads will also affect speed. Well-written code runs fast, whereas poorly written

code runs slow. Furthermore, well-written, object-oriented code will be far easier to debug and maintain.

2. Hardware specifications: Bigger, more powerful, newer servers and client computers run faster than smaller, less powerful, older ones. Also, multiprocessor machines will be an advantage.

3. Multitasking: I know a trader who used to run an Excel-based automated trading system on his desktop computer. On the same computer at the same time, he had several windows of his front-end trading platform open, was watching Bloomberg Television, was analyzing technical indicators in a charting package, surfing the Internet, and sending emails. Obviously, multitasking will slow down a trading system.

4. T1 vs. T3: T3 lines are more expensive but much faster. Also, sharing lines with other applications or other firms in the building will damage performance. One firm I talked to had only recently realized that their T1 line was for the entire floor of their building, not just their office.

5. Third-party front-end software and API: Not all front ends are created equal; some are faster than others. Also, third-party APIs may connect directly to an exchange, whereas some may connect via the front-end trading platform; another step in the process will slow things down.

6. Clearing firm's technology: Do your trades go to the clearing firm's servers first for approval? Not all clearing firms are created equal. Of course less expensive commissions may trade off against slower speed.

7. Operating system: Different Microsoft operating systems will show different performance. While UNIX is generally understood to be faster, it is more expensive to implement, maintain, and develop on.

8. Exchange technology: Some exchanges are just plain faster than others. Also, exchange price servers may show different performance than fill servers.

9. Distance from the exchange: Distance not only in terms of miles, but also in the number of technological "steps" will certainly impact speed. A trader I know spent a lot of money on fast computers, but failed to realize that his internet service provider was sending all his trades from Chicago to servers in Atlanta and back to the exchange in Chicago. The optimal solution is to have your trading system on a server in the office next to the exchange access point. Sending orders across the ocean slows things down.

10. Time of day: Trading at the open will be slower than at 1:00 in the afternoon. Fast markets will slow things down.

41.5.   Getting It Right

The hardest part of programming a financial trading system is understanding the complexity of the system prior to coding. Finance is one of the few industries with as many acronyms and industry-specific jargon as information technology. As a result, things get lost in translation. Confusion about system design is the norm.

The field of software design and project management in finance is still in the early stage of evolution as compared to other fields of engineering. Take F16 fighter planes, for example, they have 2000 to 4000 moving parts, but large-scale trading systems can easily have at least 10,000 moving parts when the "if," "case," "do until," ADO.NET, and other features are taken as moving parts. But traders always demand everything the next day when money is at stake. This view is common in the trading community, but is not at all common in the broader software community. Software for fighters never fails.

Computer codes in aviation, automotive controls, machining, and multiple other fields are just as complex as in trading, but they don't fail, as systems in trading too often do. The main difference between fighter systems and trading systems is management's willingness to spend the time and resources to properly design and build the software, especially the users tolerance of failure. Fighter pilots will wait until the system works properly every time.

In finance, too many decision makers are unwilling to invest the time required to design stable systems. This unwillingness is usually due to a belief that new trading strategies will work for only the first people who find them and for only a small amount of time. This belief forces management to shorten the development cycle by cutting back on the design stages of the project.

The K|V Methodology holds that stable trading systems can work for long periods of time and produce reliable returns. Trading systems based on random events perform erratically and eventually fail. Traders that fail blame their computer system rather than accepting that failure was the result of a poor underlying strategy, math, or software design. A properly designed system will eliminate most of the problems of randomness.

The money managers that have earned successful track records by building a robust system using computer software have been very patient in the building of the system. The problem with financial markets is that unlike manufacturing, it may take a lifetime for the market to clearly identify the algorithmic trading Warren Buffets. Trading system developers have to deal with both cultures.

Given these facts, what is the solution to this problem? The solution is to accept the fact that (1) we are making software and (2) that the software just happens to operate in the trading world. We then need to accept the best knowledge from the software field. Frederick P. Brooks clearly stated the role of software requirements regarding the success of a completed software system in his classic essay, "No Silver Bullet: Essence and Accidents of Software Engineer" in IEEE Computer magazine in April 1987.

> The hardest single part of building a software system is deciding precisely what to build. No other part of the conceptual work is as difficult as establishing the detailed technical requirements, including all of the interfaces to people, to machines, and to other software systems. No other part of the work so cripples the resulting system if done wrong. No other part is more difficult to rectify later.

The best of breed requirements and development methods firmly state that you need to first build a vision document and then a scope document prior to starting the programming of the system. In finance, you should build complete prototypes using the K|V method. The main difference between the basic vision and scope documents in industry and the K|V documents for finance is the level of detailed required for the calculation and data areas.

41.6. Logic Leaks

Take, for example, a simple moving average crossover system. When the fast-moving average crosses over the long-moving average to the upside, this is bullish. When the fast-moving average crosses over to the downside, this is bearish. Simple, right? Let's examine the logic implications. Every time our trading system receives a price update from the market, it must "rethink" everything. That is, it must recalculate the moving averages and understand the new state of the situation. What are these states? From lowest to highest the relationships are:

1. Price, short MA, long MA.
2. Price, long MA, short MA.
3. Long MA, price, short MA.
4. Long MA, short MA, price.
5. Short MA, price, long MA.
6. Short MA, long MA, price.

Now consider also that we may or may not have a position on long or short. So, multiply these six states by 3 for 18 possible total states, as we could be long, short, or flat for each of the aforementioned states. Also, our system must be able to "see" crossovers. If the previous state was that the short MA was above the long MA but, upon recalculation, the short MA is now below the long MA, we have to raise a flag indicating a bearish (or, alternatively, a bullish) signal. One last thing, MAs are one thing, but we trade prices, and when we take a position, we should bracket it with a target price and a stop price, but not just any stop price, a trailing stop price. One last thing, what happens if you get a partial fill and then a state changes? Do you cancel the remainder?

This is a lot of logic and a lot of "if" statements or "case" statements in code. Often trading logic turns into a spaghetti bowl of logical comparisons. If any potential state is unaccounted for, the trading system will fail.

I recommend in the strongest way possible that you map all of your logic before you start coding. There is too much at stake. You must be sure that all states are accounted for and that all logical outcomes are handled. Once you've started coding it's too late; you will not be able to figure it out on the fly.

Make a logic map as part of your project documentation. Any change to the logic must first be changed in your logic map because changes will have unthought of implications other places in your code. Logic leaks lead to losses.

41.7.   Ten Things That Affect the Profitability of a Trading System

What factors affect the profitability of an automated trading system? Here is a list of the 10 things in no particular order.

1. System speed: A particular high-frequency trading algorithm may be profitable at high speeds (i.e., at a low mean and narrow the dispersion of decision and messaging times), but not at slower mean speeds or higher standard deviations.
2. Trade selection algorithm: Obviously, having a good trade selection algorithm is important. Trades with favorable, statistically proven, expected payoffs are better. Standard deviation of payoffs should also be considered. However, how to prove these things is another question!

3. Commissions and exchange fees: If a particular high-frequency trading strategy shows an average profit of \$1.00 per contract traded and the round turn commission is \$1.10, you will have a difficult time making money.

4. Margin rates: The same can be said for margin rates as for commissions and exchange fees.

5. Taxes: Hedge funds seeking a competitive advantage often move offshore to the Cayman Islands or Gibralter to take advantage of opportunities for tax savings. This can make the difference.

6. Order management algorithms: For high-frequency systems trading on exchanges using a first-in/first-out matching algorithm, limit orders are options on queue position. Some exchanges use a pro-rata algorithm for matching orders, which should cause you to think differently about your order management techniques and to what extent they impact success. Optimizing order management algorithms for partial fills and time and volumes can make the difference between success and failure.

7. Efficiency of development: Speed and cost of development impact the long-term success of a system. Since no trading strategy will be successful forever, the faster and cheaper you can get a system up and running the better opportunity you will have over the long term.

8. Efficiency of management: The more efficient markets become, the more cost minimization will become a competitive advantage.

9. Efficiency of redevelopment and improvement: A trading system life can be extended if they are allowed to evolve. Firms that implement a system of continuous improvement will be at a competitive advantage.

10. Risk management: As with trade selection algorithms, risk management algorithms are an important piece of the success of a trading system. Understanding when it's time to shut a system down is also important.

41.8. Summary

This chapter looked at several issues regarding trading system development, including buy vs. build scenarios, data mapping issues, a overview of the discussion of system speed (which goes way beyond software architecture to include network speed and COTS software), trade-offs between system speed and development time and expense, issues pertaining to profitability (which again goes beyond C++), and management issues for ensuring properly functioning systems. I have provided this chapter to illustrate how coding trading logic in VC++.NET fits within the context of the much larger topic of how to build profitable trading systems, which in the end is the real discussion to have.

CHAPTER ✦ 42

K|V Trading System Development Methodology

Let's consider two theoretical questions. (1) Let's assume for a minute that all markets are perfectly efficient, but that windows of opportunity here and there open and close. These windows remain open for let's say 1 year. Who wins under this scenario?

Clearly, firms that can rapidly investigate hundreds of market opportunities, the windows, will succeed at the expense of those who are slower and less efficient. If at any given time 1000 windows exist and only 10 or so are open, the faster we can examine the opportunities and either discard them as unprofitable or keep and exploit them the better off we will be.

(2) Let's assume again that all markets are just plain perfectly efficient, period. Who wins under this scenario?

Clearly again, firms that minimize new trading system development and ongoing management costs will be able to provide better returns relative to those that don't or can't.

Under these two theoretical environments, the ability to quickly and at low cost evaluate rule-based trading opportunities will be a significant competitive advantage. As a result, efficient development and management processes will in the future be an increasingly important piece of successful business models in the money management industry, be it traditional mutual funds, hedge funds, or proprietary trading. In the future and for your firm, development of and adherence to a systematic process of trading system evaluation and implementation will drive the competitive advantage.

Several steps are involved in creating a quantitatively based trading system, and a colleague of mine, Dr. Andrew Kumiega, and I have created a methodology encompassing many of these necessary steps. Our methodology consists of four stages—research and documentation of calculations; back testing; implementation; and portfolio and risk management—and should, furthermore, ensure rapidity, desired by senior management, and consistent quality standards, desired by financial engineers.

This methodology, which we call the K|V Trading System Development Methology, combines a new product development process with the well-known waterfall and spiral software development methodologies into a single paradigm for trading system development. While the four stages progress in a traditional waterfall, four elements are connected in a spiral structure within each phase. At the completion of each stage is a gate, a management meeting where a decision must be made to kill the project altogether, return to a previous stage, put the project on hold, or continue to the next stage of development. (K|V borrows the gate concept from a new product development methodology known as the Stage-Gate method.[1])

Gates act as checkpoints along the process. They check whether the business reasons for developing the trading system are still valid. If the project is allowed to continue or is sent back to a previous stage, the gate meeting should also outline the plan for moving through the subsequent stage, define the expected deliverables, and evaluate the criteria at the next gate meeting. Criteria for each gate should include a check on the deliverables, minimum standards, potential for profitability, competitive advantage, technical feasibility, scalability, and risk. Essentially, at each successive gate management must make a progressively stronger commitment to the project. In the end, well-organized and well-run gate meetings will weed out the losers and permit worthwhile projects to continue toward completion.

Upon completion of the fourth and final stage, the K|V model requires that we repeat the entire four-stage waterfall for continuous improvement. Here are the four stages of the K|V methodology and their respective components.

Stage I. Research and Document Calculations

1. Describe Trading Idea
2. Research Quantitative Methods
3. Prototype in Modeling Software
4. Check Performance

Gate 1

Stage II. Back Test

1. Gather Historical Data
2. Develop Cleaning Algorithms
3. Perform in Sample/out of Sample Tests
4. Shadow Trade and Check Performance

Gate 2

Stage III. Implement

1. Build Software Requirements Specification (SRS) Document
2. Design and Document System Architecture
3. Program and Document the System
4. Probationary Trade and Check Performance

Gate 3

Stage IV. Manage Portfolio and Risk

1. Monitor Portfolio Statistics
2. Perform Risk Calculations
3. Document Profit and Loss Attribution
4. Determine Causes of Variation in Performance

Repeat the entire waterfall process for continuous improvement.

---

[1] Stage-Gate is a registered trademark of R.G. Cooper & Associates Consultants, Inc., a member company of the Product Development Institute. See www.prod-dev.com.

Even before we can enter the K|V process, however, we must develop a money document, so let's back up for a minute.

42.1. The Money Document

Trading and money management is a business, and in order to succeed in the trading business, we need to raise R&D as well as trading capital from either inside or outside our firm. Either way, we will need to describe in a persuasive manner why our proposed system has a competitive advantage and is therefore worthy of risk capital. As with most business proposals, a focused, professional business plan is essential to attract capital, especially in a start-up stage.

As a template, we present the Money Document, which is the primary deliverable created before fully laying out a trading system's business plan. A well-done Money Document will serve as a Vision and Scope Document for the development process by outlining the business goals of a proposed trading system in a clear and concise fashion in order to persuade management or outside investors (i.e., collectively, customers) to provide the initial capital needed for research and subsequently for development of a trading system according to the four-stage K|V model. The Money Document answers the fundamental question, "Is this a business?"

The Money Document is a lens that forces unfocused teams to concentrate on building a business. The resources allocated to a project, subsequent to the delivery of a Money Document and management approval, will permit entry into the K|V development process (see Figure 42-1).

42.2. Research and Document Calculations

It is more fun to do than to plan. This very human trait is only driven out by years of schooling and experience. The problem with planning in the markets is twofold: (1) most traders prefer to trade rather than plan and (2) most planners never get the opportunity to trade since the management in financial firms generally rises from the trading ranks. Consequently, proprietary trading and money management firms tend to optimize for the short term, building trading systems that are not sufficiently unique and are hard to explain to customers.

Systems developed in this way do not generally result in maintainable excess returns and are very often not scalable. This in part explains why the vast majority of money managers underperform their benchmark index and why so many hedge funds close each year for underperformance. Complex systems that offer longer term opportunities are built one step at a time and evolve along the way as new knowledge is gained.

42.2.1. Describe the Trading Idea

This first step is often the hardest one. The more complex the trading idea, the more difficult it becomes to communicate it clearly. Before any development on a system begins, we must be able to fully articulate the business logic and quantitative methods of the system. We have, though, already started the description process; the description created for the Money Document will serve as a starting point.

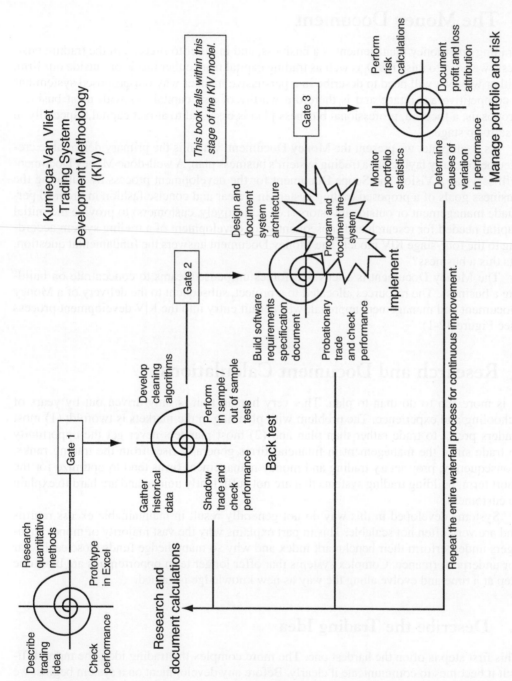

FIGURE 42-1

42.2.2. Research Quantitative Methods

Very rarely do we dream up completely new trading ideas. Rather, we build on ideas of the past and add new twists. As a result, the next step is to research existing mathematical models. This research may be in the form of derivation of proprietary algorithms or the application of publicly available research from journals, books, the Internet, or white papers. Furthermore, this research may also include gaining an understanding of the methodologies of other successful systems. The goal of research is to speed and refine our path to the best trading algorithms, which will form the basis of a Business Rules Catalog for the system. Furthermore, building and maintaining a proprietary library of unique quantitative methods are important to the long-term success of a firm.

42.2.3. Prototype in Modeling Software

Excel (and other modeling software such as Matlab, Mathematica, and QAI) is the most rapid development environment for testing trading ideas. The goal of prototyping is to quickly build several generations in order to evaluate whether a particular idea warrants further investigation.

Many times a trading idea is immediately built into a trading system if confidence is high that the trader, along with the system, will make money. The problem with this type of development is that it may not be well defined. Prototyping enables us to clearly define algorithms, Graphical User Interface (GUI), and data requirements and to develop a working application for regression testing in later stages. These prototypes will form the foundation of the Software Requirements Specification document.

42.2.4. Check Performance

Many systems cannot have their true performance tested in Excel. However, we will still use Excel prototypes as a starting point in the discussion of how we are going to measure the performance of the system. Without a clear plan on how to test, we cannot proceed to the next stage. If at any point in this or any other of the four stages performance testing shows system failure, K|V necessitates a kill decision or a looping back to a previous stage. The goal is to quickly stop development on trading systems with a low probability of success.

42.2.5. Gate 1

In order to pass through Gate 1, several criteria must be met. Should these criteria be met to the satisfaction of the customer, development will be allowed to proceed to Stage II.

This gate will prevent development of the trading system from moving to the back testing stage until the required activities and deliverables have been completed in a quality manner. Furthermore, at the gate meeting we will chart the path ahead by ensuring that plans and budgets have been made for the back testing stage.

We will use the term "well defined" to mean that a trading system has passed through this first gate. The implicit assumption is that the methodology has been rigorously followed in a fashion.

42.3.   Back Test

Successful system analysis and design necessitate research into past market movements as a way to analyze and validate a system—a process called back testing. A back test is a simulation and statistical analysis of a trading system's inputs and outputs against historical data. Specific back testing methodologies are dependent on the nature of the system under consideration. Whatever the case, back testing is based on statistical measures and should result in performance in excess of the traditional market buy and hold sample paths method. Proper back testing will not only confirm the validity and accuracy of a system's algorithms, but also the risks and variability of returns and rewards of competing alternative algorithms.

42.3.1.   Gather Historical Data

Once the initial prototype has shown a system to be worthy of further investment of time and resources, the real task of back testing begins. Prior to building and implementing the system, we must test it over a relatively large set of historical data, preferably for a large sample of instruments. As a result, we need to build a customized database or purchase a software tool that allows for back testing.

While it may seem elementary, investigating the availability of data is very important. Required data may either not exist or be prohibitively expensive based on the prospective returns of the trading system.

42.3.2.   Develop Cleaning Algorithms

One of the major obstacles to building a profitable trading system is dirty data. Virtually all data contain errors, even data purchased from reliable vendors. As a result, the identification and removal or correction of errors and, more importantly known, "as-of" issues in the calculation data is very important. Development of a Data Transformation Management System (DTMS) that scans data for errors and irregularities is essential.

A DTMS should implement data-cleaning algorithms that can operate on live time as well as historical data. Algorithms that cannot be performed in real time prior to trade selection should not be considered lest the cleaned, historical data will skew the results. The cleaning algorithms will be added to the Business Rules Catalog begun in K|V Stage I.

42.3.3.   Perform in-Sample/out-of-Sample Tests

Performing a proper in-sample/out-of-sample test is perhaps the most critical step in the process. Financial engineers are keenly aware of the extent to which in-sample results may differ from out-of-sample results, and trading algorithms must be examined against both before progressing to the implementation stage. A well-developed system will perform similarly out of sample as it does in sample so it is of utmost importance to save some of the historical data for out-of-sample testing. Such a test will result in one of three outcomes for a trading system:

1. Profitable both in sample and out of sample.
2. Profitable in sample, but not out of sample.
3. Unprofitable both in sample and out of sample.

If the system shows sufficient performance both in sample and out of sample, it will very likely receive capital to begin implementation and trading as soon as possible. If a system shows acceptable performance only in sample, it will likely be allocated additional resources for further research. If, however, the system proves to have unsatisfactory performance in sample as well as out of sample, it should likely be scrapped altogether.

42.3.4. Shadow Trade and/or Check Performance

At this point, the K|V model acknowledges that traders may very well request to trade the prototype. However, it should be understood that the only purpose this serves should be to fully understand the performance monitoring tools that are required by management in later stages. Be aware that the profit and loss (P&L) of probationary or shadow trading may not be indicative of the P&L of the completed system. Probationary trading may occur for a limited period of time and with a small amount of capital in order to more fully understand the behavior of the system and, as mentioned, to understand what tools will be needed by management. Shadow trading should nevertheless occur with dummy or simulated trades. As before, checking the performance of the system will prevent additional time and resources from being spent on unprofitable projects. We may need to loop back to the initial research stage and reassess the quantitative methods and algorithms.

42.3.5. Gate 2

As with Gate 1, Gate 2 has several questions we must answer before proceeding to Stage III. If the questions are answered to the satisfaction of the customer, development will be allowed to proceed to Stage III.

This gate will prevent development of the trading system from moving to the implementation stage until the required back testing activities and deliverables have been completed in a quality manner. Furthermore, at the gate meeting we will chart the path ahead by ensuring that plans and budgets have been made for the implementation stage.

42.4. Implement

Building a working trading system (either partially or fully automated) is really a software development project. As a result, implementation will require an object-oriented design, connectivity between and interoperability with disparate software and hardware systems for trade execution, and other processes such as connection to an optimization engine and data storage. This will require the creation of plans and blueprints before programming in a language such as C++, Visual C++.NET, or C# begins.

42.4.1. Build Software Requirements Specification Document

The purpose of a Software Requirements Specification (SRS) is to fully define the functionalities and performance requirements of the trading system. The SRS document will allow a team of programmers to quickly build the system with the correct functionalities and to the proper specifications.

As with all high-level documents in engineering, we expect these to be revised in an orderly process as we spiral through the development. This is no different than with the revision process of quality management using ISO 9000.

Prior to coding a trading system we will have essentially completed a project Vision and Scope Document in the form of a Money Document, which should define at a high level the key objectives of the project in order to obtain approval for resources for development and implementation. The Software Requirements Specification will include all of the required features and functionalities and all of the items that a software engineer will need to design, build, and modify the production system. The SRS should clearly define the steps for the project along with documenting all of the detailed information about the trading algorithms, including data dictionary, data flow maps, GUI requirements, error handling maps, and report generation maps. Fortunately, much of this work will already be done and the Software Requirements Specification document will largely be based on the prototypes and descriptions created in earlier stages of development.

42.4.2.   Design and Document System Architecture

The System Architecture Document is a blueprint of the hardware and software that form the architecture of the trading system, including financial calculations, real-time data and user interfaces, order routing connections, reporting functionalities, and any other necessary processes.

Building a trading system in code is a bit like building a building. The bigger and more complex the building, the more important blueprints are to the success of the project. Likewise, the more complex a trading system becomes, the more important it is to create detailed architectural plans, using an agreed-upon set of notations, as with Unified Modeling Language (UML). Through the use of UML, programming problems can be solved in an object-oriented way before programming begins. Some software components of the trading system may be purchased from third-party vendors. Much of the new development may be in the form of glue code, computer programming code that is written to connect reused commercial off-the-shelf applications.

42.4.3.   Program and Document the System

Once the hardware is built and network connections are completed, the process of construction will be a step-by-step march through the Software Architecture Document. Since the Software Architecture Document will be evolving, the ideal solution is to continue to add and refine it as the system is built. It should be noted that programming the system also includes proper software testing.

The data maps will continue to grow along with adding new dictionaries to clearly show the calculation of each field, where it came from, and where it is used. The GUI section also will grow to include a screen shot of each UI form. The error-handling section will continue to grow to list all known open issues. (There will be multiple other errors handlers placed into the code, but the main calculational error handlers should be placed in the Software Requirements Specification document.)

Finally, once a GUI or report is finalized in the Software Requirements Specification, a user manual should be produced to allow a junior trader to operate the system and a junior programmer to maintain it. While junior level people are not overseeing the system, the documentation should be placed at that level. It is assumed that since the systems we are building are proprietary in nature, we will not need complete user documentation.

42.4.4. Begin Probationary Trading and Check Performance

Once the system has been built, we will trade on a probationary basis, with small size. The main purpose of probationary trading is to find any design flaws in the trading algorithm or the trading system prior to investing the full sum, officially beginning the track record period, or managing customer funds. The second purpose of probationary trading is to allow the trader/money manager time to use the trading tools and to determine what additional tools need to be built to properly manage the market risk produced by the trading system. At this point, the returns of the system will be similar to those of the final product.

42.4.5. Gate 3

As with Gates 1 and 2, Gate 3 has several questions we must answer before proceeding to Stage IV. If the questions are answered to the satisfaction of the customer, development will be allowed to proceed.

This gate will prevent development of the trading system from moving to the final stage until the required activities and deliverables have been completed in a quality manner. Furthermore, at the gate meeting we will chart the path ahead by ensuring that plans and budgets have been made for the next stage. Successful passage through Gate 3 permits full implementation of the system and full investment.

42.5. Manage Portfolio and Risk

Portfolios of securities and derivatives require constant monitoring, and so successful operation of a trading system necessitates that periodic reports be generated to show the performance of the working system. These reports will present the portfolio performance statistics and risk calculations and provide documentation of the attribution of gains and losses. Furthermore, reports should present a determination of the causes of variation from the expected results and an action plan to deal with those variations.

42.5.1. Monitor Portfolio Statistics

A system for monitoring and reporting portfolio statistics, trade limits, and risk factors must be implemented. Essentially, these reports will help us understand whether the system is working within specifications and the parameters of the back test.

42.5.2. Perform Risk Calculations

Risk calculations and reports will give management a snapshot of the returns and potential losses and drawdowns on an absolute basis and relative to the benchmark over a given time horizon. Essentially, these reports will help us understand how the system is performing relative to the market and to the rest of the industry. However, while methods for dealing with extraordinary occurrences may be built into a trading system, gaps may render them useless.

42.5.3.   Document Profit and Loss Attribution

A good way to monitor the success of a system is to keep track of individual trades and their respective payoffs. These will be valuable when reevaluating the underlying premise for the system relative to a benchmark.

One of the most overlooked concepts in trading system design is the requirement that effectively every system should have a benchmark. Using a portfolio attribution system, we can clearly identify the returns above or below the benchmark. To make sure that the trading system consistently outperforms its benchmark, we need to perform attribution analysis on the portfolio as well as the benchmark itself.

42.5.4.   Determine Causes of Variation in Performance

After the attribution analysis and we understand all of the bets we are placing to beat the benchmark, we need to employ one final set of tools. These tools are based on process control theory—quality, statistics, ANOVA, and design of experiments.

The goal of these tools is to determine the causes of variance in the returns of our portfolio. If a process runs out of control, then a cause of that condition can be found. If we can find the cause, we can fix the process and theoretically have less variance than the benchmark.

Successful trading systems will not be so forever. Eventually, the market closes the door on every trade. As a result, systems will need to be continuously tweaked and eventually scrapped. The goal is to quickly stop trading systems that lose their edge before they cause large losses.

42.5.5.   Repeat the Entire Waterfall Process for Continuous Improvement (Kaizen)

Think of the steps in the K|V model as a continuous, never-ending spiral. Once we reach the end of the process, we start again to improve our system with new refinements or creation of new ideas altogether.

Continuous improvement consists of an ongoing effort toward bettering our trading system. When applied to a trading environment, a continuous improvement strategy involves management and quantitative analysts and traders and programmers, working in teams, working together to make small improvements continuously. It is top-level management's responsibility to cultivate a professional environment that engenders continuous improvement. A culture of sustained continuous improvement will focus efforts on eliminating waste in all trading systems and processes of a trading organization. Intelligent leadership should guide and encourage trading teams to continuously improve profitability, reduce risk, increase efficiency, and reduce costs.

Through small innovations from research and entrepreneurial activity, trading firms can discover breakthrough ideas. These ideas include, among other things, the creation of new trade selection algorithms, application of existing systems to new markets, and implementation of new technologies for more efficient trade execution.

42.6. Summary

The K|V Trading System Development Methodology consists of four stages, which each consist of four steps. If you intend to build a trading system, it is a good idea to plan before you build, and K|V can serve as the foundation of your plan.

I once met an investment banker who wished to start a hedge fund. He asked me what I thought he should do. "I don't need something that works, I just need something I can sell," he said. If he used the K|V methodology, he could do both!

trade selection algorithm, application of existing systems to new markets, and implementation of new technologies for more efficient trade execution.

42.6. Summary

The KJV Trading System Development Methodology consists of four stages, which each consist of four steps. If you intend to build a trading system it is a good idea to plan before you build, and KJV can serve as the foundation of your plan.

I once met an investment banker who wished to start a hedge fund. He asked me what I thought he should do. "I don't need something that works, I just need something I can sell," he said. If he used the KJV methodology, he could do both.

CHAPTER ◆ 43

Automated Trading System Classes

Objects in our trading system represent real-world things, and since trading has been going on for centuries, the basic objects used to build an automated system are easily recognizable. While many of these objects may be contained within a third-party application programming interface (API), it may still be necessary to create our own. In any case, to illustrate the rationale for and functionalities of the objects, I will discuss them each here.

43.1. Instrument Class

An Instrument object represents a tradable security or derivative. When building trading systems, you may prefer to encapsulate the complexities of the API connection within an Instrument object. That way as the programmer you will have more control over program flow, and should a new version of the API be released or should you switch APIs down the road, you won't need to tear apart your entire application. Trading systems that are shot through with API calls are difficult to understand, debug, and update.

Here is the Instrument class we will use for a single threaded system in a later chapter. Again, note that all of the TraderAPI calls lie within this class, both for price updates through the TraderAPI::InstrObjClass and for order entry through the TraderAPI::OrderSet class. Most of the code here simply encapsulates the TraderAPI connection code from a previous chapter.

Instrument.h

```
#pragma once
#include "Delegates.h"

using namespace System;
using namespace TraderAPI;

ref class Instrument
{
private:
```

```
        InstrObjClass ^m_Instr;
        InstrNotifyClass ^m_Notify;
        OrderSetClass ^m_OrderSet;

        void OnNotifyUpdate(InstrNotifyClass ^, InstrObjClass ^);
        void OnOrderFillData(FillObj ^);

        int m_TickSize;
        int m_Bid;
        int m_Ask;
public:
        Instrument(String ^, String ^, String ^);
        ~Instrument();

        event FillEventHandler ^OnFill;
        event PriceUpdateEventHandler ^OnPriceUpdate;

        bool EnterMarketOrder(String ^, int, String ^);
        bool CancelOrder(String ^);

        int get_Bid();
        int get_Ask();
        int get_TickSize();
        int get_NetPos();
};
```

Instrument.cpp

```
#include "StdAfx.h"
#include ".\instrument.h"

Instrument::Instrument(String ^m_P, String ^m_C, String ^m_Filter)
{
    // Open the connection to TraderAPI.
    m_Instr=gcnew InstrObjClass;

    m_Notify=dynamic_cast< InstrNotifyClass ^ >(m_Instr->CreateNotifyObj);
    m_Notify->EnablePriceUpdates=true;
    m_Notify->UpdateFilter=m_Filter;
    m_Notify->OnNotifyUpdate+=gcnew InstrNotifyClass::OnNotifyUpdateEventHandler
                            (this, &Instrument::OnNotifyUpdate);

    m_Instr->Exchange="CME-SIM";
    m_Instr->Product=m_P;
    m_Instr->Contract=m_C;
    m_Instr->ProdType="FUTURE";
    m_Instr->Open(true);
```

```
    m_OrderSet=gcnew OrderSetClass;
    m_OrderSet->set_Set("MAXORDERS", 1000);
    m_OrderSet->set_Set("MAXORDERQTY", 1000);
    m_OrderSet->set_Set("MAXWORKING", 1000);
    m_OrderSet->set_Set("MAXPOSITION", 1000);
    m_OrderSet->EnableOrderAutoDelete=true;
    m_OrderSet->EnableOrderFillData=true;
    m_OrderSet->EnableOrderSend=true;
    m_OrderSet->OnOrderFillData+=gcnew OrderSetClass::OnOrderFillDataEventHandler(
                              this, &Instrument::OnOrderFillData);
    m_OrderSet->Open(true);
    m_Instr->OrderSet=m_OrderSet;
}

Instrument::~Instrument(void)
{

    m_OrderSet->EnableOrderSend=false;
    m_OrderSet->OnOrderFillData-=gcnew OrderSetClass::OnOrderFillDataEventHandler(
                              this, &Instrument::OnOrderFillData);
    m_Notify->OnNotifyUpdate-=gcnew InstrNotifyClass::OnNotifyUpdateEventHandler(
                              this, &Instrument::OnNotifyUpdate);

    m_Notify=nullptr;
    m_Instr=nullptr;
    m_OrderSet=nullptr;
}

void Instrument::OnNotifyUpdate(InstrNotifyClass ^pNotify, InstrObjClass ^pInstr)
{
    // We are interested in getting every tick.
    // Notice the chunky call to API here.
    Object ^m_Data=pInstr->get_Get("LAST,LASTQTY");

    Tick m_Tick;
    m_Tick.Time=DateTime::Now;
    m_Tick.Price=Convert::ToInt32(safe_cast< array< String ^ > >(m_Data)[0]);
    m_Tick.Qty=Convert::ToInt32(safe_cast< array< String ^ > >(m_Data)[1]);

    OnPriceUpdate(m_Tick);
}
bool Instrument::EnterMarketOrder(String ^m_BS, int m_Qty, String ^m_FFT)
{
    try
    {
        OrderProfileClass ^m_Profile=gcnew OrderProfileClass;
        m_Profile->Instrument=m_Instr;
        m_Profile->set_Set("ACCT", "12345");
        m_Profile->set_Set("BUYSELL", m_BS);
        m_Profile->set_Set("ORDERTYPE", "M");
        m_Profile->set_Set("ORDERQTY", m_Qty.ToString());
        m_Profile->set_Set("FFT3", m_FFT);
```

```
            __int64 m_Result=m_OrderSet->SendOrder(m_Profile);
            return true;
        }
    catch(Exception ^e)
        {
            return false;
        }
}


bool Instrument::CancelOrder(String ^m_Key)
{
    try
        {
            m_OrderSet->Cancel(m_Key);
            return true;
        }
    catch(Exception ^e)
        {
            return false;
        }
}


void Instrument::OnOrderFillData(FillObj ^m_Fill)
{
    // Chunky call to API here. Could use SystemEventArgs object to contain data.
    array< String ^ > ^FillData=safe_cast< array< String ^ > ^ >(
                    m_Fill->get_Get("PRODUCT,KEY,BUYSELL,QTY,PRICE,TIME"));

    OnFill(FillData[0], FillData[1], FillData[2], Convert::ToInt32(FillData[3]),
                    Convert::ToInt32(FillData[4]), FillData[5]);
}


int Instrument::get_TickSize()
{
    return m_Instr->TickSize;
}


int Instrument::get_Bid()
{
    return m_Bid;
}


int Instrument::get_Ask()
{
    return m_Ask;
}
```

```
int Instrument::get_NetPos()
{
    return Convert::ToInt32(m_Instr->get_Get("NETPOS"));
}
```

Tradable securities and derivatives are always changing—bid and ask prices change, trades go off, and the quantities to buy or sell on the different price levels change constantly. An important question to ask is when do we want to receive updates? In general we prefer to receive as few updates as possible, only when important new information is available. For example, in a technical analysis system, we want to know about trades going off. We may not care if the quantity on the bid changes. TraderAPI and many industry APIs allow us to filter updates.

Those updates may have to go to more than one place. Say, for example, we are keeping track of multiple positions and orders and calculating several indicators in real time. One part of our program may need new data to calculate a moving average, while another part may need the update to check and see if a target price has been hit. The multicast update OnPriceUpate and OnFill delegates allow for this.

43.2. Order Class

An Order object represents a working order at the exchange. Generally, an order will consist mostly of data members, including the unique identifier (an order key, number, or ID), whether it is a buy or sell order, the quantity, the limit or stop price, an optional free form text (FFT), and possibly the tick size for the instrument.

What's more important, however, is what can happen to an order. They can be filled or partially filled; they can be canceled as market conditions change; they may need to be canceled after a given time interval; or they may be rejected for some reason (e.g., the exchange is down or your clearing firm cancels it). Real-time order management can be very tricky. Too often, a full investigation of order management logic is not performed. Questions to the following questions must be answered:

- Will it be a limit or a market order?
- If it is a limit, what will the price be?
- If it is a market order, do you care if the market gaps up and you get filled 5 ticks higher?
- How long will you leave your order out there?
- What if you get partially filled?
- How long will you leave a partially filled order out there?
- Will you use stop/market orders or stop/limits?

None of these questions are new to trading, but every possible logical outcome must be thought through before coding a trading can start.

In the case of time limits on orders, it would be necessary to add a timer object to the order itself. That way, the order itself can notify the application that it is time to cancel it.

As discussed in a previous chapter, for high-frequency systems trading on exchanges using a first-in, first-out matching algorithm, limit orders represent options on queue position. Having a limit order at a position at or near the front of a long queue is valuable. Having an order at or near the back may have little value, as you may likely get filled just as the market moves against you. Some exchanges use a pro-rata algorithm for matching orders, which should cause you to rethink your order management techniques. Optimizing order management algorithms for partial fills and time and volumes can make the difference between success and failure.

43.3.   Order Book

A simple order book (or order set) might be only a collection of orders. One hashtable (or two—one for working bids and one for working orders) works well, as the exchange or your API will assign unique keys. However, in the case where orders must be sequential, SortedLists are better.

In the case of market making systems, where you have working orders at each price level, you can manage a bid orders SortedList and an ask orders SortedList. The logic works smoothly in this case because canceling an inside market order will always be at index 0; the same can be said for fills. Canceled or filled orders can be removed from the SortedList, leaving the new inside market at positions 0.

43.4.   Bracket

A bracket object will consist of a target price and a stop price for an open position. Each bracket object will need to be made aware of price changes in the market and if the stop or target is hit, either enter an order to close the position itself or notify the system manager of the order requirements. Stop prices in a bracket object may be made to be trailing stops, so as the price of the instrument moves in our favor, the stop price is raised.

Because the trading systems presented in the book allow for only one open position at any given time, bracket objects will not be used. In the simple case, a stop price and a limit price variable can be set.

43.5.   Tick

Keeping track of ticks is often important, especially for technical analysis systems. Usually a simple tick class will consist of time, price, and quantity data members.

43.6.   Tick or Bar Collection

A tick collection is usually an array or queue of the last n number of ticks or bars. We can iterate or enumerate through the queue to calculate all kinds of technical indicators.

43.7.   Bar

Some technical analysis systems make use of bars, which include an opening price, a high price, a low price, a closing price, and the volume for either time-incremented bars or tick-incremented ones.

43.8.   System Manager

The system manager object contains the trade selection, order management, and position management logic of the trading system. All price updates from the instruments feed into the OnInstrumentUpdate method and fill updates into the OnInstrumentFill methods.

In the case of a two instrument system, any time the price of either of the instruments changes, the same OnInstrumentMethod will run in order to recalculate the spread price, check to see if any working orders are affected, or if any stops or limits are hit. Normally, the fill updates from the two instruments will be handled by separate methods, as fills in one may require an order to be sent in the other.

When trading logic is long and involved, it may be necessary or at least advisable to segregate trade selection logic, order management logic, and risk management logic into their own classes.

Also, if trading data need to be written to a database, these activities should be performed by separate objects, preferably also on a separate thread. Better yet, have the database activities performed on a separate server altogether.

43.9.   Graphical User Interface

The graphical user interface (GUI) will show important data and states that exist within the trading system, including the relevant real-time price data, network connection alerts, position updates, indicator updates, and the like. A GUI should also include controls to manipulate whatever dynamic inputs may be part of the system. For example, the number of ticks for the stop and limit prices, any indicators that may be changed (e.g., 30 tick moving average), instrument parameters (e.g., symbols, expirations), and, importantly, a shutdown button. There are several things to consider when shutting down a trading system.

- Do you want to cancel working orders?
- Do you want to flatten open positions?
- Be sure to turn state variables off and kill all risky objects.
- Be sure to abort all threads safely.
- You do *not* want objects out there sending in orders without a reference to them. Even if they are subject to garbage collection at some point in the future, that may not happen for a while. Be sure to explicitly delete and dereference objects and force garbage collection.

Be aware though that updating a GUI has performance implications, so in general do as little of it as possible and do it preferably on a separate, lower priority thread than those threads that perform real-time data updates and calculations. Better yet, have the GUI activities performed on a separate, client machine altogether.

43.10.   Summary

This chapter touched on some of the important ideas around the organization of trading system code into classes. Trading systems can become spaghetti very quickly and spaghetti turns into logic leaks, where potential outcomes are not accounted for, which leads to trading losses. Before coding and testing of an automated trading system begin, a software requirements specification document and software architecture document should be completed along with Excel prototypes so that all stakeholders understand the scope of the project. The software architecture document should have blueprints of the objects and their functionalities laid out. The software requirements specification and the Excel prototypes should cover all calculations and every logical outcome of price movements and order and position management.

CHAPTER • 44

Single-Threaded, Technical Analysis System

The single-threaded trading system in this chapter is based on a simple moving average crossover algorithm and uses the Instrument class presented in the ATS Objects chapter (Chapter 43), along with a Form1 class, a SystemManager class, and other .h files shown later.

The TraderAPI objects are contained within the Instrument class, which notifies the SystemManager with new price and trade fill data. The SystemManager controls all the business logic and sends data to the Form1 user interface (Figure 44-1).

Our Form1 object, shown in Figure 44-2, allows the user to change dynamic inputs within the trading logic—the number of ShortMA ticks, LongMA ticks, the Target price in ticks above or below the position price, the Stop price in ticks above or below the position price, and Quantity—through NumericUpDown controls.

The strategy will be to monitor the Nasdaq 100 E-Mini futures contracts for trades executed and to calculate a short (fast) and a long (slow) moving average. When the short MA, say 5 ticks, crosses over the long MA, say 20 ticks, to the upside, we will consider this a bullish signal and take a long position. The system will bracket the position with a target price above the buy price and a stop price below it. The user can define the number of ticks for the target and stop and the size of the position. When the short MA crosses back over the long MA, this will be a bearish signal and the system will close an open long position if there is one and take a new short position, with the target now below the sell price and the stop above it.

You will notice in this sample trading system that for simplicity I have not followed the K|V Trading System Development Methodology discussed earlier. In the real world, you should follow a development methodology to prototype and test the trading logic to ensure profitable implementation. (This chapter only shows the software architecture of a very simple, client-based trading system. It goes without saying that in the real world this trading system will not make money!)

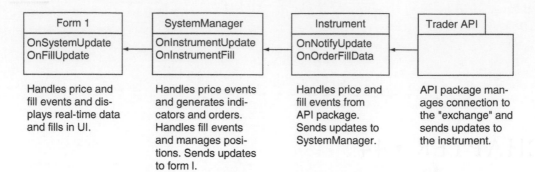

FIGURE 44-1

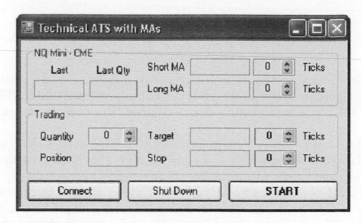

FIGURE 44-2

44.1.   Sample Code: TechincalSystem_Example

Here are the delegates we will use in the program.

```
Delegates.h

#pragma once
#include "Tick.h"

// User defined delegates
delegate void PriceUpdateEventHandler(Tick);
delegate void FillEventHandler(String ^, String ^, String ^, int, int, String ^);
delegate void SystemUpdateEventHandler(double, double, double, double,
                                       double, double);
```

Enumerations make the trading logic much easier to read.

```
Enums.h
#pragma once

enum class MA_State
{
    // ABOVE means that the short MA is above the long MA
    // BELOW means that the short MA is below the long MA
    ABOVE, BELOW
};


enum class Position
{
    FLAT, LONG, SHORT
};
```

Tick objects will contain the information about trades that happen in the instrument.

```
Tick.h
#pragma once
using namespace System;

value struct Tick
{
    DateTime Time;
    int Price;
    int Qty;
};
```

In this simple trading system, the SystemManager class is where all the action is. Upon receiving a new Tick in the OnInstrumentUpdate method, which handles the OnPriceUpdate event in the Instrument, the SystemManager object adds the Tick to the TickList and checks to see if a target or stop has been hit on an open order. Then it recalculates the moving averages. Next, it checks to see if there has been a crossover. If so, it places an order. Finally, it updates Form1.

```
SystemManager.h
#pragma once
#include "Instrument.h"
#include "Delegates.h"
#include "Tick.h"
#include "Enums.h"

using namespace System::Collections;

ref class SystemManager
{
private:
        Instrument ^m_Instrument;
```

```
        SortedList ^m_TickList;

        void OnInstrumentUpdate(Tick);
        void OnInstrumentFill(String ^, String ^, String ^, int, int, String ^);

        bool m_Go;
        bool m_Start;

        double m_LongMA;
        double m_ShortMA;
        int m_LongMATicks;
        int m_ShortMATicks;
        double m_Position;

        MA_State m_State;

        int m_Qty;


        int m_Target;
        int m_Stop;
        int m_TargetTicks;
        int m_StopTicks;
public:
        SystemManager();
        ~SystemManager();

        event SystemUpdateEventHandler ^OnSystemUpdate;
        event FillEventHandler ^OnFill;

        void StartStop();

        property int Qty
        {
            int get()
            {
                return m_Qty;
            }
            void set(int value)
            {
                m_Qty=value;
            }
        }
        property int StopTicks
        {
            int get()
            {
                return m_StopTicks;
            }
            void set(int value)
```

```
            {
                m_StopTicks = value;
            }
        }
        property int TargetTicks
        {
            int get()
            {
                return m_TargetTicks;
            }
            void set(int value)
            {
                m_TargetTicks = value;
            }
        }
        property int ShortMATicks
        {
            int get()
            {
                return m_ShortMATicks;
            }
            void set(int value)
            {
                m_ShortMATicks = value;
            }
        }
        property int LongMATicks
        {
            int get()
            {
                return m_LongMATicks;
            }
            void set(int value)
            {
                m_LongMATicks = value;
            }
        }
};
```

```
SystemManager.cpp

#include "StdAfx.h"
#include ".\systemmanager.h"

SystemManager::SystemManager()
{
    // Create a new Instrument object.
    m_Instrument = gcnew Instrument("NQ", "Sep06", "LAST,LASTQTY");
```

```
      m_Instrument->OnPriceUpdate += gcnew PriceUpdateEventHandler(this,
                                     &SystemManager::OnInstrumentUpdate);
      m_Instrument->OnFill += gcnew FillEventHandler(this,
                              &SystemManager::OnInstrumentFill);

      // Create a new SortedList to hold the Tick objects.
      m_TickList = gcnew SortedList;

      m_Position = 0;
      m_Go = false;
}

SystemManager::~SystemManager()
{
      m_Go = false;
      delete m_Instrument;
      m_Instrument->OnPriceUpdate -= gcnew PriceUpdateEventHandler(this,
                                     &SystemManager::OnInstrumentUpdate);
      m_Instrument->OnFill -= gcnew FillEventHandler(this,
                              &SystemManager::OnInstrumentFill);
      m_Instrument = nullptr;
}

void SystemManager::OnInstrumentUpdate(Tick m_Tick)
{
      //Add the tick object to the SortedList.
      m_TickList->Add(m_Tick.Time.Now, m_Tick);

      m_LongMA = 0;
      m_ShortMA = 0;

      if (m_Go)
      {
          // If we already have a position on, and have either met our target
          // or stop price, get out.
          if (m_Position > 0 && (m_Tick.Price > m_Target || m_Tick.Price < m_Stop))
          {
              bool m_Bool = m_Instrument->EnterMarketOrder("S", m_Qty, "TARGET/STOP OUT");
          }
          if (m_Position < 0 && (m_Tick.Price < m_Target || m_Tick.Price > m_Stop))
          {
              bool m_Bool = m_Instrument->EnterMarketOrder("B", m_Qty, "TARGET/STOP OUT");
          }

          if (m_TickList->Count > m_LongMATicks)
          {
              //Calculate the long moving average.
              for (int x = m_TickList->Count - m_LongMATicks;
                   x <= m_TickList->Count - 1; x++)
```

```
    {
        m_LongMA+=safe_cast< Tick >(m_TickList->GetByIndex(x)).Price;
    }
    m_LongMA/=m_LongMATicks;

    //Calculate the short moving average.
    for (int x=m_TickList->Count - m_ShortMATicks;
            x <= m_TickList->Count - 1; x++)
    {
        m_ShortMA+=safe_cast< Tick >(m_TickList->GetByIndex(x)).Price;
    }
    m_ShortMA/=m_ShortMATicks;

    // First time only and on reset, set initial state.
    if (m_Start)
    {
        if (m_ShortMA > m_LongMA)
            m_State=MA_State::ABOVE;
        else
            m_State=MA_State::BELOW;
            m_Start=false;
    }

    // Has there been a crossover up?
    if (m_ShortMA > m_LongMA && m_State == MA_State::BELOW)
    {
        // Change state.
        m_State=MA_State::ABOVE;

        // If we are already short, first get flat.
        if (m_Position < 0)
        {
            bool m_Bool=m_Instrument->EnterMarketOrder("B", m_Qty, "GET OUT");
        }
        // Go long.
        bool m_Bool=m_Instrument->EnterMarketOrder("B", m_Qty, "OPEN");

        // Set target price and stop loss price.
        m_Target=m_Tick.Price+m_TargetTicks * m_Instrument->get_TickSize();
        m_Stop=m_Tick.Price-m_StopTicks * m_Instrument->get_TickSize();
    }
    // Has there been a crossover down?
    if (m_ShortMA < m_LongMA && m_State == MA_State::ABOVE)
    {
        // Change state.
        m_State=MA_State::BELOW;

        // If we are already long, first get flat.
        if (m_Position > 0)
        {
```

```
                    bool m_Bool=m_Instrument->EnterMarketOrder("S", m_Qty, "GET OUT");
                }
                // Go short.
                bool m_Bool=m_Instrument->EnterMarketOrder("S", m_Qty, "OPEN");

                // Set target price and stop loss price.
                m_Target=m_Tick.Price - m_TargetTicks * m_Instrument->get_TickSize();
                m_Stop=m_Tick.Price + m_StopTicks * m_Instrument->get_TickSize();
            }
        }
    }
    //Send the data to the GUI.
    OnSystemUpdate(m_Tick.Price, m_Tick.Qty, m_LongMA, m_ShortMA, m_Target, m_Stop);
}

void SystemManager::OnInstrumentFill(String ^m_Product, String ^m_Key, String ^m_BS,
                                     int m_Q, int m_Px, String ^m_Time)
{

            // Update position.
            if (m_BS == "B")
            {
                m_Position+=m_Q;
            }
            else
            {
                m_Position-=m_Q;
            }
            // Send the data to the GUI.
            OnFill(m_Product, m_Key, m_BS, m_Q, m_Px, m_Position.ToString());
}

void SystemManager::StartStop()
{
            if (m_Go==false)
            {
                m_Go=true;
                m_Start=true;
            }
            else
            {
                m_Go=false;
            }
}
```

When a fill is received, the OnInstrumentFill method will increment the position by the quantity of the fill and update the Form1. Note also the use of the StartStop method. By using a m_Go state variable, we can turn off order entry, but still allow for the addition of new price updates to the TickList.

```cpp
Form1.h

#pragma once
#include "SystemManager.h"

namespace TechnicalSystem_Example {

using namespace System;
using namespace System::ComponentModel;
using namespace System::Collections;
using namespace System::Windows::Forms;
using namespace System::Data;
using namespace System::Drawing;

public ref class Form1 : public System::Windows::Forms::Form
{

// Windows generate code in here.

private: SystemManager ^m_Manager;

private: System::Void button1_Click(…)
{
    if (m_Manager==nullptr)
    {
        m_Manager=gcnew SystemManager;
        m_Manager->OnSystemUpdate+=gcnew SystemUpdateEventHandler(this,
                              &Form1::OnSystemUpdate);
            m_Manager->OnFill+=gcnew FillEventHandler(this, &Form1::OnFillUpdate);

            m_Manager->Qty=Convert::ToInt32(numericUpDown1->Value);
            m_Manager->ShortMATicks=Convert::ToInt32(numericUpDown2->Value);
            m_Manager->LongMATicks=Convert::ToInt32(numericUpDown3->Value);
            m_Manager->TargetTicks=Convert::ToInt32(numericUpDown4->Value);
            m_Manager->StopTicks=Convert::ToInt32(numericUpDown5->Value);
            textBox8->AppendText(Environment::NewLine);
    }
}
private: void OnSystemUpdate(double m_Price, double m_Qty, double m_LongMA,
                       double m_ShortMA, double m_Target, double m_Stop)
{
    // Event handler prints the data to the GUI.
    textBox1->Text=m_Price.ToString();
    textBox2->Text=m_LongMA.ToString("####");
    textBox3->Text=m_ShortMA.ToString("####");
    textBox4->Text=m_Target.ToString();
    textBox5->Text=m_Stop.ToString();
    textBox6->Text=m_Qty.ToString();
}
```

```
private: void OnFillUpdate(String ^m_Product, String ^m_Key, String ^m_BS,
                           int m_Q, int m_Px, String ^m_Pos)


{
    textBox7->Text=m_Pos;
    textBox8->AppendText(m_BS + " " + m_Q.ToString() + " " + m_Px.ToString() +
                         Environment::NewLine);
}
private: System::Void button2_Click(…)
{
    if (m_Manager!=nullptr)
    {
        delete m_Manager;
        m_Manager=nullptr;
        GC::Collect();
    }
}
private: System::Void button3_Click(…)
{
    if (m_Manager!=nullptr)
    {
        m_Manager->StartStop();
        if (button3->Text=="START")
            button3->Text="STOP";
        else
            button3->Text="START";
    }
}
private: System::Void numericUpDown1_ValueChanged(…)
{
    if (m_Manager!=nullptr)
    {
        m_Manager->Qty=Convert::ToInt32(numericUpDown1->Value);
    }
}
private: System::Void numericUpDown2_ValueChanged(…)
{
    if (m_Manager!=nullptr)
    {
        m_Manager->ShortMATicks=Convert::ToInt32(numericUpDown2->Value);
    }
}
private: System::Void numericUpDown3_ValueChanged(…)
{
    if (m_Manager!=nullptr)
    {
        m_Manager->LongMATicks=Convert::ToInt32(numericUpDown3->Value);
    }
}
```

```
private: System::Void numericUpDown4_ValueChanged(…)
{
    if (m_Manager != nullptr)
    {
        m_Manager->TargetTicks = Convert::ToInt32(numericUpDown4->Value);
    }
}
private: System::Void numericUpDown5_ValueChanged(…)
{
    if (m_Manager != nullptr)
    {
        m_Manager->StopTicks = Convert::ToInt32(numericUpDown5->Value);
    }
}
};
}
```

44.2. Summary

This chapter looked at a very simple, single-threaded trading system using a moving average crossover algorithm. As you can see, even a very simple system can be very large in number of lines of code. Notice, however, that the use of proper variable naming and the use of enumerations make the trading logic (in the OnInstrumentUpdate method) easy to read.

The object-oriented structure of the system is the thing to understand here. The form, the SystemManager, and the Instrument all provide different services to the overall functioning of the system. From here, our systems can get more complex and incorporate more systems and more threads, but the basic outline will remain the same. The brains of the system are encapsulated within the SystemManager. A bigger system with more instruments and more complex algorithms may be large enough that the SystemManager may consist of a package of classes rather than a single one. Also, we have left out any database connectivity. In the real world, keeping a record of trades is of course necessary. Your vendor's application programming interface may provide this functionality.

CHAPTER • 45

Producer/Consumer Design Pattern

Multithreaded trading systems often make use of the producer/consumer design pattern consisting of a producer object on one thread that generates data and a consumer object on another thread that consumes that data. The producer and consumer share data through a common buffer, a memory location. The two objects, though, are producing and consuming data at different rates. This brings up a nontrivial discussion: given that our trading algorithms create a latency in the system, what does it mean to be "real time"? It's possible that during our computations, our system could fall behind. A corollary is this: would we be willing to forego some data to ensure that current data are as up to date (or up to the nanosecond) as possible?

In trading systems, the nature of the system would lead us to the correct conclusion. Let's say that our system uses volume-weighted average price in its calculation. Under this scenario, because we need the price and volume of every trade, we may be willing to allow our system to fall behind in the event that a hundred ticks happen at once. As an alternative, let's assume that our system uses a statistical arbitrage calculation where we are comparing prices of two instruments. Under this scenario now, we would not be so concerned about missing market data as long as we have the most recent information.

45.1.   Sample Code: ProducerConsumer_Example

This chapter presents alternative views of the producer/consumer design pattern for each of these situations—get every tick or get only the latest tick.

45.1.1.   Get Every Tick

We can use System::Collections::Queues, which use circular arrays, to store producer-generated market data in the order it is received for sequential processing by the consumer. In this implementation of the producer/consumer pattern using a shared semaphore, our consumer thread will wait for the producer thread to generate data. When data are generated (in this case, random integers at random time intervals), our producer will add that data to the queue and then signal the consumer thread by releasing the semaphore. The consumer will then be allowed to consume data from the queue (Figure 45-1).

In this example, the consumer thread is put to sleep for half a second to simulate some time-consuming process. Because of this delay, the consumer thread will fall behind; data generated by the producer will keep piling up in the queue. Figure 45-2 shows produced data in the Output window (the column on the left) while consumed data are shown in the form.

The ProducerConsumerObjects class contains a public static queue and semaphore. Both the Producer and the Consumer classes will have access to these objects. The Producer will add data to the queue and signal the Consumer by releasing the semaphore.

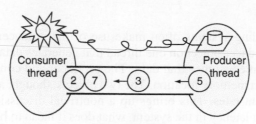

FIGURE 45-1

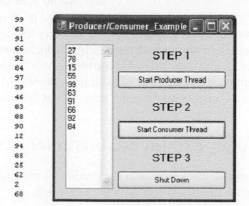

FIGURE 45-2

```
ProducerConsumerObjects.h
#pragma once

using namespace System::Collections;
using namespace System::Threading;
```

```
ref class ProducerConsumerObjects
{
public:
    static Queue ^DataQueue=Queue::Synchronized(gcnew Queue);
    static Semaphore ^ConsumerSemaphore=gcnew Semaphore(0, 999);
};
```

The Producer class contains a Timer and a Random to effect the generation of random integers between 0 and 100 and random time intervals from 0 to 1000 milliseconds.

Producer.h

```
#pragma once
#include "ProducerConsumerObjects.h"
#include "Delegates.h"

using namespace System;
using namespace System::Threading;
using namespace System::Diagnostics;
using namespace System::Windows::Forms;

ref class Producer : public ApplicationContext
{
private:
    int m_Data;

    Random ^m_Random;
    System::Windows::Forms::Timer ^m_Timer;
    void OnTimerTick(Object ^, System::EventArgs ^);

public:
    Producer();
    int get_Data();
};
```

When the random time interval elapses, the Timer::Tick event will fire, which is handled by the OnTimerTick method. In this method, a random integer is generated and added to the queue. Then ConsumerSemaphore→Release is called to signal the Consumer that new data exist in the queue.

Producer.cpp

```
#include "StdAfx.h"
#include ".\Producer.h"

Producer::Producer()
{
    // Random number generator will produce data and time intervals.
```

```
        m_Random=gcnew Random(DateTime::Now.Millisecond);


        m_Timer=gcnew System::Windows::Forms::Timer();
        m_Timer->Tick+=gcnew EventHandler(this, &Producer::OnTimerTick);
        m_Timer->Interval=1000;
        m_Timer->Enabled=true;
}

void Producer::OnTimerTick(Object ^Source, System::EventArgs ^e)
{
        // Add the new data to the queue.
        int m_Data=m_Random->Next(100);
        // Obtain a lock on the queue.
        Monitor::Enter(ProducerConsumerObjects::DataQueue);
        ProducerConsumerObjects:: DataQueue->Enqueue(m_Data);
        Monitor::Exit(ProducerConsumerObjects::DataQueue);

        // To see the ticks being generated by the Producer Thread,
        // write to Output window.
        Debug::WriteLine(m_Data);

        // Signal the Consumer Thread that new price has been received.
        ProducerConsumerObjects:: ConsumerSemaphore->Release(1);

        // Set random time interval for next tick.
        m_Timer->Interval=m_Random->Next(1000);
}

int Producer::get_Data()
{
        return m_Data;
}
```

The Consumer class, constructed on the main thread, contains the Producer object, which will run on its own separate thread as an application. The consumer thread runs within the Consumer object.

```
Consumer.h
#pragma once
#include "ProducerConsumerObjects.h"
#include "Producer.h"

using namespace System;
using namespace System::Threading;
using namespace System::Windows::Forms;

ref class Consumer
{
```

```
private:
    Thread ^m_ConsumerThread;
    Thread ^m_ProducerThread;
    Form ^m_Form;

    void RunConsumer();
    void RunProducer();

public:
    Consumer(Form ^);
    ~Consumer();

    void Go();
    UpdateEventHandler ^OnDataUpdate;
};
```

Within the Consumer, we run the Producer thread and the consumer thread. The consumer thread, which starts at the RunConsumer method, is blocked at the ConsumerSemaphore→ WaitOne() call until a signal is received from the Producer. When the Producer signals the Consumer, data are dequeued, some work is simulated (Thread::Sleep(500)), and the form is updated asynchronously on the main thread.

Consumer.cpp

```
#include <stdafx.h>
#include "Consumer.h"

Consumer::Consumer(Form ^m_F)
{
    m_Form=m_F;

    // Run Producer Thread.
    m_ProducerThread=gcnew Thread(gcnew ThreadStart(this, &Consumer::RunProducer));

    m_ProducerThread->Name="Producer Thread";
    m_ProducerThread->Start();
}

Consumer::^Consumer()
{
    m_ConsumerThread->Abort("TERMINATE Consumer");
    m_ConsumerThread->Join();

    m_ProducerThread->Abort("TERMINATE Producer");
    m_ProducerThread->Join();
}
```

```
void Consumer::RunProducer()
{
    // Start new message loop on the Producer Thread.
    Application::Run(gcnew Producer);
}
void Consumer::Go()
{
    // Start the Consumer Thread.
    m_ConsumerThread=gcnew Thread(gcnew ThreadStart(this, &Consumer::RunConsumer));

    m_ConsumerThread->Name="Consumer Thread";
    m_ConsumerThread->Start();
}


void Consumer::RunConsumer()
{
    while (true)
    {
        // Consumer Thread waits here until the Producer Thread
        // signals that new data has been received.
        ProducerConsumerObjects::ConsumerSemaphore->WaitOne();

        // Obtain a lock on the queue and get the new data.
        Monitor::Enter(ProducerConsumerObjects::DataQueue);
        int m_Data=(int)ProducerConsumerObjects:: DataQueue->Dequeue();
        Monitor::Exit(ProducerConsumerObjects::DataQueue);

        // Simulate some work, so Consumer Thread falls behind.
        Thread::Sleep(500);

        // Update the form on the main thread.
        m_Form->BeginInvoke(OnDataUpdate, m_Data);
    }
}
```

```
Delegates.h

#pragma once
delegate void UpdateEventHandler(int);
```

In the user interface just shown, we include three buttons. Button1 will allow for creation of the Consumer and Producer objects, at which time the producer thread will start generating data. The second button will start the consumer thread. The third will shut down the system and abort the threads.

Form1.h

```cpp
#pragma once
#include "Consumer.h"

namespace ConsumerProducer_Example
{
using namespace System;
using namespace System::ComponentModel;
using namespace System::Collections;
using namespace System::Windows::Forms;
using namespace System::Data;
using namespace System::Drawing;
using namespace System::Threading;

public ref class Form1 : public System::Windows::Forms::Form
{
// Windows generated code in here.

Consumer ^m_Consumer;

private: System::Void button1_Click(…)
{
    m_Consumer=gcnew Consumer(this);
    m_Consumer->OnDataUpdate+=gcnew UpdateEventHandler(this,
                            Form1::OnUpdateEventHandler);
}

private: System::Void button2_Click(…)
{
    m_Consumer->Go();
}

public: void OnUpdateEventHandler(int m_Data)
{
    textBox1->AppendText(m_Data.ToString() + Environment::NewLine);
}

private: System::Void button3_Click(…)
{
    delete m_Consumer;
    m_Consumer=nullptr;
    GC::Collect();
}
};
}
```

45.1.2.   Get Only the Latest Tick

In this alternative to the design given earlier, this design omits the queue and only updates a data member of the Producer class. When the Consumer receives the signal, it calls the Producer's get_Data method for retrieval. If the Consumer is busy when new data are generated, the Producer simply overwrites the previous data. This way, the Consumer is always guaranteed to receive the most up-to-date information (Figure 45-3).

You will notice that at times the Consumer is faster than the Producer, causing an update when none is necessary. In other words, the signals are stacking up, but data are not. If this is a problem, one simple way to control it is to have the consumer first check the newness of the data before proceeding. Figure 45-4 shows produced data in the Output window (the column on the left) while consumed data are shown in the form.

Here, the Producer::OnTimerTick method has been changed to only update the m_Data member and then signal the Consumer.

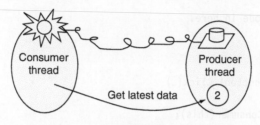

FIGURE 45-3

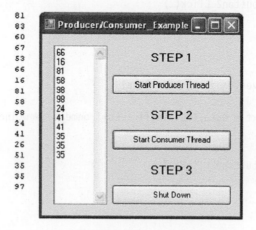

FIGURE 45-4

```
Producer.cpp

void Producer::OnTimerTick(Object ^Source, System::EventArgs ^e)
{
    // Update the new data.
    m_Data=m_Random->Next(100);

    // To see the ticks being generated by the Producer Thread,
    // write to output window.
    Debug::WriteLine(m_Data);
     // Signal the Consumer Thread that new price has been received.
    ProducerConsumerObjects::ConsumerSemaphore->Release(1);

    // Set random time interval for next tick.
    m_Timer->Interval=m_Random->Next(1000);
}
```

The Consumer will get the latest data via the Producer::get_Data method.

```
Consumer.cpp

void Consumer::RunConsumer()
{
    while (true)
    {
        // Consumer Thread waits here until the Producer Thread
        // signals that new data has been received.
        ProducerConsumerObjects::ConsumerSemaphore->WaitOne();

        // Get the latest data from the Producer.
        int m_Data=m_Producer->get_Data();

        // Simulate some work, so Consumer Thread falls behind.
        Thread::Sleep(500);

        // Update the form on the main thread.
        m_Form->BeginInvoke(OnDataUpdate, m_Data);
    }
}
```

45.2. Summary

This chapter looked at the Producer/Consumer design pattern. It is important for trading system development since such systems contain threads that are receiving real-time market data for consumption by other threads that encapsulate trade selection, order management, and risk management algorithms. Chapter 46 uses this pattern to build a statistical arbitrage trading system.

CHAPTER • 46

Multithreaded, Statistical Arbitrage System

The multithreaded trading system in this chapter is based on a statistical arbitrage of the E-Mini S&P 500 (ES) and the E-Mini Nasdaq 100 futures contracts using a z-transform procedure. This application also uses the Instrument class presented in the ATS Objects chapter, but with some minor changes to incorporate the Producer/Consumer design pattern discussed earlier. Also, we will use a form and a SystemManager as shown later.

The SystemManager controls all the business logic, calling the static CalcNormalized Price method of the NormCalc class, and sends data to the Form1 user interface. Unlike the technical system presented earlier, this application will run the user interface on its own thread, calculations on another thread, and real-time data generators (two Instrument objects) each on their own threads (Figure 46-1).

Our Form1 object, shown here, for simplicity does not allow the user to change any inputs within the trading logic, but will show the real-time price updates, including the spread price, and the positions and stop price. The dataGridView object will show the fills (Figure 46-2).

In this system, which method is running on which thread is not always clear. When the application loads, a new thread, the Main Thread, starts with a new instance of Form1. When the Connect button is clicked, a new SystemManager object is created on the Main Thread and two new threads, RTDThread_A and RTDThread_B, run applications with new instances of the Instrument class: one for ES and one for NQ (Figure 46-3).

When the Strategy Thread needs to execute a trade, it will call the EnterLimitOrder or EnterMarketOrder method of the appropriate instrument. While the Instruments are running on their own RTD threads, these methods will nonetheless run on the Strategy Thread. When the Instrument_A (ES) or Instrument_B (NQ) receives a fill update from the application programming interface, they will raise their OnFill event, which are handled by the SystemManager's OnFill_AEventHandler and OnFill_BEventHandler. These methods will execute on the corresponding RTDThread_A or RTDThread_B. Updates to the UI will always run, by necessity, on the lower priority Main Thread. Now let's take a look at our statistical arbitrage strategy.

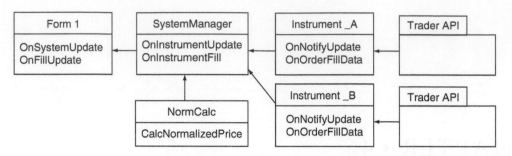

FIGURE 46-1

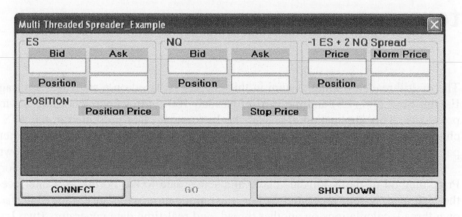

FIGURE 46-2

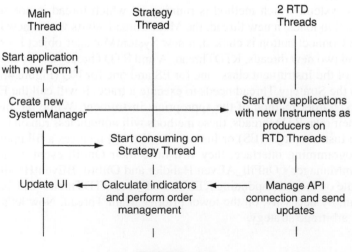

FIGURE 46-3

Arbitrarily and for simplicity, I will define the price of the ratio spread as follows:

$$\Delta = \text{Price}_{spread} = -1 \times \text{ES Bid} + 2 \times \text{NQ Ask}$$

so that

$$1704.00 = -1 \times 1258.00 + 2 \times 1481.00$$

Using the z-transform method form from Stephane Reverre's *The Complete Arbitrage Deskbook* (McGraw Hill, 2004, p. 476), we calculate the normalized price as

$$\Delta_{norm} = (\Delta - MA_{30}(\Delta)) / \sigma_{30}(\Delta)$$

- Δ_{norm} prices will be distributed normally, expressing the price in terms of standard deviation.
- MA_{30} is defined as the 30 spread-price-change moving average. Unlike the technical analysis system that listened for ticks (i.e., trades executing in the market), this system will only listen for changes in the bid and ask prices of the instruments.
- Also, a long position in the spread is defined as short 1 ES and long 2 NQs. A short position then is defined as long 1 ES and short 2 NQs.

The strategy will be to monitor the spread price and calculate the normalized price. When Δ_{norm} exceeds 2, we will consider this a bearish signal as we expect a reversion down to the mean, 0, and attempt to enter a short position. Rather than simply taking the market price, however, we will enter limit order in ES to buy 1 contract on the bid. Should we get filled, the system will immediately sell 2 NQ at the market.

Alternatively, when Δ_{norm} is less than -2, we will consider this a bullish signal as we expect to see a reversion up the mean. In this case the system will attempt to sell 1 ES on the offer. If the passive sell order is hit, we will immediately take the market price and buy 2 NQs. Should we miss the trade, i.e., if the passive limit order does not get hit and Δ_{norm} reverts back above or below our -2 or 2 threshold, we will cancel the order and wait for another opportunity. Arbitrarily again, I have hard coded the stop price at 4 ticks. The target price will be a Δ_{norm} of 0, at which time the positions in each contract will be flattened.

You will notice in this trading system that again I have not followed the K|V Trading System Development Methodology. In the real world, you should follow a development methodology to prototype and test the trading logic to ensure profitable implementation. This chapter shows the software architecture of a very simple, multithreaded, client-based trading system. (As this chapter only shows the software architecture of a very simple, client-based trading system, it goes without saying that in the real world this trading system will not make money!)

46.1. Sample Code: Spreader_Example

Let's review the changes to the Instrument class. Because our Instruments will run as applications, we need to inherit from ApplicationContext.

```
ref class Instrument : public ApplicationContext
```

We will need to manage our working limit orders. We will add an EnterLimitOrderMethod that will return an Order object to our Instrument class.

```
Order ^EnterLimitOrder(String ^, int, int, String ^);
```

```
Order ^Instrument::EnterLimitOrder(String ^m_BS, int m_Px, int m_Qty, String ^m_FFT)
{
    // This method will run on the Strategy thread.
    try
    {
        OrderProfileClass ^m_Profile=gcnew OrderProfileClass;
        m_Profile->Instrument=m_Instr;
        m_Profile->set_Set("ACCT", "12345");
        m_Profile->set_Set("BUYSELL", m_BS);
        m_Profile->set_Set("ORDERTYPE", "L");
        m_Profile->set_Set("LIMIT", m_Px.ToString());
        m_Profile->set_Set("ORDERQTY", m_Qty.ToString());
        m_Profile->set_Set("FFT3", m_FFT);
        __int64 m_Result=m_OrderSet->SendOrder(m_Profile);
        return gcnew Order(m_Profile->get_GetLast("SITEORDERKEY"), m_Px);
    }
    catch (Exception ^e)
    {
        return nullptr;
    }
}
```

The OnNotifyUpdate method has changed to incorporate the Producer/Consumer design pattern. Because we are not concerned with getting every tick, no queue will be used to store the data. Our main concern is that our system is as up to the nanosecond as possible.

```
void Instrument::OnNotifyUpdate(InstrNotifyClass ^pNotify, InstrObjClass ^pInstr)
{
    // We are only interested in the most recent tick.
    // Notice the chunky call to API here.
    // This method will run on the RTD Thread.
    Object ^m_Data=pInstr->get_Get("BID, ASK");

    m_Bid=Convert::ToInt32(safe_cast< array< String ^ > >(m_Data)[0]);
    m_Ask=Convert::ToInt32(safe_cast< array< String ^ > >(m_Data)[1]);

    TickData::ConsumerSemaphore->Release(1);
}
```

The delegates we are using are contained in the Delegates.h file.

```
Delegates.h
#pragma once

using namespace System;

delegate void UpdateEventHandler();
delegate void FillEventHandler(String ^, String^, String ^, int, int, String ^);
```

A simple Order object will contain the information we need about a working limit order in the market.

```
Order.h
#pragma once

using namespace System;

// This class contains information about a working limit order.
ref class Order
{
private:
    String ^m_Key;
    int m_Price;
public:
    Order(String ^key, int price) : m_Key(key), m_Price(price) {}
    String ^get_Key()
    {
        return m_Key;
    }
    int get_Price()
    {
        return m_Price;
    }
};
```

Our public static Semaphore, ConsumerSemaphore, will be a member of the TickData class for lack of a better name.

```
TickData.h
#pragma once

using namespace System::Collections;
using namespace System::Threading;

ref class TickData
{
public:
```

```
        static Semaphore ^ConsumerSemaphore=gcnew Semaphore(0, 999);
};
```

In this simple trading system, like the last, the SystemManager class is where all the action is. Upon receiving a signal that nice bid/ask data are available in the RunStrategy method, the SystemManager will grab the new data and calculate the normalized spread price. It will then check to see if a stop or a target has been hit. Next, if we are working an order and the normalized price has already crossed back over the threshold, cancel the working order. In the next step, the strategy thread will check to see if there is a new indication to enter and order. Finally, it updates the form.

```
SystemManager.h

#include "NormCalc.h"
#include "Order.h"
#include "Position.h"

using namespace System;
using namespace System::Threading;
using namespace System::Diagnostics;
using namespace System::Windows::Forms;

ref class SystemManager
{
private:
    Thread ^m_StrategyThread;
    Thread ^m_RTDThread_A;
    Thread ^m_RTDThread_B;
    Form ^m_Form;

    Instrument ^m_Instrument_A;
    Instrument ^m_Instrument_B;

    SortedList ^m_BuyOrderBook;
    SortedList ^m_SellOrderBook;

    ArrayList ^m_PriceList;

    int m_Bid_A;
    int m_Ask_A;
    int m_Bid_B;
    int m_Ask_B;
    int m_SpreadPrice;
    double m_NormPrice;
    int m_FillPrice_A;
    int m_SpreadPosPrice;
    int m_StopPrice;

    Position m_SpreadPos;
    Position m_Pos_A;
```

```
    Position m_Pos_B;
    void RunStrategy();
    void RunRTD_A();
    void RunRTD_B();
    void OnFill_AEventHandler(String ^, String ^, String ^, int, int, String ^);
    void OnFill_BEventHandler(String ^, String ^, String ^, int, int, String ^);

public:
    SystemManager(Form ^);
    ~SystemManager();
    void Go();

    int get_Bid_A() {return m_Bid_A;}
    int get_Ask_A() {return m_Ask_A;}
    int get_Bid_B() {return m_Bid_B;}
    int get_Ask_B() {return m_Ask_B;}
    int get_SpreadPx() {return m_SpreadPrice;}
    double get_NormPx() {return m_NormPrice;}
    int get_StopPx() {return m_StopPrice;}
    int get_SpreadPosPx() {return m_SpreadPosPrice;}
    int get_Pos_A() {return m_Instrument_A->get_NetPos();}
    int get_Pos_B() {return m_Instrument_B->get_NetPos();}
    Position get_SpreadPos() {return m_SpreadPos;}

    UpdateEventHandler ^OnPriceUpdate;
    FillEventHandler ^OnFillUpdate;
};
```

SystemManager.cpp
```
#include <stdafx.h>
#include "SystemManager.h"

SystemManager::SystemManager(Form ^m_F)
{
    m_Form=m_F;

    // Start RTD Thread for instrument A (ES).
    m_RTDThread_A=gcnew Thread(gcnew ThreadStart(this, &SystemManager::RunRTD_A));
    m_RTDThread_A->Priority=ThreadPriority::Highest;
    m_RTDThread_A->Name="RTD Thread A";
    m_RTDThread_A->Start();

    // Start RTD Thread for instrument B (NQ).
    m_RTDThread_B=gcnew Thread(gcnew ThreadStart(this, &SystemManager::RunRTD_B));
    m_RTDThread_A->Priority=ThreadPriority::Highest;
    m_RTDThread_B->Name="RTD Thread B";
    m_RTDThread_B->Start();

    // SortedLists will keep track of working orders in the market.
    m_BuyOrderBook=gcnew SortedList;
    m_SellOrderBook=gcnew SortedList;
```

```cpp
    // An ArrayList will keep track of the last 30 bid/ask changes.
    m_PriceList=gcnew ArrayList;

    // Start with flat positions, obviously.
    m_SpreadPos=Position::FLAT;
    m_Pos_A=Position::FLAT;
    m_Pos_B=Position::FLAT;
}


SystemManager::~SystemManager()
{
    // Kill all threads.
    if (m_StrategyThread != nullptr)
    {
        m_StrategyThread->Abort("TERMINATE Strategy");
        m_StrategyThread->Join();
    }
    if (m_RTDThread_A != nullptr)
    {
        m_RTDThread_A->Abort("TERMINATE RTD A");
        m_RTDThread_A->Join();
        m_RTDThread_B->Abort("TERMINATE RTD B");
        m_RTDThread_B->Join();
    }
    m_Instrument_A=nullptr;
    m_Instrument_B=nullptr;
}


void SystemManager::RunRTD_A()
{
    try
    {
        // Create new Instrument object and subscribe to the fill event.
        m_Instrument_A=gcnew Instrument("ES", "Sep06", "BID,ASK");
        m_Instrument_A->OnFill+=gcnew FillEventHandler(this,
                                &SystemManager::OnFill_AEventHandler);

        // Start a new message loop for RTD for instrument A (ES).
        Application::Run(m_Instrument_A);
    }
    catch (Exception ^e)
    {
        // Debug::WriteLine(e->Message);
    }
}


void SystemManager::RunRTD_B()
{
```

```
    try
    {
        // Create new Instrument object and subscribe to fill event.
        m_Instrument_B=gcnew Instrument("NQ", "Sep06", "BID,ASK");
        m_Instrument_B->OnFill+=gcnew FillEventHandler(this,
                                &SystemManager::OnFill_BEventHandler);

        // Start a new message loop for RTD for instrument A (NQ).
        Application::Run(m_Instrument_B);
    }
    catch (Exception ^e)
    {
        // Debug::WriteLine(e->Message);
    }
}

void SystemManager::Go()
{
    // Start the strategy on its own, highest priority thread.
    m_StrategyThread=gcnew Thread(gcnew ThreadStart(this, &SystemManager::RunStrategy));
    m_StrategyThread->Priority=ThreadPriority::Highest;
    m_StrategyThread->Name="Strategy Thread";
    m_StrategyThread->Start();
}

void SystemManager::RunStrategy()
{
// Strategy will recalculate any time there is a change in the
// bid or ask of either instrument A (ES) or B (NQ).
// This method will run on the Strategy Thread using the
// producer/consumer design pattern.

    while (1)
    {
        TickData::ConsumerSemaphore->WaitOne();

        // Get latest Bid/Ask data.
        m_Bid_A=m_Instrument_A->get_Bid();
        m_Ask_A=m_Instrument_A->get_Ask();

        m_Bid_B=m_Instrument_B->get_Bid();
        m_Ask_B=m_Instrument_B->get_Ask();

        // Calculate the spread Bid/Ask for 1×2 and add it to the list.
        m_SpreadPrice=-1 * m_Bid_A + 2 * m_Ask_B;
        m_PriceList->Add(m_SpreadPrice);

        // Calculate the normalized price.
        m_NormPrice=NormCalc::CalcNormalizedPrice(m_PriceList);
```

```
// Have we hit a stop or have we hit our target? If so, close positions.
if (m_SpreadPos == Position::LONG &&
    (m_SpreadPrice <= m_StopPrice || m_NormPrice > 0))
{
    bool m_Bool=m_Instrument_A->EnterMarketOrder("B", 1, "CLOSE");
    m_Bool=m_Instrument_B->EnterMarketOrder("S", 2, "CLOSE");
}
if (m_SpreadPos == Position::SHORT &&
    (m_SpreadPrice >= m_StopPrice || m_NormPrice < 0))
{
    bool m_Bool=m_Instrument_A->EnterMarketOrder("S", 1, "CLOSE");
    m_Bool=m_Instrument_B->EnterMarketOrder("B", 2, "CLOSE");
}


// If the reason for buying or selling the spread no longer exists,
// cancel the working order. i.e. if we missed the trade, cancel it.
if (m_NormPrice < 2 && m_BuyOrderBook->Count > 0)
{
    // Cancel buy order and remove from order book.
    m_Instrument_A->CancelOrder(safe_cast< Order ^ >(
                          m_BuyOrderBook->GetByIndex(0))->get_Key());
    m_BuyOrderBook->RemoveAt(0);
}
if (m_NormPrice > -2 && m_SellOrderBook->Count > 0)
{
    // Cancel sell order and remove from order book.
    m_Instrument_A->CancelOrder(safe_cast< Order ^ >(
                          m_SellOrderBook->GetByIndex(0))->get_Key());
    m_SellOrderBook->RemoveAt(0);
}


// Make a decision as to whether or not to enter a trade.
// Make a long trade in A if normalized price > 2 and we are
// flat and not already working an order.
// Enter order method calls run on the Strategy thread.
if (m_NormPrice > 2 &&
    m_Pos_A == Position::FLAT &&
    m_BuyOrderBook->Count == 0)
{
    // Try to buy 1 on the bid.
    Order ^m_Order=m_Instrument_A->EnterLimitOrder("B", m_Bid_A, 1, "OPEN");
    m_BuyOrderBook->Add(m_Order->get_Key(), m_Order);
}


// Make a short in A if normalized price < -2 and we are flat and not already
// working an order.
if (m_NormPrice < -2 &&
    m_Pos_A == Position::FLAT &&
    m_SellOrderBook->Count == 0)
```

```
        {
            // Try to sell 1 on the ask.
            Order ^m_Order=m_Instrument_A->EnterLimitOrder("S", m_Ask_A, 1, "OPEN");
            m_SellOrderBook->Add(m_Order->get_Key(), m_Order);
        }
        // Update the form on the main thread.
        m_Form->BeginInvoke(OnPriceUpdate);
    }
}


void SystemManager::OnFill_AEventHandler(String ^m_Product, String ^m_Key,
                                         String ^m_BuySell, int m_Qty ,
                                         int m_Price, String ^m_Time)
{
    // When fill is received in A (ES), enter market order in B (NQ).
    // This method will run on the RTD thread.
    m_FillPrice_A=m_Price;

    if (m_Pos_A == Position::FLAT)
    {
        // This is an openning trade. Place trade in Instrument_B (NQ)
        // in the opposite direction.
        if (m_BuySell == "B")
        {
            m_Pos_A=Position::LONG;
            m_BuyOrderBook->Remove(m_Key);
            bool m_Bool=m_Instrument_B->EnterMarketOrder("S", 2 , "OPEN");
        }
        else
        {
            m_Pos_A=Position::SHORT;
            m_SellOrderBook->Remove(m_Key);
            bool m_Bool=m_Instrument_B->EnterMarketOrder("B", 2, "OPEN");
        }
    }
    else
    {
        // This is a closing trade.
        m_Pos_A=Position::FLAT;
    }
    // Update form on Main thread.
    m_Form->BeginInvoke(OnFillUpdate, m_Product, m_Key, m_BuySell, m_Qty, m_Price, m_Time);
}

void SystemManager::OnFill_BEventHandler(String ^m_Product, String ^m_Key,
                                         String ^m_BuySell, int m_Qty,
                                         int m_Price, String ^m_Time)
```

```
{
    // When fill is received in B, update spread position and set bracket.
    // This method will run on the RTD thread.

    if (m_Pos_B == Position::FLAT)
    {

        // This is an openning trade.
        if (m_BuySell == "B")
        {
            m_Pos_B=Position::LONG;
        }
        else
        {
            m_Pos_B=Position::SHORT;
        }


        // Set spread position, spread price and stop price.
        if (m_Pos_A == Position::LONG && m_Pos_B == Position::SHORT)
        {
            m_SpreadPos=Position::SHORT;
            m_SpreadPosPrice=-1 * m_FillPrice_A + 2 * m_Price;
            m_StopPrice=m_SpreadPosPrice + 4 * m_Instrument_A->get_TickSize();
        }


        if (m_Pos_A == Position::SHORT && m_Pos_B == Position::LONG)
        {
            m_SpreadPos=Position::LONG;
            m_SpreadPosPrice=-1 * m_FillPrice_A + 2 * m_Price;
            m_StopPrice=m_SpreadPosPrice -4 * m_Instrument_A->get_TickSize();
        }
    }
    else
    {
        // This is a closing trade.
        m_Pos_B=Position::FLAT;
        if (m_Pos_A == Position::FLAT && m_Pos_B == Position::FLAT)
        {
            m_SpreadPos=Position::FLAT;
            m_StopPrice=0;
            m_SpreadPosPrice=0;
        }
    }
    // Update the form on the Main thread.
    m_Form->BeginInvoke(OnFillUpdate, m_Product, m_Key, m_BuySell,
                        m_Qty, m_Price, m_Time);
}
```

Note the two fill event handlers that run on the RTD thread, but nonetheless update SystemManager data members used in the trading strategy logic in the RunStrategy method.

To make the trading logic more logical, I have chosen to segregate a portion of the algorithm for calculating the normalized price into a static method.

```
NormCalc.h

#pragma once

using namespace System::Collections;

ref class NormCalc
{
public:
    static double CalcNormalizedPrice(ArrayList ^m_List)
    {

        // This method will run on the Strategy thread.
        double m_Mean=0;
        double m_StDev=0;
        if (m_List->Count == 30)
        {

            // Calculate the 30 tick MA.
            for(int x=0; x < 30; x++)
            {
                m_Mean+=Convert::ToDouble(m_List[x]);
            }
            m_Mean /= 30;

            // Calculate the 30 tick St Dev.
            for(int x=0; x < 30; x++)
            {
                m_StDev+=Math::Pow(Convert::ToDouble(m_List[x]) - m_Mean, 2);
            }
            m_StDev=Math::Sqrt(m_StDev/30);

            m_List->RemoveAt(0);

            // Return (LastPx - 30 tick MA)/30 tick St Dev
            return (Convert::ToDouble(m_List[28]) - m_Mean)/m_StDev;
        }
        else
        {
            return 0;
        }
    }
};
```

```
Form1.h

#pragma once
#include "SystemManager.h"

namespace ConsumerProducer_Example
{
using namespace System;
using namespace System::ComponentModel;
using namespace System::Collections;
using namespace System::Windows::Forms;
using namespace System::Data;
using namespace System::Drawing;
using namespace System::Threading;

public ref class Form1 : public System::Windows::Forms::Form
{
// Windows generated code in here.


SystemManager ^m_Manager;
DataSet ^m_DataSet;

private: System::Void button1_Click(System::Object^ sender, System::EventArgs^ e)
{
    // Create a dataset to keep fill information
    m_FillData=gcnew DataSet;
    SetUpDataSet();

    // Create new SystemManager object and subscribe to delegates.
    m_Manager=gcnew SystemManager(this);
    m_Manager->OnInstrumentDataUpdate+=gcnew UpdateEventHandler(
                                        this, &Form1::OnUpdateEventHandler);
    m_Manager->OnFillUpdate+=gcnew FillEventHandler(
                                this, &Form1::OnFillEventHandler);

    // Set buttons for secure start up/shut down.
    button1->Enabled=false;
    button2->Enabled=true;
    this->ControlBox=false;
}

private: System::Void button2_Click(System::Object^ sender, System::EventArgs^ e)
{
    // Start the trading system.
    m_Manager->Go();
    button2->Enabled=false;
}

private: void SetUpDataSet()
```

```
{
    DataTable ^m_DataTable=gcnew DataTable("FillData");
    m_DataTable->Columns->Add(gcnew DataColumn("CONTRACT"));
    m_DataTable->Columns->Add(gcnew DataColumn("TRADEID"));
    m_DataTable->Columns->Add(gcnew DataColumn("BUYSELL"));
    m_DataTable->Columns->Add(gcnew DataColumn("QUANTITY"));
    m_DataTable->Columns->Add(gcnew DataColumn("PRICE"));
    m_DataTable->Columns->Add(gcnew DataColumn("TRADETIME"));

    m_FillData->Tables->Add(m_DataTable);

    dataGridView1->DataSource=m_FillData;
    dataGridView1->DataMember="FillData";
}

public: void OnUpdateEventHandler()
{
    // Populate the text boxes with market data.
    // This method will run on the Main thread.
    tbBid_A->Text=m_Manager->get_Bid_A().ToString();
    tbAsk_A->Text=m_Manager->get_Ask_A().ToString();
    tbBid_B->Text=m_Manager->get_Bid_B().ToString();
    tbAsk_B->Text=m_Manager->get_Ask_B().ToString();
    tbSpreadPrice->Text=m_Manager->get_SpreadPx().ToString();
    tbNormPrice->Text=m_Manager->get_NormPx().ToString("#.000");
    tbPos_A->Text=m_Manager->get_Pos_A().ToString();
    tbPos_B->Text=m_Manager->get_Pos_B().ToString();
    tbPosSpread->Text=m_Manager->get_SpreadPos().ToString();
    tbSpreadPosPx->Text=m_Manager->get_SpreadPosPx().ToString();
    tbStopPrice->Text=m_Manager->get_StopPx().ToString();
}

public: void OnFillEventHandler(String ^m_Contract, String ^m_Key,
                               String ^m_BuySell, int m_Qty,
                               int m_Price, String ^m_Time)

{
    // Add fill data to the dataset.
    // This method will run on the Main thread.
    DataRow ^m_Row=m_FillData->Tables[0]->NewRow();
    m_Row[0]=m_Contract;
    m_Row[1]=m_Key;
    m_Row[2]=m_BuySell;
    m_Row[3]=m_Qty;
    m_Row[4]=m_Price;
    m_Row[5]=m_Time;
    m_FillData->Tables[0]->Rows->Add(m_Row);
}
```

```
private: System::Void button3_Click(System::Object^ sender, System::EventArgs^ e)
{
    // Shut down system gracefully.
    if (m_Manager!=nullptr)
    {
        delete m_Manager;
        m_Manager->OnInstrumentDataUpdate-=gcnew UpdateEventHandler(
                                    this, &Form1::OnUpdateEventHandler);
        m_Manager->OnFillUpdate-=gcnew FillEventHandler(
                                this, &Form1::OnFillEventHandler);
        m_Manager=nullptr;
        GC::Collect();
    }
    this->ControlBox=true;
}
};
}
```

46.2.   Summary

This final chapter looked at the architecture of a multithreaded trading system using a variation of the Producer/Consumer design pattern. This simple trading system incorporates many of the programming topics covered earlier in the book.

46.3.   Conclusion

I once had a student in my class who had several years of experience as a programmer developing trading systems at a large hedge fund. After the last lecture, he told the class that if they learn everything in this book, they will get jobs.

In this text, I have tried to include market-driven, job-relevant information. Today's employers in the financial markets demand job readiness. If you want to get a job in the trading industry, which more and more every day is driven by automated systems, you will have to have a competitive level of knowledge of programming. As we have not covered everything in this book, I inspire you to continue your education and research in this exciting field.

Index

A

Abstract classes, 56
Abstraction, OOP relating to, 19–20
Access, 125
Access modifiers, 55, 55t
Active Template Library projects. *See* ATL
    projects
Add Method Wizard, 204
ADO.NET, 138, 243
    Microsoft relating to, 117, 119, 124
    VC++.NET relating to, 120–122
ADO.NET_Example, 120–122
Aggregate SQL functions. *See* SQL functions
Algorithmic trading systems. *See* Automated
    trading systems
Algorithms. *See also* Moving average crossover
    algorithm
    cleaning of, 248, 252
    order management, 245
    order selection, 2
    risk management, 287
    trade selection, 1, 237, 244
Aliasing, 133, 134
ANSI/ISO SQL, 125, 130, 193
APIs (application programming interfaces), 209,
    237–238, 238f, 240, 259. *See also* FASTAPI;
    TraderAPI, connecting to; Win32 API
    projects and DLLs; Winsock32 API
AppDomain, 165
Application class, 100
Application programming interfaces. *See* APIs
ApplicationContext, 291
Applications. *See also* EDAs

CLR console, 80, 84
COM, 6, 60
Arrays
    circular, 279
    marshaling of, 193–194
    VC++.NET relating to, 83–85
ASP.NET, 8
Assemblies, 8–9
    mixed, 23
AsynchEvent_Example, 80–81
Asynchronous communication, 183
Asynchronous method calls, 80
Asynchronous Programming Model, .NET
    Framework, 183, 189
Asynchronous sockets, 183
ATL (Active Template Library) projects,
    5, 204
Automated trading systems, 175, 182, 289
    building of
        buy, build v., 237–238
        data mapping relating to, 239–240, 239f,
            240f, 245
        logic leaks relating to, 243–244
    business logic of
        order management, 1, 2, 263
        position management logic, 1
        trade selection algorithms, 1, 237, 244
    classes of
        bar relating to, 264
        bracket object relating to, 264
        GUI relating to, 251, 254, 265
        instrument, 20, 20t, 259–264, 267, 277, 289,
            291, 292

Automated trading systems (*Continued*)
    order, 263–264
    order book relating to, 264
    system manager relating to, 265
    tick collection/bar collection, 264
    tick relating to, 264
  development of, 242–243
    computer science used in, 2, 237
    efficiency of, 245
    quality management used in, 2, 237
    quantitative finance used in, 2, 237
    speed of, 240–242, 241f, 244
    trading strategy used in, 2, 237, 240
  hardware relating to, 1
  profitability of, 2, 244–245
  software relating to, 1
  trigger functions relating to, 71
AVG/COUNT/MIN/MAX functions, 131–132

B

Back testing, of K/V Methodology, 247, 252
  develop cleaning algorithms, 248, 252
  gather historical data, 248, 252
  perform in sample/out of sample tests, 248,
    252–253
  shadow trade and check performance, 248, 253
Bar, 264
Bar collection, 264
BeginInvoke, 173, 174
Blittable types, 193, 209
Boolean, 61
Bracket object, 264
Brooks, Frederick P., 243
Building, of automated trading systems. *See*
  Automated trading systems
Business logic, of automated trading systems, 1, 2,
  237, 244, 263
Business Rules Catalog, 251, 252
Buy automated trading system, build v., 237–238

C

C#, 5, 6, 31, 253
C++ classes, 216
C++ DLLS, PInvoke used for, 209–216
C++ languages, 5, 31, 33, 36, 69, 253
C++ libraries, 193, 216
C++ pointer, 195
C++ project types, 5
CalcNormalizedPrice method, 289
Calculations, research and documentation of, 247,
  248, 249, 251, 266
Calculations, risk, performance of, 248, 255–256
Calling C-style functions, 209, 216
CallingConventionEnumeration, 215

Calls
  asynchronous method, 80
  chatty, 203, 209
  chunky, 203, 209
  method, 203
Casting, 61–65. *See also* Multicasting
  dynamic, 63
  safe, 64
  static, 62
Catch blocks, 103, 104, 127
Catch statements, 103, 104
Catching unmanaged C++ types, 104–105
C++/CLI, 5–6
Chatty call, 203, 209
Chicago Mercantile Exchange, 223
Chunky call, 203, 209
Circular arrays, 279
Classes. *See also* Automated trading systems;
  CPM coclasses; ManagedClass; MFC
  projects; MyClass; MyWin32ClassLibrary;
  .NET Class Libraries
  abstract and sealed, 56
  application, 100
  C++, 216
  CLR relating to, 19–23
  collection, 107–112, 113
  CollectionBase, 116
  COM, 233
  consumer, 280, 282
  convert, 61, 65
  DataSet, 115
  Debug, 12–14, 14f
  elements of, 20t
  file and directory, 99
  FileStream, 99, 101
  Futures, 21
  Instrument, 20, 20t, 259–264, 267, 277, 289,
    291, 292
  marshall, 183
  monitor, 182
  mutex, 178, 180
  .NET Socket, 183
  NetworkStream, 183
  NormCalc, 289
  object, 56, 56t
  Option, 21
  order, 263–264
  producer, 280, 281, 286
  random, 87–89, 281
  sealed, 56
  semaphore, 180, 279, 280, 293
  sorted List, 109, 110, 264
  STL collection, 113
  StreamReader, 101

StreamWriter, 99, 101
StringBuilder, 11–12
synchronization, 177–182
thread, 175
ThreadPool, 171, 175
TickData, 293
TraderAPI relating to, 224–226, 224t, 225t,
      226t, 259
WaitHandle, 178, 180
Clauses
   FROM, 126, 133
   GROUP BY, 132
   HAVING, 133
   INNER JOINT, 134, 135
   LIKE, 129–130
   ORDER BY, 129
   OUTER JOINT, 135
   WHERE, 128–129, 128t, 133, 134, 138
Cleaning algorithms, development of, 248, 252
CL.exe compiler, 7
CLI (Common Language Infrastructure), 5–6
CLR (common language runtime), 6, 15, 25, 46,
      71, 104
   classes relating to, 19–23
   garbage collection relating to, 203
   marshaling relating to, 193–194, 198
   .NET framework relating to, 8, 98, 103
   pointers relating to, 195, 196
CLR console application, 80, 84
Codes. See also Sample codes
   glue, 237, 238, 239, 239f
   managed, 193, 203
   unmanaged, 193, 209
Collection classes, 107–112, 113
CollectionBase class, 116
Collections, 107–112
   bar, 264
   garbage, 8, 9, 25, 30, 43, 48, 78, 198, 203
   generic, 110
   tick, 264
COM (Component Object Model), 203–207, 223,
      231
COM applications, 6, 60
COM classes, 233
COM dlls, 203–207
COM Interop, 193, 194, 209, 217
COM libraries, 203, 207, 217
COM objects, 203, 221
COMInterop, 203–207
Commercial-off-the-shelf software. See COTS
Commission and exchange fees, 245
Common Language Infrastructure. See CLI
Common language routine. See CLR
Communicating data, 1

Communication
   asynchronous, 183
   synchronous, 183
Communications network, for data, 237
Compiler
   CL.exe, 7
   VC++.NET, 7, 8, 67
The Complete Arbitrage Deskbook (Reverre), 291
Component Object Model. See COM
Composition, 41–48
Composition_Example, 41–44
Computer science, 2, 237
Concurrency. See Multithreading
Connecting, to managed DDLs, 199–201
Connectivity and interoperability, 1, 2, 194, 238
Constraints, 115, 116
Consumer class, 280, 282
Consumer object, 279, 282, 284
Consumer thread, 280, 280f, 283, 284, 286f
Consumer/producer design pattern, 279–287, 289,
      292, 304
ConsumerSemaphore, 293
ConsumerSemaphore÷Release, 281
ConsumerSemaphore÷WaitOne, 283
ContextBoundObjects, 178
ControllingExcel_Example, 217–220
Convert class, 61, 65
Convert_Example, 61
Converting, 61–65
COTS (commercial-off-the-shelf) software,
      237–238, 239, 245
CPM coclasses, 203
Creation
   of objects, 212
   of reference types, 25–26
   of tables, 139
   of views, 138–139
Custom marshaler, 193

D
Data
   communication of, 1
   communications network for, 237
   historical, gathering of, 248, 252
   managing of, in memory, 1
   mapping of, 239–240, 239f, 240f, 245
   retrieval of, 124
Data definition language. See DDL
Data manipulation language. See DML
Data mapping, 239–240, 239f, 240f, 245
Data source, 123
Data Transformation Management System. See
      DTMS
DataAdapter, 120, 122

Databases
    connecting to, 119–124
    finance, 122
    option.mdb, 136
    storing data in, and retrieving from, 1
    updating of, 123–124
DataColumnCollection, 116
DataColumns, 115, 116, 117
DataGridViews, 124, 289, 290f
DataReader, 119, 124
DataRelations, 115
DataRowCollection, 116–117, 122, 124
DataRows, 115, 116–117, 122
DataSet class, 115
DataSet objects, 115t, 117, 121
DataSet_Example, 116
DataSets, 115–117, 119, 120, 124
    enumeration of data in, 122
    writing XML from, 123
DataTables, 115, 116, 117, 120, 122
DateTime, 61, 91
DDL (data definition language), 125
    altering tables relating to, 140
    creating tables relating to, 139
    creating views relating to, 138–139
DDL_Example, 199–201
DDLs, managed, connecting to, 199–201
Debug builds, solution configurations for, 7
Debug class, 12–14, 14f
Debug_Example, 12–14, 14f
Decimal, 61
Delegates, 71–82, 171, 292
Delegates_Example, 72–73
Delete and dispose, 27–28, 30, 43
DELETE statement, 137–138
Development, of automated trading systems. See
    Automated trading systems
Dispose. See Delete and dispose
DISTINCT function, 132
.dll files, 199–201, 209–216, 230, 231, 233
DLL projects, 5, 6, 7
DLLImport, 209
DLLs, Win32 API projects and, 5, 204
DML (data manipulation language), 125
    LIKE clause, 129–130
    ORDER BY clause, 129
    SELECT statement, 126–129, 128t, 132–134,
        136, 138
    WHERE clause, 128–129, 128t, 133, 134, 138
Document/documentation. See K/V Methodology;
    Visual Studio Documentation; XML
    documents; XML Schema documents
Double, 61
DTMS (Data Transformation Management
    System), 252

Dynamic casting, 63
DynamicCast_Example, 62–64

E
ECMA (European Computer Manufacturers
    Association), 6
EDAs (event-driven applications), 71, 82
Efficiency, 245
Element objects, 107, 109
E-Mini Nasdaq 100, 223
E-Mini Nasdaq 100 futures contracts, 267, 289
E-Mini S&P 500, 75, 223, 289
Encapsulation, OOP relating to, 19, 21
EnterLimitOrder, 289
EnterLimitOrderMethod, 292
EnterMarketOrder, 289
Enumerations, 51–53, 109, 110
    of data in DataSets, 122
    FileMode, 100
    ProtocolType, 183
    ThreadState, 170–171, 171t
Enums_Example, 53
European Computer Manufacturers Association.
    See ECMA
Event-driven applications. See EDAs
Event-driven architecture, 1
Event_Example, 76–78
Events, 71–82, 281, 289
Excel, 119, 123, 124, 251, 266
    connecting to, 217–221
ExcelChart_Example, 220–221
Exception, 9
Exception handling, 103–105
Exceptions_Example, 103–104
Exchange fees, 245

F
FAST (FIX adapted for streaming), 151
FASTAPI, 151
FFT (free form text), 263
File and directory classes, 99
FileMode enumeration, 100
Files, .dll, 199–201, 209–216, 230,
    231, 233
FileStream class, 99, 101
FillObj, 224, 224t
Finalize method, 28, 29–30, 43, 44, 48
Finalize_Example, 29–30
Finance database, 122
Finance, quantitative, 2, 237
Financial engineering, 216
Financial information exchange protocol
    FIX, overview of, 148
    XML protocols in financial markets, 147
Financial markets, XML protocols in, 147

"Financial Numerical Recipes in C++"
    (Ødegaard), 216
FIX
    costs for, 149
    hub-and-spoke network relating to, 148–149
    overview of, 148
    point-to-point VPNs relating to, 148
FIX adapted for streaming. *See* FAST
FIX engines, 148, 149–151, 237
    capabilities of, 149, 150t
    technologies relating to, 149, 150t
    vendor support services for, 149, 150t, 151
FIX Protocol, Ltd. *See* FPL
Form1 user interface, 267, 268f, 269, 274,
    277, 289
FormsTimer_Example, 93–94
FormUpdate_Example, 172–174
FPL (FIX Protocol, Ltd.), 147, 151
Free form text. *See* FFT
FROM clause, 126, 133
Front office programming, 1
Fully qualified names, 9
Futures class, 21

G
Garbage collection, 8, 9, 25, 30, 43, 48, 78, 198
    CLR relating to, 203
Gate meeting, 248
Gates, K/V Methodology relating to, 247, 248,
    250f, 251, 253, 255
Generating random numbers, 87–89
Generic collections, 110
Generics_Example, 111–112
GetUpperBound, 83
Glue code, 237, 238, 239, 239f
Graphical User Interface. *See* GUI
GROUP BY clause, 132
GUI (Graphical User Interface), 251, 254, 265

H
Hardware, 1
Hashtable, 109
Hashtable_Example, 107–108
HAVING clause, 133
Heaps
    managed, 21–22
    unmanaged, 21–22, 44, 193
Historical data, gathering of, 248, 252
Hub-and-spoke network, 148–149

I
IConvertible interface, 61, 65
IDictionaryEnumerator, 107
IEnumerator, 107
Implementation, of K/V Methodology, 247, 253

build SRS document, 248, 251, 253–254
design and document system architecture, 248,
    254, 266
probationary trade and check performance, 248,
    255
program and document system, 248, 254–255
In sample/out of sample tests, performance of,
    248, 252–253
Inheritance, 55–60
    abstract and sealed classes relating to, 56
    access modifiers for, 55, 55t
    interfaces relating to, 58–60
    object class relating to, 56, 56t
    OOP relating to, 19, 21
    RCW relating to, 60, 203
    rules for, 55
Inheritance_Example, 56–58
INNER JOINT clause, 134, 135
INSERT statement, 136–137, 138, 140
Installation packages, 161–162
Installation_Example, 161–162
Installers, 161–162
InstrNotifyClass, 225, 225t
InstrObjClass, 224, 224t, 225, 259
Instrument class, 20, 20t, 259–264, 267, 277, 289,
    291, 292
Instrument object, 259
Instrument_A (ES), 289
Instrument_B (NQ), 289
Int16, 61
Int32, 61, 209
Int64, 61
INTC options, 134
Integers, marshaling of, 193–194
Interface. *See also* APIs; GUI
    form1 user, 267, 268f, 269, 274, 277, 289
    IConvertible, 61, 65
    inheritance relating to, 58–60
Interface_Example, 59–60
Interior pointers, 195–198
InteriorPointer_Example, 195–196
Internet, 148
Interop marshaler, 193, 209
Interop wrapper, 231
Interoperability and connectivity, 1, 2, 194, 238
IpEndPoint, 183
IsHighResolution, 92
ISO, 6
ISO 9000, 254
ISO C++ programming concepts, 2, 55, 67
ISO C++ projects, Win32 Console projects for, 5

J
JIT (Just In Time), 7, 8
Join method, 167

Joining tables
  INNER JOINT clause, 134, 135
  OUTER JOINT clause, 135
  UNION keyword, 134
Just In Time. *See* JIT

K

K/V Methodology, 243, 247–257, 250f, 267, 291
  back testing, 247, 252
    develop cleaning algorithms, 248, 252
    gather historical data, 248, 252
    perform in sample/out of sample tests, 248, 252–253
    shadow trade and check performance, 248, 253
  Business Rules Catalog relating to, 251, 252
  gates relating to, 247, 248, 250f, 251, 253, 255
  implementation, 247, 253
    build SRS document, 248, 251, 253–254
    design and document system architecture, 248, 254, 266
    probationary trade and check performance, 248, 255
    program and document system, 248, 254–255
  money document, 249
  portfolio and risk management, 247, 255
    determine causes of variation in performance, 248, 256
    document profit and loss attribution, 248, 256
    monitor portfolio statistics, 248, 255
    perform risk calculations, 248, 255–256
  research and documentation calculations, 247, 249, 266
    check performance, 248, 251
    describe trading idea, 248
    prototype in modeling software, 248, 251
    research quantitative methods, 248, 251
  System Architecture Document, 254
  Vision and Scope Document relating to, 254
  waterfall development methodology relating to, 247, 256–256
K/V Trading System Development Methodology.
  See K/V Methodology

L

LIKE clause, 129–130
LIKE operator, 129–130
LinkedList_Example, 110–111
Logic leaks, 243–244
LongMA ticks, 267

M

Main thread, 289, 290f
Managed codes, 193, 203
Managed console, 5, 6, 7

Managed DDLs, connecting to, 199–201
^Managed Handle, 16
Managed heaps, 21–22
Managed memory, 209
Managed object, 46, 48, 203
Managed stacks, 21–22
Managed types, 39
Managed wrapper, 203
ManagedArray_Example, 83–84
ManagedClass, 44
ManagedComposition_Example, 46–48
Management. *See also* DTMS; Memory
    management; OMS; Position management logic
  efficiency of, 245
  order, 1, 2, 263
  quality, 2, 237
  risk, 245, 247, 248, 255–256
Managing data, in memory, 1
Mapping. *See* Data mapping
Margin rates, 245
Marshaler
  custom, 193
  interop, 193, 209
Marshaling, 209
  of arrays, 193–194
  CLR relating to, 193–194, 198
  of integers, 193–194
  of objects, 193–194
  process of, 193–194
Marshall class, 183
Marshall::StringToHGlobalAnsi method, 193
Mathematical operations, 133
Memory location, 279
Memory management
  managed and unmanaged stacks, 21–22
  managed heaps, 21–22
  unmanaged heaps, 21–22, 44, 193
Memory, managing data in, 1
MessageBox_Example, 9–11, 10f
Messaging, 2
Method calls, 203
Methods. *See* Specific entries
MFC (MS Foundation Classes) projects, 5
Microsoft, 5, 6, 7, 75, 113, 240
  ADO.NET relating to, 117, 119, 124
  Excel relating to, 217
  Platform Invoke relating to, 209
Microsoft Intermediate Language. *See* MSIL
Microsoft Jet driver, 121
Milliseconds_Example, 91–92
Mixed assemblies, 23
Money document, 249
Monitor, 182
Monitor class, 182

Monitor::Enter method, 182
Monitoring, of portfolio statistics, 248, 255
Moving average crossover algorithm, 267, 277
MS Access, 119, 121, 139
MS Foundation Classes projects. *See* MFC projects
MS SQL Server, 119
MS Visual C++ 2005, 5
MS Visual Studio 2005, 5
MSDN Library, 7
MSIL (Microsoft Intermediate Language), 7, 8
Multicast_Example, 73–75
Multicasting, 73
Multithreaded statistical arbitrage system, 289–304
Multithreading, 2, 82, 98, 110, 165–166, 175, 182, 279
Mutex class, 178, 180
Mutex_Example, 178–180
MyClass, 26, 27, 73, 75, 78, 81, 172–174
MyCOMLibrary, 203–206, 204f, 205f
MyDelegate Handler, 72, 73
MyEventHandler, 75
MyWin32ClassLibrary, 212–214
MyWin32Library, 209–211

N

Namespaces, 9–11, 10f, 19, 166
.NET Class Libraries, 8, 9
.NET framework, 5–14, 19, 23, 60, 91, 105, 165, 203, 231. *See also* VC++.NET
  ASP.NET, 8
  CLR, 8, 98, 103
  collection classes relating to, 107–112, 113
  .NET Class Libraries, 8, 9
  STL.NET, 6, 107, 112, 113–114
.NET Framework Asynchronous Programming Model, 183, 189
.NET or "Managed" console, Windows, or DLL projects, 5, 6, 7
.NET programs, 119, 207, 223
.NET Socket class, 183
.NET types
  references, 22–23, 25–31
  unmanaged, 23
  value, 22, 33–36
NetworkStream class, 183
NetworkStream object, 183
"No Silver Bullet: Essence and Accidents of Software Engineer" (Brooks), 243
Non-XML protocol. *See* FIX
Norman, David, 1
NormCalc class, 289
Nullptr reference, 30

O

Object class, 56, 56t
Object-oriented programming. *See* OOP
Objects, 9, 19–23, 112, 259
  bracket, 264
  COM, 203, 221
  consumer, 279, 282, 284
  creation of, 212
  DataSet, 115t, 117, 121
  delete and dispose of, 27–28, 30, 43
  element, 107, 109
  instrument, 259
  managed, 46, 48, 203
  marshaling of, 193–194
  NetworkStream, 183
  OleDbConnection, 119, 121, 124
  producer, 279, 282, 284
  TraderAPI, 267
  unmanaged, 37–39, 46, 48, 203
Ødegaard, Bernt, 216
OleDbConnection objects, 119, 121, 124
OleDbDataAdaptar, 120, 121, 123, 124, 125
OleDbDataReader, 124
OleDeCommand, 136
OMS (order management system), 148
OnFill event, 289
OnFill_AEventHandler, 289, 301
OnFill_BEventHandler, 289, 301
OnInstrumentFill method, 274
OnInstrumentUpdate method, 269
OnNotifyUpdate method, 292
OnOrderFillData, 224
OnTimeTick, 281
OOP (object-oriented programming), 19–23, 41, 48
  abstraction, 19–20
  encapsulation, 19, 21
  inheritance, 19, 21
  polymorphism, 19, 21
Operator overload, 67–69, 68t
OpOverload_Example, 67–69
Option class, 21
OptionContracts, 134
Option.mdb database, 136
Options, INTC, 134
OptionTrades table, 133
Oracle, 119, 125
Order book, 264
ORDER BY clause, 129
Order classes, 263–264
Order execution, 237
Order management, 1, 2, 263
Order management algorithms, 245
Order management system. *See* OMS
Order object, 292, 293

Order selection algorithms, 2
OrderObj, 225, 225t, 226
OrderProfileClass, 225–226, 226t
OrderSetClass, 224, 225, 226, 226t, 259
Out of sample/in sample tests, performance of, 248, 252–253
OUTER JOIN clause, 135
Output streams, 99–101

P

Parameterization model, 114
Parsers, 142
PassingArrays_Example, 84–85
PassingValueTypes_Example, 35–36
Pinning pointers, 195–198
Pinning_Example, 196–198
PInvoke (Platform Invocation Services), 209–216
Platform
    unix, 240
    X_Trader, 223
Platform Invocation Services. *See* PInvoke
Platform Invoke, 194, 198, 209
PL/SQL, 125
Pointers
    C++, 195
    CLR relating to, 195, 196
    interior, 195–198
    pinning, 195–198
Point-to-point VPNs, 148
Polymorphism, OOP relating to, 19, 21
Portfolio and risk management, for K/V
        Methodology, 247, 255
    determine causes of variation in performance, 248, 256
    document profit and loss attribution, 248, 256
    monitor portfolio statistics, 248, 255
    perform risk calculations, 248, 255–256
Portfolio statistics, monitoring of, 248, 255
Position management logic, 1
Probationary trade, check performance for, 248, 255
Producer class, 280, 281, 286
Producer object, 279, 282, 284
Producer thread, 280, 280f, 283, 284, 286f
Producer/consumer design pattern, 279–287, 289, 292, 304
ProducerConsumer_Example, 279
ProducerConsumerObjects class, 280
Producer::get_Data method, 287
Producer::OnTimerTick method, 286
Professional Electronic Trading (Norman), 1
Profit and loss attribution, documentation of, 248, 256
Profitability, of automated trading systems, 2, 244–245

Properties, 49–50
Properties_Example, 49–50
Proprietary software, 237–238
ProtocolType enumeration, 183
Prototype, in modeling software, 248, 251

Q

Quality management, 2, 237
Quantitative finance, 2, 237
Quantitative methods, research in, 248, 251
QueueUserWorkItem method, 171

R

Random class, 87–89, 281
Random numbers, generation of, 87–89
Random_Example, 87
RCW (runtime callable wrapper), 60, 203
Real time, 279, 287, 289
Reference types, 22–23, 25–31. *See also* Tracking references
    creation of, 25–26
    destruction of, 27–30
    Nullptr, 30
    stack semantics for, 30
    of structures, 51, 52
ReferenceStructure_Example, 52
RefType_Example, 17, 26–27
Release builds, solution configurations for, 7
Research and documentation calculations, for K/V
        Methodology, 247, 249, 266
    check performance, 248, 251
    describe trading idea, 248
    prototype in modeling software, 248, 251
    research quantitative methods, 248, 251
Retrieval, of data, 1, 124
Reverre, Stephane, 291
Risk calculations, performance of, 248, 255–256
Risk management, 245
    portfolio and, 247, 248, 255–256
Risk management algorithms, 287
Rows, DataRowCollections, and DataRows, 116–117
RTDThread_A, 289, 290f
RTDThread_B, 289, 290f
RunConsumer method, 283
RunStrategy method, 294, 301
Runtime callable wrapper. *See* RCW

S

Safe casting, 64
SafeCast_Example, 64
Sample codes
    ADO.NET_Example, 120–122
    AsynchEvent_Example, 80–81

Composition_Example, 41–44
ControllingExcel_Example, 217–220
Convert_Example, 61
DataSet_Example, 116
DDL_Example, 199–201
Debug_Example, 12–14, 14f
Delegates_Example, 72–73
DynamicCast_Example, 62–64
Enums_Example, 53
Event_Example, 76–78
ExcelChart_Example, 220–221
Exceptions_Example, 103–104
Finalize_Example, 29–30
FormsTimer_Example, 93–94
FormUpdate_Example, 172–174
Generics_Example, 111–112
Hashtable_Example, 107–108
Inheritance_Example, 56–58
Installation_Example, 161–162
Interface_Example, 59–60
InteriorPointer_Example, 195–196
LinkedList_Example, 110–111
ManagedArray_Example, 83–84
ManagedComposition_Example, 46–48
MessageBox_Example, 9–11, 10f
Milliseconds_Example, 91–92
Monitor, 182
Multicast_Example, 73–75
Mutex_Example, 178–180
MyCOMLibrary, 203–206, 204f, 205f
MyWin32ClassLibrary, 212–214
MyWin32Library, 209–211
OpOverload_Example, 67–69
PassingArrays_Example, 84–85
PassingValueTypes_Example, 35–36
Pinning_Example, 196–198
ProducerConsumer_Example, 279
Properties_Example, 49–50
Random_Example, 87
ReferenceStructure_Example, 52
RefType_Example, 17, 26–27
SafeCast_Example, 64
Semaphore_Example, 180–182
Serialization_Example, 153–154
SortedList_Example, 109–110
Spreader_Example, 291–304
SQL_Example Windows, 128
StaticCast_Example, 62
StdNormRandom_Example, 87–89
STL_Example, 114
STL.NET_Example, 113
Stopwatch_Example, 93
StreamReader_Example, 101
StreamWriter_Example, 100

StringConcat_Example, 11–12
StringToCharArray_Example, 194
Synchronize_Example, 177–178
SynchronousClient_Example, 187–189
SynchronousServer_Example, 184–186
TechnicalSystem_Example, 268–277
TemplateFunction_Example, 16
ThreadAbort_Example, 167–169
Thread_Example, 166–167
ThreadingTimer_Example, 95–96
ThreadPool_Example, 171–172
ThreadPriority_Example, 170
TimersTimer_Example, 96–97
TrackingReference_Example, 15
TraderAPIConnection_Example, 227–230, 227f
Traders.xsd, 142–143
UnmanagedComposition_Example, 44–46
UnmanagedObject_Example, 37–39
UsingCOMDDL_Example, 207
UsingWin32Class_Example, 214–215
UsingWin32DLL_Example, 211–212
ValueStructure_Example, 51–52
ValueTypes_Example, 34–35
WindowsService_Example, 155–159
Wrapper_Example, 78–80
Xml Reader_Example, 144–146
Xml Writer_Example, 144
XTAPIConnection_Example, 231–233
SByte, 61
Sealed classes, 56
SELECT statements, 126–128, 136, 137
    FROM clause of, 126, 133
    GROUP BY clause, 132
    HAVING clause, 133
    ORDER BY clause of, 129
    WHERE clause of, 128–129, 128t, 133, 134, 138
Semaphore class, 180, 279, 280, 293
Semaphore_Example, 180–182
Serialization, 153–154
Serialization_Example, 153–154
Setup and installation packages, 161–162
Shadow trade, check performance of, 248, 253
ShortMA ticks, 267
Single, 61
Single-threaded technical analysis system, 267–277
Sockets, 183–189
Software, 1
    COTS, 237–238, 239, 245
    modeling, prototype in, 248, 251
    proprietary, 237–238
    spiral, development methodology for, 247
    third-party trading, 237
Software requirements specification document.
    See SRS document

Solution Configurations for Debug builds and
    Release builds, 7
Solutions, 5
Sorted List class, 109, 110, 264
SortedList_Example, 109–110
Speed, 7
    of development, 240–242, 241f, 244
    of system, 240–242, 241f
Spiral software development methodology, 247
Spreader_Example, 291–304
SQL (Structured Query Language), 2, 120, 125–140
SQL functions
    aggregate, 131t
        AVG/COUNT/MIN/MAX, 131–132
        SUM, 130–131, 132
    aliasing, 133, 134
    DISTINCT, 132
    joining tables, 134, 135
    mathematical operations, 133
SQL statements, 121, 125, 126, 127, 131, 133, 134
    DDL, 125
    DELETE, 137–138
    DML, 125
    INSERT, 136–137, 138, 140
    LIKE clause of, 129–130
    SELECT, 126–128, 130, 132, 134, 136
    UPDATE, 137, 138
SQL_Example Windows, 128
SRS (software requirements specification)
    document, 248, 251, 253–254
Stack semantics, for reference types, 30
Stacks
    managed, 21–22
    unmanaged, 21–22
Stage-Gate method, 248
Standard Template Library. See STL
StartStop method, 274
Statements. See Catch statements; SELECT
    statements; SQL statements
Static casting, 62
StaticCast_Example, 62
Statistical arbitrage system. See Multithreaded
    statistical arbitrage system
StdNormRandom_Example, 87–89
STL (Standard Template Library), 2
    STL.NET and, 113–114
STL collection classes, 113
STL_Example, 114
STL.NET, 6, 107, 112
    STL and, 113–114
STL.NET_Example, 113
Stopwatch, 92
Stopwatch_Example, 93
Storing data, in databases, 1

Strategy threads, 289, 290f, 294
StreamReader class, 101
StreamReader_Example, 101
StreamWriter class, 99, 101
StreamWriter_Example, 100
String ^, 61
StringBuilder class, 11–12
StringConcat_Example, 11–12
Strings, 9, 122, 193
StringToCharArray_Example, 194
Structured Query Language. See SQL
Structures
    reference types of, 51, 52
    value types of, 51–52
SUM function, 130–131, 132
Sybase, 119, 125
Symbol ES, 223
Symbol NQ, 223
Synchronization classes, 177–182
Synchronize_Example, 177–178
Synchronous communication, 183
Synchronous sockets, 183
SynchronousClient_Example, 187–189
SynchronousServer_Example, 184–186
System. See also Automated trading systems;
    DTMS; K/V Methodology; OMS
    multithreaded statistical arbitrage, 289–304
    single-threaded technical analysis, 267–277
    speed of, 240–242, 241f
System architecture, design and document for,
    248, 254, 266
System Architecture Document, 254
System manager, 265
System::Collections namespace, 107, 107t, 112, 114
System::Collections::Generic namespace, 110,
    112, 114
System::Collections::Queues, 279
System::IO namespace, 99, 101
SystemManager, 44, 75, 93, 267, 268f, 269, 277,
    289, 290f, 294
System::Threading namespace, 166, 178
System::Threading::Timer, 93, 94

T

Tables. See DDL; Joining tables; OptionTrades table
Taxes, 245
TechnicalSystem_Example, 268–277
Technologies, FIX engines relating to, 149, 150t
TemplateFunction_Example, 16
Third-party trading software, 237
Thread class, 175
Thread safety, 110, 174
Thread::Abort, 169
ThreadAbort_Example, 167–169

ThreadAbortException, 167
Thread_Example, 166–167
Threading, 165–175
Threading namespace, 166
ThreadingTimer_Example, 95–96
ThreadPool, 167, 183
ThreadPool class, 171, 175
ThreadPool_Example, 171–172
ThreadPriority, 169, 169t
ThreadPriority_Example, 170
Threads
    consumer, 280, 280f, 283, 284, 286f
    main, 289, 290f
    other, updating forms from, 172
    producer, 280, 280f, 283, 284, 286f
    strategy, 289, 290f, 294
ThreadStart, 166
Thread::Start, 167
ThreadState enumeration, 170–171, 171t
Tick collection/bar collection, 264
TickData class, 293
TickList, 274
Ticks, 264, 267, 269, 279, 281, 286
Time, 91–98
Timers, 91–98, 281. See also Sample codes
    System::Threading::Timer, 93, 94
    System::Timers::Timer, 93, 96
    System::Windows::Forms::Timer, 93
TimersTimer_Example, 96–97
Timer::Tick event, 281
TimeSpan, 91
Tracking references, 15–18
    ^Managed Handle, 16
    RefType_Example, 17, 26–27
    TemplateFunction_Example, 16
    TrackingReference_Example, 15
TrackingReference_Example, 15
Trade
    probationary, check performance for, 248, 255
    shadow, check performance of, 248, 253
Trade selection algorithms, 1, 237, 244
TraderAPI, connecting to, 233, 259–263
    classes of
        FillObj, 224, 224t
        InstrNotifyClass, 225, 225t
        InstrObjClass, 224, 224t, 225, 259
        OrderObj, 225, 225t, 226
        OrderProfileClass, 225–226, 226t
        OrderSetClass, 224, 225, 226, 226t, 259
    overview of, 223–224, 224f
    TraderAPIConnection_Example relating to,
        227–230, 227f
TraderAPI objects, 267
TraderAPIConnection_Example, 227–230, 227f

TraderAPI.dll, 230
Traders.xsd, 142–143
Trading idea, description of, 249
Trading strategies, 2, 237, 240
Trading system development. See Automated
    trading systems; K/V Methodology
Trading Technologies, Inc., 223, 231, 233
Transact-SQL, 125
Trigger functions, 71
Try..Catch block, 103

U

UInt16, 61
UInt32, 61
UInt64, 61
UML (Unified Modeling Language), 254
Unblittable types, 193
Unified Modeling Language. See UML
UNION keyword, 134
Unix platform, 240
Unmanaged C++ types, catching, 104–105
Unmanaged codes, 193, 209
Unmanaged heaps, 21–22, 44, 193
Unmanaged memory, 209
Unmanaged .NET types, 23
Unmanaged objects, 37–39, 46, 48, 203
Unmanaged stacks, 21–22
Unmanaged types, 23, 37–39
UnmanagedComposition_Example, 44–46
UnmanagedObject_Example, 37–39
UPDATE statement, 137, 138
UpdateFormEventHandler, 174
Updating forms, from other threads, 172
Updating, of databases, 123–124
UsingCOMDDL_Example, 207
UsingWin32Class_Example, 214–215
UsingWin32DLL_Example, 211–212

V

Value types, 22, 33–36
    of structures, 51–52
ValueStructure_Example, 51–52
ValueTypes_Example, 34–35
VB, 5
VC++.NET (Visual C++.NET), 1, 2, 5, 245, 253
    ADO.NET relating to, 120–122
    arrays relating to, 83–85
    benefits of, 6–7
    converting and casting relating to, 61–65
    delegates and events relating to, 71–82
    .dll files in, 199–201
    Excel relating to, 217–221
    inheritance relating to, 55–60
    namespaces relating to, 9–11, 10f

VC++.NET (Visual C++.NET), (*Continued*)
  as OOP, 19
  operator overload relating to, 67–69
  properties relating to, 49–50
  SQL relating to, 125–140
VC++.NET compiler, 7, 8, 67
Vendor support services, for FIX engines, 149,
    150t, 151
Versioning, 14
Virtual Private Networks. *See* VPNs
Vision and Scope Document, 254
Visual Basic 6.0, 5, 6
Visual C++.NET. *See* VC++.NET
Visual Studio (VS) 2005, 5, 161
Visual Studio Documentation, 9, 82, 189
Volume-weighted average price, 279
VPNs (Virtual Private Networks), point-to-point,
    148

W

WaitCallback delegate, 171
WaitHandle class, 178, 180
Waterfall development methodology, 247,
    256–256
WHERE clause, 128–129, 128t, 133, 134, 138
Win32 API projects and DLLs, 5, 204
Win32 Console projects, for ISO C++ projects, 5
WIN32 custom.dll, 209
Windows, 5, 6, 7, 165, 240
Windows .NET Integrated Development
    Environment, 240
Windows services, 155–159

Windows.Forms-based timer, 96
WindowsService_Example, 155–159
Winsock32 API, 183
Wrapper_Example, 78–80
Wrappers, 78
www.tradingtechnologies.com, 231

X

XML documents, 123
  valid, 141–142
  well-formed, 141
XML protocols, in financial markets, 147
Xml Reader_Example, 144–146
XML Schema Definition. *See* XSD
XML Schema documents, 142–146
XML Serialization, 153–154
Xml Writer_Example, 144
XmlReader, 146, 154
XmlSerializer, 153–154
XmlWriter, 146, 154
XSD (XML Schema Definition), 142, 143,
    146, 154
XTAPI, 223, 230
  connecting to, 231–233
XTAPIConnection_Example, 231–233
XTAPI.DLL, 233
X_Trader platform, 223
X_Trader Pro, 223, 231

Z

Z-transform procedure, 289, 291